Land Use and Wildlife Resources

Committee on Agricultural Land Use and Wildlife Resources

Division of Biology and Agriculture

National Research Council

NATIONAL ACADEMY OF SCIENCES
Washington, D.C.   1970

This study was supported by the United States Department of Agriculture

International Standard Book Number 0-309-01857-9

Available from:

Printing and Publishing Office
National Academy of Sciences
2101 Constitution Avenue
Washington, D.C. 20418

Library of Congress Catalog Card Number 70-607553

First printing, October 1970
Second printing, September 1971

Printed in the United States of America

Preface

In 1965, at the request of the U.S. Department of Agriculture, the National Academy of Sciences – National Research Council undertook an assessment of the impact of current agricultural practices on wildlife resources. The Committee on Agricultural Land Use and Wildlife Resources, formed to carry out this assessment, focused its attention on two general objectives:

- To evaluate the interrelations of agricultural land use and the protection and production of wildlife and other natural resources.
- To examine areas of apparent conflict between the objectives of agriculture and wildlife management, with a view to what might be done through cooperative research, education, extension, and regulatory programs toward their resolution.

It soon became clear that land and water management are inseparable and that many of the most critical problems of wildlife are involved with the extent and quality of aquatic habitats. Thus wetlands and other areas are discussed in this report as they are affected by land-use practices. The treatment does not extend to the details of fisheries management, nor is pollution as such dealt with other than in connection with activities and operations on the watershed. As for pesticides, in view of several detailed studies elsewhere available, the present review is limited to a generalized interpretation of trends.

The term wildlife is here used in a broad sense as it applies to vertebrate animals and, in particular, to those of social and economic interest. Emphasis is on mammals, birds, and fish as they have value for sport, commercial, or esthetic reasons. Other forms of life are included as appropriate.

The Committee acknowledges the contributions of Dr. Emmett L. Pinnell, University of Missouri, a member whose death in 1967 brought to premature end his efforts on behalf of the study. The Committee also expresses its appreciation for the continuing advice and assistance of a group of specialists who have provided valuable support during the study: Jack H. Berryman, USDI; Lawrence V. Compton, USDA; Frank C. Edminster, USDA; John V. Krutilla, Resources for the Future; Robert C. Otte, USDA; Kenneth W. Parker, USDA; D. I. Rasmussen, USDA; Robert F. Scott, USDI; Robert J. Smith, USDI; Harry A. Steele, USDA; V. Daniel Stiles, USDI; Albert H. Swartz, USDI; and William E. Towell, The American Forestry Association.

Initial drafts of the eight major chapters were prepared as follows, after which the Committee developed the final versions through extended discussion and debate:

Historical Perspective—Allen
Wildlife Values in a Changing World—Allen
New Patterns on Land and Water—Giles, Leedy, and Pinnell
Influences of Land Management on Wildlife—Hervey, Hill, and Leedy
Special Problems of Waters and Watersheds—Allen and Leedy
Pesticides and Wildlife—Fertig and Smith
Wildlife Damage and Control—Swanson
Legislation and Administration—Swanson

The Committee is particularly grateful to one of its members, Dr. Durward Allen, who undertook the difficult and time-consuming task of putting the individual chapters into a final manuscript and of responding to editorial suggestions on behalf of the group.

COMMITTEE ON AGRICULTURAL LAND USE
AND WILDLIFE RESOURCES

Sanford S. Atwood, *Chairman*

Durward L. Allen

Stanford N. Fertig

William L. Giles

Donald F. Hervey

Ralph R. Hill

Daniel L. Leedy

Emmett L. Pinnell

Edward H. Smith

Gustav A. Swanson

Contents

CHAPTER 1

Historical Perspective

Managing wildlife resources is largely a problem in land and water use. What can be done at present often is indicated by past events, insofar as these can be interpreted reliably. The coming of Caucasian man to North America vastly altered the complex of pristine plant-animal communities. It appears reasonable to assume that most such communities represented a stage in a developmental series of types trending toward stability. The progression of changes was monitored by climate, conditioned by the substrate, and often modified or suspended by the influences of animals or aboriginal man. Although the dynamics of natural ecosystems are too little understood, biological investigations since 1920 have revealed relationships sufficiently consistent for guidance in many aspects of resource use.

It is axiomatic that every currently living thing evolved as part of a working association of plants and animals (see Taylor, 1949). Thus, no species can now reproduce and survive in self-dependence outside such a community, each having specific relationships that limit the conditions under which it can exist. Whether it is broadly tolerant or highly specialized is likely to be reflected in its present distribution and how it has responded to alterations in environment.

PRIMITIVE CONDITIONS IN NORTH AMERICA

The record of faunal and floral events on this continent falls far short of a desirable level of detail, but major changes are fairly well known.

1

Pre-Columbian vegetation patterns probably approximated those mapped by Küchler (1964) as "potential natural vegetation." Then, as now, any large area so characterized might encompass any or all stages in the sere.

Testimony to the ultimate ascendancy of geological erosion is implicit in such formations as the ancient stubs of the Appalachians, massive river deltas, extensive loess deposits, and the slope of land from the foot of the Rockies eastward. Yet the stabilizing influence of vegetation is also manifest, and not alone in the attainment of a self-perpetuating stage. At each step of succession there is a countering and buffering of the degrading action of water, wind, heat, cold, and animal life. In terms of the general thrift and coverage of vegetation, it is hardly to be doubted that in the late fifteenth century the land surface of this continent was undergoing a slower rate of change than at any time after the white man's enterprise became effective. Marsh (1864) clearly perceived these relationships more than a century ago.

Aftermath of Glaciation

As compared with much of the earth's surface, North America is largely a young land. The final phases of continental and alpine glaciation in mid-latitudes were only 8 to 10 thousand years in the past. After recession of the ice, further climatic perturbations induced extensive biogeographic advances and retreats that left species and community isolates as witness to their passage (Sears, 1948; Deevey, 1949; Smith, 1957). Of special significance was extension of the "prairie peninsula" eastward presumably during a dry period of the Hypsithermal Interval (Gleason, 1922; Transeau, 1935; Deevey and Flint, 1957), with grassland relicts remaining to mark the way, and even a heath-adapted prairie chicken established on the Atlantic coastal barrens (Gross, 1928). As pointed out by Sears (1942), some of the evidences of past xerothermic conditions may survive from interglacial, even Tertiary, climatic episodes.

A major faunal occurrence of postglacial times was extinction of many species of North American large mammals—camels, llamas, horses, bison, muskoxen, pronghorns, stag-moose, peccaries, mammoths, mastodons, ground sloths, giant beavers, and certain carnivores (Flint, 1957; Martin, 1958-1967). The disappearance of this megafauna has not been satisfactorily explained, but it was in progress during the period of roughly 12,000 to 5,000 B.C., when early men were numerous and active. Well-developed hunting cultures were widely distributed across

the continent (Wormington, 1962; Müller-Beck, 1966) and finely
crafted clovis, Folsom, and subsequent types of projectile points were
being used against mammoths, bison, and lesser beasts. Relative to
further events, Martin (1963) surmised that

Following extinction of the large mammals the early hunters probably suffered
economic depression and a population crash. Under a climate similar to the present
and with the existing biotic zones in place, the early hunters were obliged to begin
their 7,000-year experiment with native plants, leading in the altithermal to increasingly skillful techniques of harvesting and gathering, to the domestication of
certain weedy camp-followers, and, within the last 1,000 years, to the widespread
adoption of flood plain agriculture. Many clues along the trail remain to be detected by pollen analysis and other paleoecological methods.

Certain it is that the beginnings of intensified land use in the New
World interrupted long-term biotic adjustments. In no sense were the
natural changes complete, nor was the situation static. The lag in such
processes being what it is, there is reason to suppose that the mercurial
North American climate was shifting sufficiently often to maintain a
state of flux in associations of living things. Nonetheless, bioclimatic
types were recognizable for large areas, which, under various definitions, have been described as life zones (Merriam, 1898), biomes
(Clements and Shelford, 1939), biotic associations or provinces (Vestal,
1914; Dice, 1943), biochores (Dansereau, 1957), or plant formations
(Holdridge, 1947). Questions of terminology need not confuse the
present discussion. That plant-animal associations commonly exhibit a
"continuum" of variation from one locality to another is inherent in
the distribution and complexity of environmental factors.

Disturbance Communities

As noted in the foregoing, conditions of the immediate prehistoric
period were largely an expression of postglacial vegetation successions
induced by climatic change. Associated with, or added to, this predis-
posing influence were disturbance factors responsible for recurring
cycles of developmental plant-animal communities. Weather extremes—
high winds, torrential rains, floods, drought, exceptional heat or cold—
often brought about drastic localized modifications of the biota, especially through the setting back of vegetation to early seral stages. That
animal and human activity produces similar effects is well known.

Any review of habitat requirements in birds and mammals attests
that relatively few species are characteristic of climax vegetation (see

Shelford, 1963). Certain rodents are capable of living in fully developed grassland or tundra—e.g., voles and lemmings—or in terminal forest types. Among forest species, the white-footed mouse and eastern gray squirrel may be mentioned. A few birds (woodpeckers, titmouse, chickadee) are present the year round in stabilized forests such as beech-maple or oak-hickory. Of all North American hoofed animals, probably the barren-ground caribou can most logically be considered a climax species (Leopold and Darling, 1953: 54), although it wanders over a variety of vegetation types, and especially into the sparse boreal forests for wintering.

Most of the wildlife species of major interest to man depend on a stage of vegetation below the climax, or they make use of several successional stages, or they migrate from one vegetation zone to another.* This undoubtedly was an important key to distribution in primitive times and to great changes that have taken place in recent centuries.

To generalize on a widely varied relationship, it is true that many rodents and lagomorphs, both seed- and leaf-eaters, are largely dependent on pioneer herbaceous types of vegetation. Particularly in grasslands, they respond to disturbance factors that induce the spread of forbs and annual grasses (see review by Bond, 1945), and by their own burrowing and other activities they may help to maintain such conditions, the prairie dog being an outstanding example (Koford, 1958). That there are also more subtle, long-term, cumulative effects important in the development of soils—loosening, mixing, aeration, weathering—is hardly to be doubted (Grinnell, 1923).

In each forested region of the continent there are numerous species of thicket-inhabiting or edge-dwelling birds and mammals. They spread and increase whenever the woodland canopy is opened and a subsere initiated. They depend on a transitory condition, and they will disappear with the habitat in the course of successional change. Some of the game birds well exemplify this situation. In forested areas, nearly every kind of grouse and the various races of wild turkey require that a part of the range be in herbaceous vegetation—grassy and weedy openings where the young can sun and dust and obtain their "starter" diet of insects (cf. Edminster, 1954). The brushy fringes provide many kinds of fleshy fruits, and different vegetation types may fulfill other essen-

---

*The term "climax" will be used most often in this report to designate a terminal stage in the development of vegetation under given climatic conditions. This use recognizes that in some areas such a stage may not be clear and agreed-upon, and no universally accepted definition of climax, especially as applied to ecosystems, is available (see Tansley, 1935; Clements, 1936; Whittaker, 1953).

tial functions in the life history. A similar dependence is seen in many small mammals, including mice and ground squirrels, the snowshoe hare of boreal forests, and southward many races of the cottontail. Among larger species, the deer, elk, and moose are in part browsers upon the brush ranges of secondary successions.

Modifications of vegetation have far-reaching effects in the life community. Responses occur from step to step in the energy-exchange linkage originating in the primary production of green plants. When key food supplies—such as ground-covering types of herbage—flourish, the lower consumer levels (prey animals) are nourished and increased. These, through their augmented numbers, pass on to the carnivores the benefits of favorable change. Through this universal mechanism the herbivores exert a primary control on their dependent predators. When basic conditions are altered, at least for a time, the community may take on a new aspect and composition.

Animal Influences

In every native ecosystem the animal component has played its part in annual and long-term dynamics. Some of the effects on vegetation and site were widespread and conspicuous, although relatively few can be described reliably.

On the vast majority of wooded watersheds, innumerable beaver dams were constantly renewed to produce a cycle of deadenings, ponds, meadows, and early-growth forests. The floodings and succeeding stages became habitat for waterfowl and other aquatic life, edge-inhabiting birds and mammals, and, in the North, moose and woodland caribou.

The extent of wetlands in primitive times is not likely to be fully appreciated by those accustomed only to today's scenery. Although most early observers simply took for granted what they saw, a few left valuable descriptions of conditions that were changing rapidly even a century ago. Hubbard (1887, 362 et seq.), first state geologist of Michigan, described the lowlands between Lake Erie and Saginaw Bay as one of the great beaver-trapping grounds.

To a great extent level, it is intersected by numerous water courses, which have but moderate flow. At the head-waters and small inlets of these streams the beaver established his colonies. Here he dammed the streams setting back the water over the flat lands, and creating ponds, in which were his habitations. . . . The trees were killed, the land converted into a chain of ponds and marshes, with intervening dry ridges. In time, by nature's recuperative process—the annual growth and decay of grasses and aquatic plants—these filled with muck or peat, with occasional deposits of bog lime, and the ponds and swales became dry again. . . . In a semi-circle of twelve miles around Detroit, having the river for base, and embracing about 100,000 acres, fully one-fifth part consists of marshy tracts or prairies [sic], which had their origin in the work of the beaver. A little further west, nearly one whole township, in Wayne County, is of this character.

Although the total ecological influence of beavers in aboriginal North America probably cannot be estimated today, it must have been great for a creature that ranged from south of the Rio Grande to Hudson Bay and from western Alaska to Labrador. According to Seton (1929, vol. IV, pt. 2, p. 446), the only major areas in the United States lacking beaver were the coastal region of the Southeast, including Florida, and the largely waterless deserts of the Southwest. He states that the early beaver population of the Adirondacks was estimated at 1 million, or about 60 to the square mile, and that a more recent estimate for Algonquin Park in Ontario was 50 per square mile. His extrapolation of a minimum population of 60 million in North America appears conservative.

The extensive dewatering of the land surface that has resulted from killing off of beaver, deforestation, drainage, and natural and accelerated filling is one of the most significant changes affecting wildlife since the discovery of America. Disappearance of springs, siltation of streambeds, and drying up of watercourses in summer have been especially well documented in Wisconsin (Scott and Hoveland, 1951). In degree, such changes were to be expected, but the extremes of conditions often are associated with overgrazing and destructive methods of agriculture, which will be terminated inevitably, either because they destroy productivity or as a result of land-use improvements. In forested areas a part of recent trends toward restoration of a more natural hydrology is the countrywide re-establishment and management of beavers.

The bison provides another example. There is little doubt that this animal was an important influence in determining the floral composition of the Great Plains.* Trailing and dust wallowing provided the bare soil conditions conducive to early successions of forbs and certain grasses (see Roe, 1951: 101; Weaver and Albertson, 1956: 104, 370). More especially, the extensive coverage of short grasses on the high plains was largely a result of sustained grazing by the bands and herds that shifted about in response to forage conditions. This activity fa-

---

*Here we have an example of the problems encountered in strictly defining *climax*. Said Shelford (1931): ". . . if the bison held some of the mixed prairie in a short grass stage, then short grass is the bioecological climax and its proper bioecological designation is *Bouteloua-Bison*, even though the climax with bison excluded is something different."

vored the more xeric buffalograss (*Buchloe dactyloides*) and gramas (*Bouteloua*) over the mid-grasses, which Weaver and Albertson (1956) regard as part of the "mixed prairie" climax of the high plains. Larson (1940) reviewed the early findings on this situation and discussed its conceptual semantics. Relative to the number of bison and associated species, he remarked:

A buffalo requires about the same amount and kind of feed as a cow, so it is evident that if Seton's estimate of 20 million or Clements' and Shelford's estimate of 30 million buffalo in early days on the plains is anywhere near correct these animals were sufficiently numerous, along with the 4 to 8 million antelope and extensive herds [sic] of elk, deer, and other wild animals, to hold the drier portions of the plains in a short grass stage.

It is probable that another creature, largely restricted to the eastern deciduous forest region, had important and widespread effects on vegetation and associated animal life in pre-Columbian times. That the passenger pigeon was inconceivably abundant is attested by all original descriptions. After a review of various estimates, Schorger (1955) "guessed" that there were three billion, and possibly five billion, in the primitive continental population.

The clue to ecological impacts of the pigeon lay in its association in flocks numbering many millions. In such masses it nested, fed, roosted, and migrated. The great nestings in the Lake States region covered thousands of acres of forest, loading some trees to the breaking point. A nesting in Benzie County, Michigan, in 1874 was described as "50 square miles of pigeons" (Hubbard, 1887: 308). The results of such a concentration were similar to those described by Audubon (quoted from *Ornithological Biography, 1831-1839*, by Mershon, 1907: 33) for one of the nighttime roosts in Kentucky:

The dung lay several inches deep, covering the whole extent of the roosting-place, like a bed of snow. Many trees two feet in diameter, I observed, were broken off at no great distance from the ground; and the branches of many of the largest and tallest had given way, as if the forest had been swept by a tornado. . . . The Pigeons, arriving by thousands, alighted everywhere, one above another, until solid masses as large as hogsheads were formed on the branches all around. Here and there the perches gave way under the weight with a crash, and, falling to the ground, destroyed hundreds of the birds beneath, . . .

Whether on the wintering grounds of southern states or nesting in the North, the great flocks required huge quantities of food within flying distance, which might be 50 miles (Schorger, 1955). A wide variety of tree fruits and berries were taken, but mainstays were the large mast crops of the forest, especially beech, oak, and chestnut. A visitation by millions of pigeons took the entire harvest and left little for squirrels, bears, deer, raccoons, and other wilderness mast-feeders.

Ecological effects of the passenger pigeon were drastic and often lasting (especially forest damage and overfertilization), but they were localized. The pigeons were sustained by the environment because of the erratic migration habits of the species. One-time (or perhaps periodic) concentrations occurred in a given area in response to temporarily favorable conditions (especially large food crops). Then the birds passed on, not to return in force for some years, during which the range recovered. Similar adaptations are seen in other gregarious species, notably the migratory barren-ground caribou in its use of the slow-growing lichen ranges of the Arctic (Darling, 1956).

A recognition of some of the more obvious animal influences on the North American environment in no way implies that they were unusual. In every natural community such relationships are prevalent, whether or not they are a part of our biological insight.

Fire

Of all the factors that disturb the earth's vegetation, fire is undoubtedly the one that has the greatest effect. It is the inevitable concomitant of xeric conditions, and hence is an important means by which plant communities are determined in dry climates. It is evident that the nature of soils is closely tied in with these processes, in terms of both soil development and the predisposition of sites to burning. Shantz (1954) noted that "The grasslands are of two types: (A) Those determined largely by climatic conditions and on pedocal soils, unleached and with dry subsoils, and (B) those which have replaced forests destroyed by cutting or by fire or both, or maintained against forest development by conditions favoring fire."

The American tall-grass "prairies" were an outstanding example of the latter type—a disturbance climax (disclimax of Weaver and Clements, 1938: 86 et seq.), or fire subclimax. After the introduction of heavy grazing by domestic livestock and the breaking of the prairies for farming, the extensive fires of early days were no longer possible. In the North an immediate result was widespread overgrowth of uncultivated tall-grass habitats by woodland (Gleason, 1913; McComb and Loomis, 1944; Curtis, 1959). In southern grasslands an evident trend was the thickening and spread of the mesquite savanna and other shrub types (Jackson, 1965; Lehmann, 1965; Box, 1967). Recognition of the close relationship of fire dynamics to many types of grassland is now quite general; Sauer (1950) goes so far as to say, "Suppression of fire results in gradual recolonization by woody species in every grassland known to me. I know of no basis for a climatic grassland climax, but only of a fire grass 'climax' for soils permitting deep rooting."

In all regions of the United States where pines occur, fire plays a major role in the ecology of many species of *Pinus*, as well as certain other conifers (Hanson, 1939; Garren, 1943; Little, 1953; Biswell, 1963). The practical utility of such knowledge in producing timber crops is evidenced by the fact that on national forests of the southern region in 1963 the U.S. Forest Service carried out prescribed forest management burning on 316,658 acres. In Florida burning can be controlled on some half million acres, of which an average of 83,000 acres a year are so treated (Riebold, 1964).

Through eons of evolution, fire has played its part in the speciation of many kinds of plants and animals and in the development of biotic communities. As Komarek remarked (1964):

The antiquity of fire seems apparent in that the most ancient of tree families, such as the conifers, and the apparently oldest genera of grasses, such as *Aristida, Stipa, Andropogon*, etc., have the greatest concentration of those genes responsible for resistance and adjustment to a "fire environment." In fact, it appears that during long periods of time fire type communities of plants and animals have covered vast areas of the earth's land surface.

While this factor must have been ever-present in dry climates, it is likewise influential in areas of light soil and other xeric sites in temperate and relatively moist climates. For fires to be effective in shaping the composition and aspection of vegetation, periodic dry summers may be sufficient to inhibit the growth of thicket-forming deciduous woody plants and to promote the spread of forbs, grasses, and fire-resistant trees, many of which are characteristically thick-barked.

The ecological effects of fire have been categorized by Hanson (1939) as follows:

1. Burning causes partial or complete destruction of plant and animal life, as well as dead vegetation cover.
2. Burning causes modification of atmospheric factors; light, wind, precipitation (rainfall interception).

3. Direct effect of the temperature of the fire, upon the soil, as organic and mineral contents, structure, texture, animal and plant life in the soil.

4. Effect of destruction of plant cover upon consequent soil moisture, wind and water erosion, mineral content, biotic processes in soil, pH, etc.

5. Effect of fire upon consequent plant and animal succession, relation of fire to aiding establishment of early invaders as Lodgepole pine.

6. Effect of subterranean fires upon rock formation and topography.

Lightning strikes, especially on trees or stubs, undoubtedly were a common natural cause of fires. Hanson cites sources indicating that lightning caused 41 percent of fires on and adjacent to California forests (obviously in a period when fires of human origin also were prevalent) and about 8 percent of forest fires in the nation as a whole. In his revealing study of "the natural history of lightning," Komarek (1964) demonstrated that this factor is so effective and widespread that the presence of burnable material is the only requisite for producing fires frequently enough "to have lasting effect on plant and animal communities." There can be little doubt that these effects did accumulate to a highly significant degree over large areas before the coming of men to this continent.

An appraisal of early human influences on the biota of North America must necessarily give further emphasis to the subject of fire. While the Paleo-Indians may well have had a hand directly in the disappearance of large mammals, their most far-reaching cultural impacts undoubtedly were exerted through habitat change. The great significance of burning by primitive man was described by Martin (1958):

For the ecologist and biogeographer one point remains clear. From the time of man's arrival we may assume a radical change in fire frequency. In the strict sense, theoretical climatic climax vegetation in savanna and grassland areas . . . and even in parts of the Eastern Deciduous Forest, cannot postdate man's arrival. In addition to savannas many areas of temperate forest may have been greatly modified and subclimax, consolidation, or even pioneer species favored at the expense of those typical only of climax positions in plant succession.

The antiquity of the human species in North America needs no particular discussion here (see summary by Griffin, 1967). Firm evidence supports the presence of man on this continent for the last 15,000 years, a period that began more recently than the time of maximum Wisconsin glaciation, which was about 18,000 years ago. Thus, many millenia passed during which plant-animal communities reached dynamic adjustment to intensified regimes of burning as a result of the human factor.

In an incomplete review of this subject, Stewart (1951) found "more than 200 references to Indians setting fire to vegetation in aboriginal times, and these references cover all major geographic and cultural areas." Wherever plant cover would burn, it was burned repeatedly as a part of the cultural way of life. Some of the beneficial effects probably were evident. Fires opened up thick growth where game might be hunted more easily. They brought about early green-up and improved grazing on the prairie, making areas near villages more attractive to buffalo. Fires also were the means of producing large berry crops in some situations, and they helped abate the mosquito nuisance in others. Scientific study now shows that after fires certain kinds of vegetation are more succulent and palatable, and higher in protein content, providing immediate benefits to browsing and grazing animals (Aldous, 1934; Lay, 1957).

Basic changes brought about by repeated burning and resulting in the establishment and maintenance of fire disclimax communities have been described by Sauer (1956):

Pyrophytes include woody monocotyledons, such as palms, which do not depend on a vulnerable cambium tissue, trees insulated by thick corky bark, trees and shrubs able to reproduce by sprouting, and plants with thick, hard-shelled seeds aided in germination by heat. Loss of organic matter on and in the soil may shift advantage to forms that germinate well in mineral soils, as the numerous conifers. Precocity is advantageous. The assemblages consequent upon fires are usually characterized by a reduced number of species, even by the dominance of few and single species. Minor elements in a natural flora, originally mainly confined to accidentally disturbed and exposed situations, such as windfalls and eroding slopes, have opened to them by recurrent burning the chance to spread and multiply. In most cases the shift is from mesophytic to less exacting, more xeric, forms, to those that do not require ample soil moisture and can tolerate at all times full exposure to the sun. In the long run the scales are tipped against the great, slowly maturing plants—the trees (a park land of mature trees may be the last stand of what was a complete woodland). Our eastern woodlands, at the time of white settlement, seem largely to have been in process of change to park lands.

As noted previously, changes of this nature over large areas had given character to the vegetation and animal life long before the advent of man on the American scene. The human influence was one of intensification. At all levels of culture man depends largely on early ecological successions. With the passage of time he not only adapted to regional habitats of the continent; he also made large-scale environmental changes that, at least in some cases, helped to serve his needs.

Influences of Indian Agriculture

Current archaeological concepts of cultural development among North American Paleo-Indians presume that the early hunting way of life, featuring fluted projectile points, gave way to a broader, preceramic, food-gathering trapping and hunting industry, the "Archaic." The transition probably took place from about 9000 to 6000 B.C. (Griffin, 1967). The Late Archaic, roughly 4000 to 1000 B.C., was a time of population buildup. Both along the coasts and inland, the gathering of a wide variety of mollusks for food left extensive shell middens. During this period copper came into use for weapons, tools, and ornaments, and the earliest pottery appeared.

The long-continued elaboration of food-gathering skills and environmental adaptation is indicated in Yarnell's (1964) compilation of records for the Upper Great Lakes region showing use by Indians of at least 373 native plants for some 560 purposes. Both hunting and gathering continued as part of the cultural complex in eastern North America after the introduction of agriculture about 1000 B.C. Griffin (1967) remarked that "the major impetus for agricultural development is clearly from Mexico, where agriculture already had had a long history."

Indian agriculture had particular biotic significance in the deciduous forest region of the East as a disturbance factor supplementing the widespread effects of fire. The principal crops were corn, beans, squash, pumpkins, gourds, and sunflower. Cropping was accomplished by hoeing and hilling in forest deadenings (which eventually became cleared land) created by girdling trees and burning. The agricultural period in this region was coincident with extensive mound building, an activity that reached its highest development between 100 B.C. and 300 A.D. (Griffin, 1967).

European explorers and settlers of the fifteenth century saw relatively little of the original agricultural development in eastern North America. At the time of the voyages of Columbus and immediately thereafter, introduced diseases spread rapidly among the Indians, who had minimal resistance to exotic pathogens (see Spinden, 1928; Ashburn, 1947). As Day (1953) said, "We shall never know the population of the northeastern tribes of the sixteenth century, because the white man's acquaintance with them was preceded by his diseases and his disruption of the primitive economic patterns. . . ." The process of decimation continued into historic times. Swanton (1952) cites many examples of the devastation wrought upon various tribes by smallpox and other diseases pandemic among Caucasians.

In many areas regrowth of the forest for one to two centuries had largely obscured the prehistoric openings (commonly on floodplains and river terraces) before the period of active settlement in the seventeenth and eighteenth centuries. This obviously was the situation in the regions of mound building in Ohio and Missouri. Yet remaining clearings and agricultural activity of the Indians were impressive to those who described early conditions in the historic period. When Thomas Hariot reported on several expeditions to Virginia under the direction of Sir Walter Raleigh in the 1580's, he described a great variety of both natural and agricultural foods of the natives. Accompanying Hariot's account published in London in 1588 were reproductions of on-the-scene paintings by John White. Some of these show clearings planted to agricultural crops on level lands adjoining stockaded Indian villages (Lorant, 1965).

Relative to the dependence of southeastern tribes on their cultivated crops, Swanton (1946: 256) stated that

As the harvest was seldom sufficient to last—nor was it expected to last—until another crop came in, the Indians were obliged to seek natural food supplies elsewhere and, since such supplies were not usually concentrated, this meant that the people themselves scattered about in camps where they remained until planting time. Along the coast food supplies were usually more plentiful, though the same scattering took place in search of favorite fishing grounds.

In 1773, William Bartram found extensive signs of agricultural clearings along the Altamaha River in Georgia, and, inadvertently perhaps, he described the old field plant successions that were taking them over: ". . . an ancient Indian field, verdured over with succulent grass, and chequered with coppices of fragrant shrubs . . . nearly encircled with an open forest of stately pines. . . ." And later, on lands once inhabited by the Creeks, he noted that "Their old fields and planting land extend up and down the river, fifteen or twenty miles from this [town] site" (Van Doren, 1928: 65).

Day (1953) explored the historical record in depth in appraising the influence of the Indian on northeastern forests. He concluded that fertile alluvial soils were widely used for growing maize and other crops. Clearings of the Iroquois and other tribes frequently aggregated hundreds, even thousands, of acres. Fuelwood demands near permanent villages occasioned extensive cutting, and the burning of flammable vegetation was a common practice in such environs.

On a canoe trip down the Shiawassee River in southern Michigan in 1837, Hubbard (1887) observed that

Many of the Indian clearings stretched for several continuous miles, and many acres bordering the river were covered with the luxuriant maize,—the chief cultivated food of the natives. These plantations receive the name of villages, because they are resorted to by the tribes at the periods of cultivation and harvest. But, in fact, these people had no fixed habitations, but wandered . . . from place to place, in patriarchal bands, finding such subsistence as the woods and waters afforded.

Hubbard said that little remained of original forest openings "characterized by a gravelly soil and a sparse growth of oaks and hickories" in the vicinity of Pontiac, Michigan. This was partly a result of recent cultivation and partly because of "the thick growth of small timber that has covered all the uncultivated portions since the annual fires have ceased, which kept down the underbrush."

Carrier (1923) called attention to the great value of old Indian clearings to the early colonists on the east coast. He suggested that it would have taken at least a generation of settlers to clear as much land as they found ready to use in some localities. "It was necessary for the colonists to produce food crops at once and they did not have the time to clear land before seeding." The fact that the Jamestown settlement did not have such openings available brought on the starvation conditions experienced there.

From the prairies westward the ecological effects of floodplain agriculture are difficult to appraise, since many sites could be used with a minimum of clearing, and population density in semi-arid lands must have been considerably less than in the east. Faunal relationships for the deciduous forest region seem fairly clear. A species like the heath hen depended for its existence on repeated burning in the coastal barrens from Maine to Virginia. The bobwhite quail undoubtedly extended its range wherever openings were created in the forest, and it throve on the seed-bearing herbs and brushy fringes of cultivated areas. Wherever the Indian abandoned his fields or was wiped out by disaster, the invading vegetation went through a stage highly productive of ruffed grouse, rabbits, and deer, and the openings fitted nicely into the life pattern of the wild turkey. These situations likewise supported the increase of such species as the fox squirrel, woodchuck, red fox, prairie deermouse, and crow. They were unfavorable to such woodland species as the gray squirrel, gray fox, and raven.

It is likely that the progressive breaking and thinning of forested areas from the prairies eastward largely accounts for the presence of bison as far east as Pennsylvania and Georgia. The same conditions favored elk; and large predators, notably the wolf and panther, would follow their prey in numbers and distribution.

In summary, pre-Columbian environments in the eastern half of North America were characterized by great variety in vegetation patterns and a correspondingly wide distribution of wildlife species depending on edges and subseral stages of vegetation. During two centuries after the discovery of the New World, the general decline of the aboriginal population greatly reduced human activity as a disturbance factor.* In many humid areas the forest overgrew former agricultural openings, although xeric sites continued to support fires of both natural and human origin. Early observers could not be expected to interpret the dynamics of what they saw. Nor did they often record the most significant facts about what they—like many people today— regarded as the chaos of nature. The biology of early conditions must be pieced together largely by analogy with what has been learned since 1920.

EXPLORATION AND SETTLEMENT

Early expeditions of the Spanish, French, and English to the coast of Florida and northward in the 1500's demonstrated the ineptitude of Europeans at subsisting in the American wilderness. Dependence on the Indians or on ocean transport for supplies, and resulting frequent starvation, vastly complicated the occupation of a new continent—an enterprise already in jeopardy from international rivalry and conflict (Parkman, 1895; Lorant, 1965). The first exploratory efforts were motivated by the quest for plunder and riches, but the real wealth of America was manifest to many observers, whose extravagant accounts of a heavily fruited land, rivers full of fish, rich soils, and abounding animal life led to successful colonization during the 1600's. Thereafter, however, for some 200 years the penetration of the continent was stimulated primarily by the lure of peltries, principally beaver, for which the European market was good.

The Fur Trade

The initial way to the interior was a canoe route pioneered by French traders and Jesuits via the St. Lawrence system to the Great Lakes and

---

*Referring to early historic times and population estimates of Indians by Mooney (1928), Spinden (1928) noted that the eastern agricultural area of about 1,375,000 square miles supported about 1 person to 4 square miles. In 1928 this same area was inhabited by about 90 million people—more than 65 per square mile.

the Mississippi. The official policy of the Court was to gain accessions to the Empire through granting exploitation rights, a device most profitable for France in the case of LaSalle. The first sailing ship on the Great Lakes was LaSalle's *Griffin*, which disappeared with a cargo of furs on her maiden trip back from Green Bay in 1679. La Salle reached the mouth of the Mississippi and took possession of "Louisiana" 3 years later. Plagued by disaster and faithless associates, he perished in the wilds in 1687 (Parkman, 1894). His adventures were a loss to his backers, but the dubious French title to the vast and indefinite territory of Louisiana (assumed to extend northwestward to a region called Oregon) played a key role in developments leading to the opening and occupation of the western half of the United States.

Since the English Crown had made large land grants beyond the Appalachians, there ensued decades of skirmishing and finally war with the French. Near the end of the French and Indian War (1762), with the complete loss of frontier holdings in prospect, Louis XV conveyed title to lands west of the Mississippi to Spain. The next 39 years saw a reversal of fortunes, and Spain returned Louisiana to France under Napoleon in 1800. Three years later President Jefferson purchased the Territory on behalf of his rising young nation, which by that time had occupied nearly all the area east of the Mississippi (Landstrom, 1958).

There followed the classic expedition from St. Louis to the mouth of the Columbia, carried out under the orders of Jefferson by Meriwether Lewis and William Clark from 1804 to 1806. Primary aims were the opening of travel routes and an assessment of resources; immediate interest centered on exploitation of the widely distributed and plentiful beaver (Thwaites, 1904). However, there were other motives for, and other important results of, this venture into largely unknown country.

Chief among these were scientific observations and the collection of specimens. Many specimens were lost or destroyed, but the journals of the expedition provided a wealth of new information on the fauna and flora of the region of the Upper Missouri and westward to the Pacific. Through this work the world was first reliably introduced to the grizzly bear, various races of black-tailed and white-tailed deer, kit fox, prairie dog, white-tailed jackrabbit, white-fronted goose, sage grouse, great gray owl, blue-backed salmon, and the prairie rattlesnake. The original observations on these and other fauna of the region have been extracted, classified, and indexed and are now generally available for scientific use (Burroughs, 1961).

The Lewis and Clark epic constituted the first contribution of the new government in the field of natural history and biological survey. It was likewise unique in that an officially conceived and supported exploration actually led the way into lands hitherto unknown. That this was not the usual pattern and, in particular, was not to be the case in most of the West has been emphasized by Chittenden (1935, vol. I:x):

It was the roving trader and the solitary trapper who first sought out these inhospitable wilds, traced the streams to their sources, scaled the mountain passes, and explored a boundless expanse of territory where the foot of the white man had never trodden before. The Far West became a field of romantic adventure, and developed a class of men who loved the wandering career of the native inhabitant [i.e., the Indian] rather than the toilsome lot of the industrious colonist. The type of life thus developed, though essentially evanescent, and not representing any profound national movement, was a distinct and necessary phase in the growth of this new country.

For about 40 years after Lewis and Clark the popularity of beaver hats in Britain and Europe would be the economic spur to western exploration. It was the most colorful period of American history, featuring the mountain fur trapper—lawless, incredibly durable, short-lived— a character whose ability to live off the land became legend. The fur companies, competing on every front, invested their capital, organized expeditions, built remote trading posts, held their mountain rendezvous, negotiated with the Indians, and sent down the waterways to St. Louis their annual cargoes of wilderness wealth (Chittenden, 1935).

The market was not to last, nor did the beaver in many areas. By midcentury, silk from the Orient had come into vogue as hat material and took the place of felt. On the frontier, as finer furs lost value, a trade in buffalo robes was picking up.

Westward Expansion

Now there were well-marked trails to lead settlers into the West—stockmen, farmers, speculators who would filter into every fertile valley and stake their claims on irrigation water, grazing ranges, forests, and mining lands. Railways were built across the great grassland in the 1860's, which made possible the wiping out of millions of buffalo and the eventual subjugation of the plains Indians.

In the United States, for the most part east of the Great Plains, the population was more than 23 million by 1850. By 1880 the cattle industry was taking over the central grasslands vacated by the buffalo and Indians, and population buildup westward was rapid. At that time more than 70 percent of Americans were living in rural communities. This percentage declined to 54.2 in 1910 and 48.6 in 1920, as the population passed 105 million (Edwards, 1940).

Changes on the Land

Under many types of grants and incentives, the private occupation, breaking, and clearing of huge areas had gone forward (Edwards, 1940):

It was practically impossible to have foretold in 1860 that within 30 years a half billion acres of the public domain would have been disposed of or reserved for governmental purposes. The land was considered valueless unless it was put under cultivation as rapidly as possible, and the various land acts did help to people the wilderness. To have opposed unregulated settlement would have been considered either a mad perversion or a reflection of selfish economic interest.

This was the period of heedless wiping out of wildlife and wastage of forest resources that gave rise to new and more conservative trends of thinking. The conservation movement became recognizable during the Cleveland administration when land policies were revised (1891) to abate flagrant abuses and Congress first authorized the reservation of forested areas of the public domain for public purposes. The idea of using resources "for the greatest good of the greatest number" received its greatest stimulus under Pinchot and Roosevelt.

The industrialization, mechanization, and specialization of American agriculture came rapidly after the Civil War, and the permanent land-use pattern was well established by the turn of the century. Potentially, nearly a third of the land area of the 48 contiguous states (about 600 million acres) is suited to some kind of agricultural cropping, but only about 400 million acres is actually so used (Barnes and Marschner, 1958). The widespread conversion of primitive habitats has posed the great problems, as well as many of the opportunities, in wildlife management.

Lands primarily adapted to forestry have likewise undergone extensive change. Abounding abuses in the timberlands of the nation received initial federal recognition in 1876 with the appointment in the Department of Agriculture of an agent to study forest problems. This step led to creation of the Division of Forestry in 1881 and the Forest Service in 1905. By the end of the Roosevelt administration in 1908, some 148 million acres had been reserved for national watershed and timber protection purposes.

By that time the great bulk of virgin forests in the East and Midwest had been cut, and loggers were moving into the South.

Vast areas had been converted to fire-ravaged barrens, scrub timber, and brush growth. As state and federal forestry programs expanded and became more professional, the cutovers were brought under protection and management. New crops of timber began to grow.

Effects on Wildlife

By the early 1900's, faunal conditions in much of North America bore little resemblance to the communities of early times. What may be termed "wilderness wildlife" had been greatly reduced. The panther, wolf, elk, and wild turkey were largely gone from the eastern United States, and the grizzly, antelope, and mountain sheep were disappearing in the West. Deer, beaver, black bear, and many lesser species had become locally or regionally scarce or absent. In part, this was due to lack of adequate protection, as well as to widespread changes in habitat.

In contrast, some species of birds and mammals obviously throve on the land-use changes and came to be known as farm wildlife. Bobwhite quail, cottontail rabbits, and the edge-inhabiting fox squirrel spread widely in the region formerly occupied by extensive hardwood forests. In the rail-fence era of generalized farming, they became the wildlife symbols of rural America. Other familiar creatures, including the woodchuck, prairie deermouse, field sparrow, meadowlark, and killdeer, extended their ranges into regions of new cropfields. Over the Midwest, the raven, gray squirrel (especially the black phase), and gray fox were reduced in number with the forests, while the crow, fox squirrel, and red fox increased with the openings. Commonly it was said that one creature "drove out" another. There was a general extension northward of the range of the opossum.

Effective control of forest fires became a reality in the second and third decades of the century. During this period many states were establishing agencies to administer and manage their woodlands, waters, and wildlife. In 1918 responsibility for migratory birds was assumed by the federal government, and resident wildlife came under increasingly efficient regulation by the states. As new brush-stage forests developed, whitetail deer spread northward into the Lake States and Canadian border country where moose and caribou had been the principal big game. Deer herds reached their maximum in Pennsylvania and Michigan during the thirties, and a decade later it was evident that western mule-deer and blacktails were on the increase.

Upland game birds were prominent in reflecting the changes in vegetation. When forests of northern Wisconsin and Michigan gave way to grassy burns and brushlands, the prairie chicken and sharptailed grouse spread eastward beyond Sault Ste. Marie and the Straits of Mackinac

(Schorger, 1944; Ammann, 1957). Conversely, by midcentury, with the planting of openings and regrowth of timber stands, these prairie grouse were on the decline in Michigan's Upper Peninsula. From coast to coast across the North, and southward in both eastern and western mountains, ruffed grouse spread and multiplied in the vigorous growth of cutovers, old fields, and edges. Western blue grouse responded similarly. In the central hardwoods of the East, restocking of ruffed grouse and eastern turkeys (and also deer) helped to re-establish these species where they were wiped out early in the century. In the Southwest, the Merriam and Rio Grande turkeys returned to brushlands where they had long been absent.

The development of early-stage forests was an extremely favorable condition for beavers, and they were widely restored in the thirties and forties—to the point of becoming a nuisance as they moved into agricultural areas. Largely after 1940, a general increase and spread of carnivores occurred in the eastern United States. Black bears became abundant from the Deep South to Canada. Coyotes extended their range through woodlands and semiwild country to the east coast, and raccoons and foxes increased in numbers beyond anything previously observed. The extent to which this carnivore prosperity may be attributed to habitat changes, as against long-term trends of obscure origin, is by no means certain.

These discussions have centered on striking examples of faunal change following the extensive alteration of North America as a wildlife environment. In actuality, practically the entire biota of the continent was affected and is being affected further as human populations build up. A relatively recent factor in the situation is the conscious effort toward wildlife habitat management that has developed since the mid-thirties.

LAND-USE PLANNING

The "redoing" of the American landscape has largely been a history of opportunism and short-term self-interest on the part of individuals and short-term expediency on the part of government. No doubt, extensive trial and error alone would eventually bring about a durable and productive use pattern for the various regions. This was the manner in which early crop specialization developed. But errors are costly, and obviously a better approach utilizes the application of science and technology. Edwards (1940) noted that the "agricultural revolution" was accompanied by a quickening of the tendency for certain agricultural crops and commodities to dominate in the regions naturally suited to their production. In its Yearbooks for 1921 through 1925 the Department of Agriculture provided a notable series of articles which include historical descriptions, both textual and graphic, of the westward movement and current location of the agricultural crops and products of the United States.

Our commonest miscalculation has always been to overuse the land, especially during intervals of exceptionally favorable weather. Even the disastrous drought years of the thirties did not result in complete adjustment of cropping demands to soil-climate limitations. Chepil (1957) described the situation 20 years later:

Large acreages suited only to permanent grass or forests are still devoted to cultivated crops. In the Great Plains alone about 14 million acres not suited for permanent cultivation were cultivated in 1955. Much of this land offers low returns and is subject to severe erosion even in average years.

The overuse momentum of the last century was widely evident as farmers attempted to cultivate areas cleared by lumbering and fires. The most knowledgeable agriculturists recognized the quality difference between "pine land" and "hardwood land." But pioneer settlers commonly had little familiarity with the soil they wished to till, and their only sources of guidance were the representations of speculators or state land agents. In the three upper Lake States—Michigan, Wisconsin, and Minnesota—more than 38 million acres of the public domain were granted to the states (Lee and Wooten, 1958), and "these States quickly disposed of the land in order to get settlers on the land and to get cash for public improvements."

Many a homestead was hewn out of the forest edge where, in a later generation, crumbling buildings would bear witness to the tragedy of misled optimism. Through tax reversions, "The Lake States began to see much land moving back into State ownership in the 1920's. They suddenly became the unwilling owners of millions of acres of cutover land and abandoned farms because the private owners could no longer make a living . . ." (Lee and Wooten, 1958).

The almost universal tendency toward overgrazing by the world's nonnomadic pastoralists has been discussed by Darling (1956). The market-grazing economy on western ranges is a convincing example. When, in 1936, Secretary of Agriculture Wallace sent to the President a report on the first comprehensive study of public and private grazing lands (U.S. Forest Service, 1936), he commented that "the general public knows less of the range resource, and as a result has been and is less concerned about its condition and conservation, than any of our other important natural resources." The report noted that nearly 40 percent of the land area of the 48 states is available for livestock grazing, about half being privately owned. Through neglect and overstocking, "Range depletion on the public domain and grazing districts averages 67 percent, on private, Indian, and State and county lands about half, and on national forests about 30 percent." Passage of the Taylor Grazing Act in 1934, followed by this historic Forest Service report, initiated a new era in which better practices gradually became established.

As the errors of guesswork became manifest and studies of soil and its cover made headway, it became clear that farsighted government action would be necessary to avoid the continuation of economic and social disruption through unwise land use. In the ultimate resolution of factors, a durable husbandry must demand only the kind and quantity of products that can be yielded in perpetuity. As Shantz (1954) stated the case:

Ecology should establish the proper balance of priorities of production. This planning should be based on the natural resource of climate, topography, soil, plant cover, animal population, and finally on the needs of the dependent human society. . . . Few lands can be given over to a single crop or to local or temporary needs.

In many states the need was recognized for determining the production potential of lands and the reorientation of uses. Land economics surveys were carried out and in some cases zoning regulations were adopted (see Smith, 1926). By 1948, 34 states had enabling legislation on zoning, and in eight states there were counties with specific rural zoning restrictions. Among leading states in this field, Wisconsin used zoning ordinances in combination with the State Forest Crop Law to close some 5 million acres of forest land to agricultural development (Ruess et al., 1948). The limited-use capability of certain sites and soils was the basis for allocating them to extensive, as opposed to intensive, cropping. On new land-utilization maps these submarginal tracts were assigned to forestry and recreation. Many such lands would be incorporated into fish and wildlife restoration areas, especially under programs spurred by the availability of federal aid funds provided in acts of 1937 and 1950.

Largely in response to destructive cutting, forest fires, and the tax reversion process, New York's justly famous Forest Preserve was established by an act of 1885, the provisions of which became a part of the state constitution (Lee and Wooten, 1958). The Adirondack and

Catskill Forest Preserve, nearly 2.5 million acres, was placed in protective custody of the state for public uses and ". . . shall be forever kept as wild forest lands. They shall not be leased, sold, or exchanged, or be taken by any corporation, public or private, nor shall the timber thereon be sold, removed or destroyed. . . ." The primary benefits from this area were to be watershed protection and recreation—certainly a conservative appraisal of land-use capability.

As noted by Marsh and Gibbons (1940), millions of acres of former cropland were so extensively damaged by erosion as to be submarginal for agriculture. "On much of this the forest is creeping back. Some day these lands may again be needed for cultivation; meanwhile, there may be no better or cheaper means for rebuilding them than restoration to forests."

The long-term hazards of grain farming on what had been the central grasslands were evident in the dry thirties, and Thornthwaite (1941) summarized concepts strongly conditioned by the immediate past:

In a semiarid climate like that of the Great Plains, wide climatic fluctuations are to be expected. Although it is not yet possible to forecast a specific drought year, it is possible to determine drought frequency and the probability of its occurrence. A stable economy can be achieved only if agriculture is adapted to the entire range of climatic conditions. This would necessitate returning to a grazing economy, in which pasturing of cattle on the natural and restored range is supplemented by the production of forage and feed crops in areas where flood irrigation is possible, and elsewhere in the rainy years on soils that are resistant to deterioration by wind and water. Such a change in land use requires an increase in the size of farms to a point where cultivation and grazing can both be controlled.

It is well known that the most extensive and thorough application of land-use capability principles has been by the Soil Conservation Service. At the inception of this program in 1933, it was evident that there must be a systematic and objective basis for appraising sites of different potential on the same cropping unit. This realization led to the development of eight capability classes (Hockensmith and Steele, 1943) by means of which a land-use plan of the farm could be drawn. The significance of this approach in the management of wildlife is discussed in Chapter 4.

It is inherent in such a system that the most intensive management a site can sustain (for a yield of plant and animal products) should be determined scientifically on a basis of soil, topography, and climate. The individual operator cannot do this for himself, so it becomes a function of public programs where, logically, ultimate public welfare is an important frame of reference. In the final analysis, considerations of demand and marketability are involved, and the question of what an area *can* produce becomes one of what it *should* produce. In this connection the influences of a growing population and a changing technology pose problems with which we shall be particularly concerned in chapters to follow.

BIOLOGICAL INTERPRETATION OF HISTORY

The history of our land and wildlife, interpreted in the context of modern ecological knowledge, is a study of "management experiments" on a vast scale. Unfortunately, there were no controls, and often the records are poor. Conclusions must be regarded in some degree as provisional.

There can be no doubt, however, concerning the key role played by vegetation in determining the nature of animal communities and the density of populations. We may accept it as elementary in wildlife management that a desired species must be produced by first understanding its place in the succession of communities and then finding the means of renewing, through effective and practicable kinds of "disturbance," the conditions in which it lives. Every environmental change must be viewed as a balance of values, for the processes that wipe out one organism may well benefit another. As Marsh (1864) said, ". . . in the husbandry of Nature there are no fallows."

Wildlife management of the past was extensive and largely fortuitous. Now, and in time to come, for the service of vastly more people, it must be intensive and purposeful. Opportunities for the kinds of recreation that depend on privacy are being diminished at the source. Somewhere a balance of values must be struck as we fashion our way of life for the future. In this endeavor it is a major asset to have a correct appraisal of what has happened in the past.

REFERENCES

Aldous, A. E. 1934. Effects of burning on Kansas bluestem pastures. Kan. Agr. Exp. Sta. Tech. Bull. 38.

Ammann, G. A. 1957. The prairie grouse of Michigan. Mich. Dep. Conserv. Game Div. 200 p.

Ashburn, P. M. 1947. The ranks of death: a medical history of the conquest of America. Coward-McCann, New York. 298 p.

Barnes, C. P., and F. J. Marschner. 1958. Our wealth of land resources. p. 10-18, *In* Land. The yearbook of agriculture 1958. U.S. Department of Agriculture. U.S. Government Printing Office, Washington, D.C.

Biswell, H. H. 1963. Research in wildland fire ecology in California. Tall Timbers Fire Ecol. Conf. Proc., 2d Annu. Conf.

Bond, R. M. 1945. Range rodents and plant succession. 10th N. Amer. Wildl. Conf. Trans.

Box, T. W. 1967. Brush, fire, and west Texas rangeland. Tall Timbers Fire Ecol. Conf. Proc., 6th Annu. Conf.

Burroughs, R. D. 1961. The natural history of the Lewis and Clark Expedition. Michigan State University Press, East Lansing.

Carrier, L. 1923. The beginnings of agriculture in America. McGraw-Hill Book Co., New York. 323 p.

Chepil, W. S. 1957. Erosion of soil by wind, p. 308-314. *In* Soil. The yearbook of agriculture 1957. U.S. Department of Agriculture. U.S. Government Printing Office, Washington, D.C.

Chittenden, H. M. 1935. The American fur trade of the far west. Barnes & Noble, New York. 2 vol.

Clements, F. E. 1936. Nature and structure of the climax. J. Ecol. 24:252-284.

Clements, F. E., and V. E. Shelford. 1939. Bio-ecology. John Wiley & Sons, New York. 425 p.

Curtis, J. T. 1959. The vegetation of Wisconsin. University of Wisconsin Press, Madison. 657 p.

Dansereau, P. 1957. Biogeography: an ecological perspective. Ronald Press, New York. 394 p.

Darling, F. F. 1956. Man's ecological dominance through domesticated animals on wild lands, p. 778-787. *In* W. L. Thomas (ed.) Man's role in changing the face of the earth. University of Chicago Press, Chicago.

Day, G. M. 1953. The Indian as an ecological factor in the northeastern forest. Ecology 34(2):329-346.

Deevey, E. S. 1949. Biogeography of the pleistocene (Part 1: Europe and North America). Geol. Soc. Amer. Bull. 60:1315-1416.

Deevey, E. S., and R. F. Flint. 1957. Postglacial hypsithermal interval. Science 125:182-184.

Dice, L. R. 1943. The biotic provinces of North America. University of Michigan Press, Ann Arbor. 78 p.

Edminster, F. C. 1954. American game birds. C. Scribner's Sons, New York. 590 p.

Edwards, E. E. 1940. American agriculture—the first 300 years, p. 171-276. *In* Farmers in a changing world. The yearbook of agriculture 1940. U.S. Department of Agriculture. U.S. Government Printing Office, Washington, D.C.

Flint, R. F. 1957. Glacial and pleistocene geology. John Wiley & Sons, New York. 553 p.

Garren, K. H. 1943. Effects of fire on the vegetation of the southeastern U.S. Bot. Rev. 9:617-654.

Gleason, H. A. 1913. Relation of forest distribution and prairie fires in the middle west. Torreya 13:173-181.

Gleason, H. A. 1922. The vegetational history of the Middle West. Ass. Amer. Geogr. Annu. 12:39-85.

Griffin, J. B. 1967. Eastern North American archaeology: a summary. Science 156:175-191.

Grinnell, J. 1923. The burrowing rodents of California as agents in soil formation. J. Mamm. 4:137-149.

Gross, A. O. 1928. The heath hen. Boston Soc. Natur. Hist. Memoirs 6(4):491-588.

Hanson, H. C. 1939. Fire in land use and management. Amer. Midl. Nat. 21:415-434.

Hockensmith, R. D., and J. G. Steele. 1943. Classifying land for conservation farming. U.S. Dep. Agr. Farmers' Bull. 1853.

Holdridge, L. R. 1947. Determination of world plant formations from simple climatic data. Science 105:367-368.

Hubbard, B. 1887. Memorials of a half-century. G. P. Putnam, New York. 581 p.

Jackson, A. S. 1965. Wildfires in the Great Plains grassland. Tall Timbers Fire Ecol. Conf. Proc., 4th Annu. Conf.

Koford, C. B. 1958. Prairie dogs, whitefaces, and blue grama. J. Wildl. Manage. 3:78.

Komarek, E. V. 1964. The natural history of lightning. Tall Timbers Fire Ecol. Conf. Proc., 3d Annu. Conf.

Küchler, A. W. 1964. Potential natural vegetation of the coterminous U.S. Amer. Geogr. Soc. Spec. Publ. 36. 116 p.

Landstrom, K. L. 1958. How we acquired our landed estate, p. 19-27. *In* Land. The yearbook of agriculture 1958. U.S. Department of Agriculture. U.S. Government Printing Office, Washington, D.C.

Larson, F. 1940. The role of bison in maintaining the short grass plains. Ecology 21(2):113-121.

Lay, D. W. 1957. Browse quality and the effects of prescribed burning in southern pine forests. J. Forestry 55(5):342-347.

Lee, A. T. M., and H. H. Wooten. 1958. The management of state lands, p. 72-86. *In* Land. The yearbook of agriculture 1958. U.S. Department of Agriculture. U.S. Government Printing Office, Washington, D.C.

Lehmann, V. W. 1965. Fire in the range of Attwater's prairie chicken. Tall Timbers Fire Ecol. Conf. Proc., 4th Annu. Conf.

Leopold, A. S., and F. F. Darling. 1953. Wildlife in Alaska. Ronald Press, New York, 129 p.

Little, S., Jr. 1953. Prescribed burning as a tool of forest management in the Northeastern states. J. Forestry 51(7):496-500.

Lorant, S. (ed.). 1965. The new world; the first pictures of America. Duell, Sloan & Pearce, New York. 292 p.

McComb, A. L., and W. E. Loomis. 1944. Subclimax prairie. Torrey Bot. Club Bull. 71:46-76.

Marsh, G. P. 1864. Man and nature: physical geography as modified by human action. C. Scribner's, New York. 560 p.

Marsh, R. E., and W. H. Gibbons. 1940. Forest-resource conservation, p. 458-488. *In* Farmers in a changing world. The yearbook of agriculture 1940. U.S. Department of Agriculture. U.S. Government Printing Office, Washington, D.C.

Martin, P. S. 1958. Pleistocene ecology and biogeography of North America, p. 375-420. *In* C. Hubbs (ed.). Zoogeography. Amer. Ass. Advan. Sci. Publ. 51. Washington, D.C.

Martin, P. S. 1963. The last 10,000 years. University of Arizona Press, Tucson. 87 p.

Martin, P. S. 1967. Pleistocene overkill. Natur. Hist. 76(10):32-38.

Merriam, C. H. 1898. Life zones and crop zones of the U.S. Bur. Biol. Surv. Bull. 10. 79 p.

Mershon, W. B. 1907. The passenger pigeon. Outing Publ. Co., New York. 225 p.

Mooney, J. 1928. The aboriginal population of America north of Mexico. Smithsonian Misc. Coll. 80(7). 40 p.

Müller-Beck, H. 1966. Paleohunters in America: origins and diffusion. Science 152(3726):1191-1209.

Parkman, F. 1894. LaSalle and the discovery of the Great West. Little, Brown & Co., Boston. 483 p.

Parkman, F. 1895. Pioneers of France in the new world. Little, Brown & Co., Boston. 473 p.

Riebold, R. J. 1964. Large-scale prescribed burning. Tall Timbers Fire Ecol. Conf. Proc., 3d Annu. Conf.

Roe, F. G. 1951. The North American buffalo. University of Toronto Press, Ontario, Canada. 957 p.

Ruess, L. A., H. H. Wooten, and F. J. Marschner. 1948. Inventory of major land uses, United States. U.S. Dep. Agr. Misc. Publ. 663. U.S. Government Printing Office, Washington, D.C. 89 p.

Sauer, C. O. 1950. Grassland climax, fire, and man. J. Range Manage. 3(1):16-21.

Sauer, C. O. 1956. The agency of man on the earth, p. 49-69. In W. L. Thomas (ed.), Man's role in changing the face of the earth. University of Chicago Press, Chicago.

Schorger, A. W. 1944. The prairie chicken and sharp-tailed grouse in early Wisconsin. Wis. Acad. Sci. Trans. 35:1-59.

Schorger, A. W. 1955. The passenger pigeon: its natural history and extinction. University of Wisconsin Press, Madison. 424 p.

Scott, W. E., and N. H. Hoveland. 1951. Report to the people of Wisconsin on cover destruction, habitat improvement and watershed problems of the state in 1950. Wis. Conserv. Bull. 16(2):3-77.

Sears, P. B. 1942. Xerothermic theory. Bot. Rev. 8(10):708-736.

Sears, P. B. 1948. Forest sequence and climatic change in northeastern North America since early Wisconsin time. Ecology 29:326-333.

Seton, E. T. 1929. Lives of game animals. Doubleday, Garden City, N.Y. 4 vol.

Shantz, H. L. 1954. The place of grasslands in the earth's cover of vegetation. Ecology 35(2):143-145.

Shelford, V. E. 1931. Some concepts of bioecology. Ecology 12:455-467.

Shelford, V. E. 1963. The ecology of North America. University of Illinois Press, Urbana. 610 p.

Smith, P. W. 1957. An analysis of post-Wisconsin biogeography of the prairie peninsula region based on distributional phenomena among terrestrial vertebrate populations. Ecology 38:205-218.

Smith, R. A. 1926. The land-economic survey in Michigan. Roosevelt Wildl. Bull. 3(4):679-692.

Spinden, H. J. 1928. The population of ancient America. Geogr. Rev. 18:641-660.

Stewart, O. C. 1951. Burning and natural vegetation in the United States. Geogr. Rev. 41:317-320.

Swanton, J. R. 1946. The Indians of southeastern United States. Bur. Amer. Ethnol. Bull. 137.

Swanton, J. R. 1952. The Indian tribes of North America. Bur. Amer. Ethnol. Bull. 145.

Tansley, A. G. 1935. The use and abuse of vegetational concepts and terms. Ecology 16(3):284-307.

Taylor, W. P. 1949. The biotic community concept as applied in historical geology. Tex. J. Sci. 1(1):34-40.

Thornthwaite, C. W. 1941. Climate and settlement in the Great Plains, p. 177-187. *In* Climate and man. The yearbook of agriculture 1941. U.S. Department of Agriculture. U.S. Government Printing Office, Washington, D.C.

Thwaites, R. G. 1904. The original journals of the Lewis and Clark expedition. Dodd, Mead & Co., New York.

Transeau, E. N. 1935. The prairie peninsula. Ecology 16(3):423-437.

U.S. Forest Service. 1936. The western range, p. 620. *In* Senate Doc. 199, 74th Congr., 2d Sess. U.S. Government Printing Office, Washington, D.C.

Van Doren, M. (ed.). 1928. The travels of William Bartram. Dover Publ., New York. 414 p.

Vestal, A. G. 1914. Internal relations of terrestrial associations. Amer. Natur. 48:413-445.

Weaver, J. E., and F. W. Albertson. 1956. Grasslands of the Great Plains. Johnson Publ. Co., Lincoln, Nebr. 395 p.

Weaver, J. E., and F. E. Clements. 1938. Plant ecology. McGraw-Hill Book Co., New York. 601 p.

Whittaker, R. H. 1953. A consideration of climax theory: the climax as a population and pattern. Ecology Monogr. 23:41-78.

Wormington, H. M. 1962. A survey of early American prehistory. Amer. Sci. 50(1):230-242.

Yarnell, A. R. 1964. Aboriginal relationships between culture and plant life in the Upper Great Lakes region. Univ. Mich. Mus. Anthrop. Pap. 23. 218 p.

CHAPTER 2

Wildlife Values in a Changing World

The question of how to use wildlife resources has many biological and economic facets, and ways of considering it are heavily influenced by tradition. Assumptions about the benefits of public management programs vary widely. At one extreme we have dollar-oriented standards that can become exploitive and shortsighted. At the opposite extreme are socially important esthetic values not easily measured or expressed. Some uses of wildlife are intensive and must be subject to control. Others are casual, nonconsumptive, and productive of mass benefits.

Management in the public interest must be based on an understanding of our long-term predispositions, changing social and environmental conditions, and the best possible appraisal of expectations for the future. This chapter reviews wildlife values as a means of defining realistic objectives for handling wildlife resources in the modern world.

HUMAN SUBSISTENCE BY GATHERING AND HUNTING

Wild plants and animals were the primordial food supply of mankind. Although omnivorous feeding permitted man to adapt to a wide range of habitats, the exploitation of indigenous foods by primitive methods must have required favorable conditions and relative abundance. Thus, some environments were habitable only seasonally and some not at all. Sauer (1947) stated:

As far as we know, men always preferred to form communities and were sedentary as their food supply permitted. We may judge that when skills were minimal the community usually was small. Except for rich collecting grounds on bays and estuaries, half a dozen or at most a dozen families could make full use of the food supply within convenient foraging distance.

Vicissitudes of the food-gathering life are evident in the account of Alvar Nunez, survivor of the Narvaez expedition, which met disaster on the coast of east Texas in 1528. Nunez spent 4 years among Indians of the coastal region and told of their expedients in living off the land (Hallenbeck, 1940). Some tribes moved to river mouths and fed on oysters 2 to 3 months in early spring. For about a month, blackberries were the principal dependence. Fish, occasional game animals, and various roots were eaten. At times, spiders, worms, lizards, salamanders, snakes, "even earth and wood" were the means of survival. Fruits of every kind were taken as they appeared, and in late summer there was a general movement to the prickly-pear (tuna) thickets. All tribes fed on the plentiful fruit and pads of this cactus until pecans ripened in the bottoms in fall. Beginning with groves near the sea, the nut harvest was taken progressively upstream during winter months. In some areas the beans of mesquite were an important staple.

In marginal habitats, primitive men have been characteristically few and frequently have lived a hand-to-mouth existence. Among early explorers of the Great Basin the low estate of the so-called Digger Indians (several tribes) was well known. They utilized a wide variety of roots, seeds, and small animals, including grasshoppers. Wissler (1940) remarked that "they deserve our respect, because they solved the problem of existence in such a forbidding environment, were too busy feeding themselves to engage in continual war and to conduct long, involved ceremonies."

When European adventurers came to North America in the 1500's, they soon learned that subsisting on the native fauna and flora could involve primitive skills of a high order. The newcomers were largely without the implements of their own civilization, and their pioneering arts were minimal. Too often the supplies from home did not arrive, and the beneficence of the Indians was uncertain—frequently with good reason (Lorant, 1965). In extensive wanderings through southeastern forests, plentifully supplied with game and other indigenous foods, DeSoto's numerous company drove before it a herd of hogs to furnish a part of its livelihood.

Graham (1947) noted that the English and Dutch colonists were commoners who knew little of hunting and fishing and could not take advantage of food supplies in the woodlands, streams, and coastal waters surrounding them.

Living off the land was more foreign to them than it is to most urban dwellers of America today. The time of the pioneer was yet to be, and living in the wilderness was something Americans had not accomplished. . . . With the help and example of the Indians and through perseverance and experience, the settlers did learn in time to adapt themselves to the new conditions. . . .

In testimony to the white man's capacity for learning, the hardy fur trappers of the early nineteenth century were more than a match for the Indian on his own ground. No more resourceful or capable men ever subsisted in the wilderness than the "mountain men" who explored the West for beaver and incidentally opened it for settlement.

MAN IN THE FOOD CHAIN

The most strategic situations for early man undoubtedly were those where he could live primarily as a carnivore. An abundant game supply appears almost invariably to have produced the cultural skills required for its exploitation. The highly developed hunting cultures that were dependent on the Pleistocene megafauna about 10,000 years ago were mentioned in Chapter 1. That stone-age men dealt effectively with every kind of big game, including mammoths and mastodons, is evident. Martin (1967) attributes the extinction of more than 100 species of large mammals during about 1,000 years to the predatory activities of late paleolithic hunters.

In places and times of abundance, the carnivorous habit supports a high standard of living. The ability of plains Indians to exploit the practically unlimited buffalo resource after obtaining horses in the 1700's is an outstanding example in North America (Ewers, 1955; Roe, 1955). However, the plant-animal biomass necessary to support a carnivore at the end of a relatively long food chain is necessarily much greater than the plant biomass from which a well-adapted herbivore can live. Sauer (1947: 25) commented on the change in diet at the primitive cultural level in these terms:

As in modern agriculture, so in early collecting, a shift from animal to plant food yielded more calories per unit of surface. As man became more vegetarian in habit, he could support larger numbers of his kind. Every increase in his skill of reducing forest area, of harvesting seed, of digging roots, of cooking, of storage, raised the ceiling of population for him and, in most instances, exerted selective pressure in favor of the plants most useful to himself.

It probably is a realistic view that men as hunters and food gatherers were skimming a thin cream off the more productive areas of the earth's surface. Within the limits of primitive capabilities, they adapted to certain environments that they were unable to change beneficially.

In the course of a long period in post-Pleistocene times, the harvest of certain wild food plants by the Indians became controlled husbandry and eventually developed into a specialized and highly successful agriculture (Carrier, 1923: 109). As mentioned previously, at the time of white settlement on the east coast, it was the adoption of both native methods and native plant resources that made existence possible for Europeans in the New World. The hill culture of corn and other crops was peculiar to this continent and became the foundation for many American agronomic practices. The extent of our modern dependence on this aboriginal foundation was described by Edwards (1940: 174):

... the economic plants domesticated by the American Indian and taken over by the white man constitute, according to a reliable estimate, approximately four-sevenths of the present total agricultural production of the United States, measured in farm values. ... the most important are maize or corn, cotton (the New World species, *Gossypium barbadense* Linn.), peanuts, pumpkins, squashes, beans, potatoes, sweetpotatoes, tobacco, and tomatoes.

In the not-too-distant past, all mankind was dependent on the wild fauna and flora. The relationship was elemental and total. By converting wild species into forms specialized to artificial conditions that only man can maintain, we have mass-produced and stabilized the food supply, thus broadening the resource base upon which human populations can expand.

More particularly, it is evident that men can be most abundant if they are willing to restrict their diet and live primarily on such grains as wheat or rice. When people feed plant products to livestock and eat the animals, they go back to a longer food chain and thus cannot provide for maximum numbers. The possibility of supporting an over-population of human beings on a diet compounded directly of algae— the primary green-cell producers on which much of the earth's life depends—has long been of interest to theoreticians, but the idea has few practical implications.

COMMERCE AND ATTITUDES

In Chapter 1 we noted that commercial incentives provided by the fur trade were the immediate lure that took men into the American hinterlands. By adopting Indian gathering and hunting methods, the frontiersman was able to extract some of his livelihood from the primitive environment. Then, through a new system of agriculture, he gained the first effective control over his New World resources. As the original scenery disappeared and cropping took over large areas, there were corresponding economic, social, and political gains.

Thus, in large measure, "progress" was bought through the toilsome erasure of aboriginal conditions—a process that came to be looked upon as the natural course of events. Deeply ingrained in the American character is an attitude that all resources should be developed for their highest production of consumer goods. Areas not so treated are regarded as "idle," their existence being in some degree a reflection on the industry of potential entrepreneurs. Inherent wilderness values and even the most patent beauties of nature have been held in slight regard by the settlers and developers of land. Edwards (1940: 172) characterized the outlook of the colonial farmer, observing that:

His was a struggle to procure the basic necessities. To be sure, he usually did gain some comforts over and above a rudimentary existence, but he lacked the time or the stimulus to develop an interest in the aesthetic or the philosophical. There is no indication of his having an appreciation even of the glorious settings which nature had provided as the scene of his activities.

It is understandable if few people (other than an occasional Thoreau) felt regrets over the disappearance of tall grass, large trees, and certain animal life. That these commodities did disappear was mere evidence that they had been "used"—in the context of the biblical injunction that man should multiply and subdue the earth. Complacency over this situation was abetted by the undeniable fact that, often enough, nothing at all could be done about it.

Originally the commercialization of any product of the land was taken for granted as routine business. The regulation of wildlife uses has become effective gradually since colonial times. As human numbers expanded to alter the environment and as competition for wild land resources built up, the social implications of individual freedom in such matters became evident.

Hardin (1968) has likened the situation of our natural resources to that of a commons used as a community pasture. The individual owner of livestock can show a clear and measurable profit each time he adds an animal to his herd and takes a greater share of the common resource. When grazing pressure gets too high and degrades the pasturage, it affects him immediately only to a limited extent, because the cost of shortage is shared by all the owners. Thus, there is no future in the free use of a commons.

Ways to Extinction

Almost without exception in modern times, wherever wildlife was readily available for uncontrolled use, the growth of human population and exploitation of wildlife for profit created an unsupportable demand. The history of many extinctions and jeopardized species in recent centuries attests to this fact, although two other conditions were likely to be involved, either singly or in combination. Such species were sometimes specialized in ways that made them vulnerable, or they were adapted to primitive habitats that were fated for destruction.

The passenger pigeon (Chapter 1) provides a classic example of all three factors at work, the clue to its original success being its extreme gregariousness (Griscom, 1946). Schorger (1955) concluded that a pair normally reared but one young per year, yet the survival rate permitted a prehistoric buildup to inconceivable abundance. Evidently the great flocks shifted about so far and so often that natural enemies could not increase effectively. In addition, frequent movements to fresh ranges may have been beneficial in terms of disease epidemiology.

The huge flights made it necessary to find each year, somewhere in the East, extensive forests bearing thousands of tons of mast, as well as abundant berry crops for late-summer feeding in the North. When nesting concentrations came under ever-increasing human exploitation for the market, and eastern woodlands were broken up for farming, the annual regime of the pigeons was destroyed. The bird was behaviorally dependent on overflowing numbers. It throve under social conditions that few, if any, other species could have tolerated. Passenger pigeons were not able to live and breed a pair at a time, like the mourning dove. With the disappearance of the great flocks in the 1880's, this species steadily declined to extinction.

The wiping out of the plains bison in the 1870's and 1880's has been abundantly documented (Branch, 1929; Roe, 1951; Allen, 1962). The buffalo bands required an extensive range over which they could move freely, taking forage that would be renewed by adequate intervals of rest. The need for space was critical, and after the white man came, there never was any question of the ultimate fate of the buffalo.

Yet it was the guns of the hide hunters that cleared the grassland before it was converted to farms and ranches.

In this case, failure of the government to control the killing was well-considered policy. The self-supporting traffic in skins and other products provided the means of removing both the bison and the Indian who depended on it from land being allocated to other uses. In little more than a decade a population of wild buffalo numbering in the millions was eliminated. The simple fact of availability evidently attracted a continuous increase in hunters and guaranteed the result. In the face of a specialized enemy, factors of density dependence did not operate to save a few buffalo, as they might have in the case of a smaller animal in a more protective habitat.

Only in the far north of Canada, in Wood Buffalo National Park, do major numbers of buffalo survive today in the presence of their natural predator, the wolf (Fuller, 1962). Even there, conditions are altered by a heavy incidence of introduced disease. Both of these points have relevance to all our efforts to preserve endangered wildlife. It is inevitably true that no wild species can be preserved effectively outside a biotic community in which it can occupy its natural niche and perform its biological functions. Thus, the buffalo in fenced pastures, immune to the selectivity of natural mortality, will inevitably undergo an artificially redirected speciation. The animal of the future will not be what it was under primitive conditions. One might paraphrase by saying that if the bison is to remain a bison, it must live with the wolf.

Both habitat conditions and unregulated shooting have been important in deciding the status of our grassland grouse (see U.S. Bureau of Sport Fisheries and Wildlife, 1966a). The various prairie chickens illustrate the trends. The heath hen was a species whose demise probably can be ascribed primarily to the gun, and especially to market hunting. This bird was dependent for survival on frequently burned barrens along the Atlantic coast from Maine to Virginia (Gross, 1928). The sandy soils of its habitat were of little value for agriculture, although the area occupied may well have been attenuated by settlements.

Despite this, it is likely that enough of the mainland habitat remained well into this century, and possibly to the present, to support small populations if the birds had not been wiped out to supply the game markets of a century ago. It is true that the species was fully protected from shooting on the island of Martha's Vineyard, and its final disappearance from that area probably can be ascribed to successional changes in vegetation too effectively protected from fire.

In Texas the Attwater prairie chicken, although now protected from hunting, has been reduced in numbers to the danger point by the progressive conversion of its grassland habitat to cropland. The greater and lesser prairie chickens are being similarly affected by the disappearance of native vegetation.

On the central prairies and plains, grassland birds were heavily hunted in the late 1800's, but they withstood the toll because of the vastness of their range. In spring, the slaughter featured eskimo curlews that migrated in leisurely fashion northward from the Texas coast, where they arrived after a flight from Argentina (Forbush, 1912; Swenk, 1916). This species was especially vulnerable to shooting, and large numbers were taken on the prairies for both sport and the market.

The arctic nesting ground of the eskimo curlew was largely undisturbed, and in late summer there was a general movement of old and young southeastward to the Maritime Provinces, where great flocks fed on the abundant berry crops of coastal muskegs. There the birds fattened and provided seemingly unlimited hunting to gunners from all over the world. The fall migration was over water to the coast of Brazil, thence to the pampas of Argentina, where the wintering population was harried by more hunting.

Three shooting seasons a year steadily reduced this species from a population numbered in millions to its present status of extreme rarity, or possible extinction—this in spite of an isolated and relatively secure nesting range. The fact that protection would have required an international effort may have helped to discourage any attempt to salvage the bird.

It was a lethal trait of the curlews that they would circle and hover over birds that had been shot, thus exposing the survivors to another volley. Similar tactics contributed to the decimation of flocks of the Carolina parakeet. This North American parrot nested in deep swamps, but it was attracted to dooryards by domestic fruits, which it damaged. Confirming the effects of shooting, the extinction of this bird in the early 1900's largely antedated the cutting of extensive bottomland forests. In fact, another species found in such habitat, the ivory-billed woodpecker, has barely managed to escape total destruction. Both of these wilderness dwellers were obviously ill-adapted to survive the buildup of human populations (Greenway, 1958), although protection from direct killing and the reservation of some high-quality range probably could have preserved small populations.

Of all North American birds, the California condor has the slowest rate of increase, maturing at about 6 years and producing only one young in 2 years (Koford, 1953). Its numbers have declined to about 40, and with the growth of human population in the Los Angeles area, the outlook is not favorable. Losses from even occasional shooting are not readily replaced, and the extensive wild areas required by the species for breeding and feeding are undergoing progressive attrition. Condors seem especially vulnerable to human disturbance of any kind, and the necessary degree of protection has not been achieved (McMillan, 1968). This, the largest bird of flight on the continent, must be regarded as a spectacular showpiece of the primitive that is likely to be swamped by the rising tide of human activity in the only region where it might be preserved.

The trumpeter swan (Banko, 1960) and whooping crane (Allen, 1952) were large, conspicuous, and edible. The skins of the former were an early article of commerce. These birds were obvious targets for unbridled gunnery on the grasslands and northward. In the contiguous 48 states they disappeared wherever the land was settled, a result made permanent by the progressive drainage of large nesting marshes. Both species have survived by virtue of fairly effective recent protection against hunting and the existence of remote undisturbed units of nesting environment. The swan has been re-established in scattered breeding sites from Yellowstone Park and South Dakota to Alaska and is reasonably secure in its present status of 4,000 to 5,000 birds. The crane, numbering less than 50, is in greater danger, especially on migrations between the small Gulf Coast wintering area (Aransas National Wildlife Refuge) and the breeding marshes in the Northwest Territories. Like the condor, this impressive bird must be regarded as a rare showpiece for which a special dispensation in land and protection is necessary if it is to survive.

Some of the foregoing examples clearly indicate the role of public demand in the absence of harvest regulations. An available resource attracts exploitation to the point where competition for the harvest may eliminate the last of a population. It became evident in the first decade of this century that both the sea otter and the northern fur seal were in this position. An international agreement in 1911 gave protection to both species and was the means of reversing the downward trend and restoring their populations to productivity. In the absence of such measures, the southern fur seals disappeared from most of their former ranges.

Studies of rare and vanishing wildlife now are going forward in the Bureau of Sport Fisheries and Wildlife with a view to salvaging the remnant populations of specialized wilderness creatures needing emergency measures (U.S. Bureau of Sport Fisheries and Wildlife, 1966a; Linduska, 1967). The Secretary of the Interior recognizes 78 species of endangered birds, mammals, reptiles, and fish, and many of them could disappear in the onrush of development and intensified use of land and water. In a measure, old trends are still with us. There seem to be no local economic incentives for the preservation of the Texas coastal prairie chicken and the Attwater prairie chicken. Continued poisoning of rodents on remaining grasslands could destroy the last remaining black-footed ferrets. Nominally protected alligators are supporting a vigorous poaching industry because there is a legal market for the hides of crocodilians. Despite many unfavorable trends, it may be said, however, that for the first time in history there is systematic governmental attention and concern for vanishing species. A reasonable effort of this kind in the past could have avoided costly errors.

Jeopardy of the Migrants

The development of international conventions for protecting migratory birds was one of the major management successes in the history of wildlife on this continent. Waterfowl, in particular, were historically popular as game and in great demand on the markets. Canvasbacks and other prized ducks were long featured on the menus of resort hotels, and professional hunters enjoyed profitable fall and spring shooting on such famous grounds as Currituck Sound, Maryland's Eastern Shore, the Erie marshes, the St. Clair flats, and the Kankakee marsh.

Waterfowl are particularly vulnerable because of their repeated reconcentration on water areas as they run the gauntlet of gunnery from Canada southward to wintering grounds in southern states or Latin America. Early in this century many devices were used to attract and slaughter birds during seasonal migrations. Live decoys and baiting were in common use, and professional market hunters in the United States and Mexico decimated whole flocks with punt guns and batteries (see Day, 1959). So well established were these practices, and the ways of life that depended on them, that more than a quarter of a century after passage of the Migratory Bird Treaty Act of 1918, federal enforcement officers were still faced with flagrant lawlessness in certain famous shooting areas.

There has been a growing recognition that waterfowl are endangered by the decline of wetland habitat, and large segments of the continental population are reduced drastically during periodic droughts. Hunting is the one mortality factor that can be managed in some degree on a year-to-year basis. The history of regulations has been one of steadily increasing restrictions and growing attention to the special needs of individual species. Management is complicated by the inability of hunters to identify birds either in the field or in the hand, and also by the fact that wetlands have diminished for hunters just as they have for ducks.

Many hazards attend today's waterfowl resource. Without strenuous efforts by both the states and the federal government to curb the excesses of earlier times, many more species of wildfowl might well be destroyed or reduced to rarity.

Wild Commodities Today

With lessons of the past in mind, we have put restraints on commercialization of wild creatures. The free-and-easy attitudes of early times have given way to a rigorous control over taking and selling most species. We still have legal markets for a few wildlife products, including a highly discriminatory and regulated commercial fishery in which the aim of study and management is sustained yield. In fact, it is highly probable that productivity in this field can be expanded with further research on oceanic resources. Landings of fish and other aquatic life in 1965 were 4.8 billion pounds, with an initial value of $445.7 million (Lyles, 1965). At the federal level the industry is served by the Bureau of Commercial Fisheries, and state agencies control their own internal problems.

Fish resources readily available to the general public are usually cropped for sport fishing purposes. Where a choice exists, the modern appraisal is likely to assume that a recreational fish harvest produces more benefits than a purely commercial enterprise. Dollar income to someone is involved in both (discussed later in this chapter in connection with the national survey of sport fishing and hunting).

Wild fur represents another kind of wildlife crop that has been on the market since prehistoric times. In 1967, a year of low prices, the annual summary of the U.S. Bureau of Sport Fisheries and Wildlife (1968) indicated a minimum raw fur value of more than $12 million. The most important single species is muskrat, of which the annual catch is 4 to 5 million pelts. The fur industry is not large, and it evidently is in long-term decline in the face of continued development of competing synthetic products.

RECREATION: THE NEW PERSPECTIVE

The increase of leisure time in our culture and the progressively greater mobility of the individual have combined to promote the use of outdoor areas of every description. While this is commonly assumed to be a development of the period after World War II, the recognition of outdoor recreation as socially and economically important can more properly be ascribed to the years after World War I. The National Conference on Outdoor Recreation was organized among several citizen associations in 1924, the initial purpose being to survey local, state, and national parks, playgrounds, forests, waters, and other types of reservations (Wharton *et al.*, 1928). It was in the preceding 10 years, said the report, that "motor-born [sic] recreation has permeated the Federal land fabric affecting vitally all but a few classifications." The trends in public demand and government programs were sufficiently clear at that time for the report to assert:

It will be seen that, while belated in some respects, the reservation and administration of public lands for aesthetic enjoyment, historic or scientific appreciation, or economic use has now become an established Federal policy.

With regard to unique scenery or vegetation, exceptional animal life such as big game, or wilderness areas:

These are assets which man cannot provide but which he can preserve and enjoy to supplement and complement the more intensive forms of popular recreation incident to congested communities.

The Outdoor Recreation Resources Review Commission and Its Consequences

Although interrupted and obscured by depression and war, the new appreciation of the importance of outdoor recreation continued to grow, and public agencies at all levels found ways to include it within their land-use purview. This trend became particularly evident with the increase of city populations during the fifties, and it culminated in 1958 with the creation by Congress of the Outdoor Recreation Resources Review Commission (ORRRC). The charge of the commission was to survey our needs and recommend ways to meet them. After 3 years of study, it submitted the report to Congress and the President in January 1962 (Rockefeller *et al.*, 1962).

Projections for the future indicated that, while the population might double by the year 2000, the need for outdoor recreation was likely to triple—an estimate that undoubtedly was conservative. The greatest interest of the public in outdoor activities centered on the simple pastimes of driving, walking, swimming, and picnicking. The need for increased opportunities for these pursuits was greatest near large cities, and lands and waters currently available clearly were inadequate.

The commission pointed out a basic need for more information on the social and economic significance of recreation, and recommended the establishment of a new bureau to monitor such a program. It found that many types of both public and private land could furnish benefits of this kind without impairing major land-use programs. Public interest was obviously greatest in attractive water areas. In 1960 about 90 percent of the American people sought some kind of outdoor activity, and their recreational pursuits were the basis of a $20 billion market in goods and services.

During the 1960's there were many moves, both administrative and legislative, to implement the ORRRC recommendations. The Bureau of Outdoor Recreation was established under the Secretary of the Interior in 1962, and a year later its organic act was signed into law (PL 88-29). The bureau has no land-management responsibilities, being concerned with fact-finding and planning, and it administers the Land and Water Conservation Fund Act of 1965. Under this statute federal grants in aid are made to states and their political subdivisions for planning, acquiring, and developing outdoor recreation projects.

In succeeding years, Congress and the President moved ahead with many measures concerned with the American out-of-doors. There was an obviously enhanced interest in providing for national parks, seashores, trails, wilderness, rivers, reservoir areas, wildlife refuges, and endangered species. Conservation of the environment through pollution control and other means, and the preservation of natural beauty, became major issues.

While citizens of this nation are as much interested as ever in extracting the means of subsistence and industrial support from their environment, the pressures of population and the deterioration of land, water, and air have become increasingly evident. Outdoor activities that once were taken for granted now come at a premium, and there is overwhelming consensus that they are worth the cost of preservation and restoration. This concern of the general public has been reflected in the willingness of citizens to be taxed to support such efforts. As of 1966, at least 24 states had issued bonds, or had authority to do so, for financing such programs. In the period 1960-1965, eight states placed referenda before their voters requesting authority to raise capital for outdoor recreation investments. All eight were approved, by an average majority of 63 percent, and the bond issues totaled $454.5 million.

The new position of outdoor recreation in our culture means that wildlife must have a new and improved standing among renewable resources. Its chief significance for the foreseeable future will be as a recreational resource.

Difficulties in Acquiring Land

In 1967 the Bureau of Outdoor Recreation reported on the rapid escalation of land prices affecting acquisition programs for recreation. The bureau predicted the inadequacy of the Land and Water Conservation Fund to meet outdoor recreation needs in the next decade and stated:

There has been a steady upward trend in land values almost everywhere in the Nation. Land values appear generally to be rising, on the average, from 5 percent to 10 percent annually. And the prices of lands suitable for public recreation use and administration are rising at a considerably higher rate.

A 7 percent annual rate of increase in land prices will double the cost in 10 years. At this rate, $100 million would be needed a decade hence to buy what $50 million will buy now. A higher rate of increase shortens the period during which the cost would double.

Speculation in land is occurring at numerous proposed and authorized public recreation areas. Land price escalation is primarily the result of:

1. A rising trend in land values generally throughout the Nation;

2. Keen competition between individuals, developers, and public agencies for prime recreation lands, particularly those which are water oriented; and

3. The upgrading of lands as a result of change in use, i.e., in many cases from normal agricultural land to prime recreation land with frontage on water or easy access thereto.

With a fast-growing population and increasing scarcity of land for all purposes, the steady and oftentimes spectacular increase in the value of land suitable for outdoor recreation is expected to continue.

On the basis of preliminary data supplied by the Economic Research Service of the U.S. Department of Agriculture, the U.S. Bureau of Outdoor Recreation (1967) showed that, as of March 1965, the estimated value of recreation land having direct access to water was about $1,370 per acre, nationally, and for recreation land without direct access to water, $530 per acre.

One way to minimize the cost of acquiring federal land is to move quickly after a project has been approved. The Congress set a precedent of this kind in 1967 by, in effect, taking possession of the included private lands when the act creating the Redwoods National Park was passed.

FISHING AND HUNTING SURVEYS

Although this report does not encompass fish management problems in any detail, in some contexts fish may conveniently be included with other products of land and water. Fishing and hunting are pursuits amid natural or seminatural scenes whereby men recreate for fun something akin to ancient patterns of the chase. Perhaps berry picking, nut gathering, and mushroom hunting have a similar relationship to the one-time arts of food-plant harvest.

Of 12 outdoor pastimes included in the ORRRC survey, fishing ranked fourth, with 25 percent of the people participating, and hunting ranked eighth, with 12 percent participating. Thus, it might be said that substantial minorities engage in these sports, which are less casual than some other outdoor activities since they usually require licenses and special gear and are subject to definite regulation. Through license fees and taxes on supplies and equipment, hunters and fishermen have helped support both state and federal programs for preserving and managing wildlife.

The first national survey of fishing and hunting was made in connection with the census in 1955. Surveys have been made and published by the Bureau of Sport Fisheries and Wildlife at 5-year intervals since then. Beginning in 1965, the tabulations were limited to fishermen and hunters who devote at least 3 days or spend at least $5 on these sports during the year. This excludes the occasional participant.

In 1965, sport fishermen numbered 28.3 million and spent more than 522 million days in the field. The fishing trips involved some 22.1 billion passenger-miles of auto travel. About one fifth of the fishing was done in salt water, and about 5 million fishermen used small ponds on farms and ranches. Slightly more than 3 million of those fishing were between 9 and 11 years old.

Statistics on hunting give similar clues to the social implications of the sport. Hunters in 1965 numbered about 13.5 million (roughly half the number of fishermen). They spent 185.8 million days in the field and drove 8.4 billion passenger-miles by auto. There were 10.5 million small game hunters and 6.5 million big game hunters—of course, with considerable overlap. There were only 10 percent as many hunters in the 9-11 age group as there were fishermen.

The above figures and many more on the total fishing and hunting effort by the public are contributing to a greatly improved understanding of these outdoor activities. It is evident, for example, that major participation in both cases is by people in small cities and in rural areas, bespeaking the increasing isolation from the natural scene of the residents of large metropolitan districts. Since people tend to be unconcerned about things they do not understand, valid questions are raised about the degree of sophistication in outdoor affairs that can be expected of an increasingly urbanized society. There are substantial indications of the relative growth of nonconsumptive uses of wildlife. For example, in the 3 years following the 1965 survey, the sale of hunting licenses remained about the same, whereas membership in the National Audubon Society more than doubled. Figures obtained by the Bureau of Outdoor Recreation in connection with the 1965 census indicated that there are 8 million birdwatchers and 3 million wildlife photographers in the nation. In 1967, there were 140 million visitors to areas in the national park system—nearly a threefold increase since 1950.

Markets for Gear and Services

The recent fishing and hunting surveys have shown clearly that these activities are supporting a substantial annual business turnover in goods and services. Expenditures in all categories for the 1965 census aggregated more than $4 billion for the 33 million "serious" anglers and hunters involved (U.S. Bureau of Sport Fisheries and Wildlife, 1966b). The mean expenditure by sport fishermen per recreation-day was $5.60 and by hunters, $6.03.

As a major part of the fiscal support of management programs, the states collected $138 million in fishing and hunting license fees in 1965. Sportsmen paid $28 million in federal excise taxes on equipment and supplies. These funds reached the state programs through the Federal Aid to Fish and Wildlife Restoration Programs of the Bureau of Sport Fisheries and Wildlife.

Before the collection of such information, it was not possible to estimate accurately how much fishing and hunting were contributing to the large business base of outdoor recreation and the "tourist" industry. Since this is now measurable, it is frequently cited in justification for properly maintaining and managing the renewable wildlife resources involved. It should be pointed out, however, that overemphasis on dollar values could lead to underestimating elusive but much greater social values. The problems of cities are in large degree produced by the overconcentration of people. The role that outdoor relaxation will play in countering undesirable density effects is not clear at present, but in the interest of erring on the "safe" side, it must be assumed to be large.

How much value fish and game have to an individual landowner is likely to depend on the kind of land he has, whether the farm is also a family home, and the degree of sophistication of the proprietor as an outdoorsman. As a scenic amenity, wildlife in general can be important nearly anywhere, but fishing and hunting are marketable only where high quality in one form or another can be demonstrated.

Artificially stocked fishponds and game preserves are increasingly popular near large cities, and various incidental services (e.g., guides and dogs) are usually provided along with fishing or hunting privileges. Frequently the "results" of this kind of fishing or hunting are guaranteed in one way or another.

Incentives and Realities

Dependence for sport on wild stocks of fish or game is a different matter. Some areas are productive enough to enable an owner to charge for access to his property and obtain an adequate return for his effort. But the yield of "average" fishing waters or game lands is not high in comparison with yields of other crops. Referring to this situation in the introduction to a government publication (Miller and Powell, 1942), W. L. McAtee made an evaluation that is as good today as it was when it was written:

The aggregate of wildlife on agricultural lands of the United States is large and its estimated value is very impressive. Hence enthusiasts have suggested that returns from wildlife management may be an important source of revenue to farmers. Locally, worthwhile revenue may be obtained, but the country is vast, and the values, however large, when spread over the whole, become very thin. Hunters are so numerous that the game harvest of a State distributed among them could supply each with only a fraction of a single specimen of some of the species most sought. If the return to the hunter is small, then that to the farmer cannot be great. Again, high-class agricultural land can hardly be devoted to such a distinctly low-income crop as wildlife. Only inferior lands can be used and their productivity of wildlife as of other crops is low.

Miller and Powell (op. cit.) recognized the need for substantial landowner incentives if wildlife is to be managed on private lands. They noted, however, that the effectiveness of available incentives is likely to depend greatly on the views of the individual.

Administrative officials, the public, the farmers, and the sportsmen must be taught to realize that the recreational, social, and esthetic values of wildlife greatly exceed its economic value; and that wildlife is a natural resource that all have a right to enjoy. The rights of individuals must be respected and protected even if this restricts public utilization of wildlife. The user must become willing to pay an increased amount and the farmer must be willing to accept a large part of the return for his efforts on behalf of wildlife in the form of such intangibles as recreational, esthetic, and social enjoyment.

On this basis it is assumed that the appreciation and use of wildlife values will require an educational effort applied to both the public and the landowner, and that the returns in public benefits are worth the effort. It may also be inferred that the demand for free public hunting will continue, at least in "low-pressure" areas, but as a minimum condition its perpetuation will require the effective protection of landowner rights.

If these conditions apply to a large part of our private wildlife-producing lands, another situation also needs to be recognized. Certain critically important and highly productive wildlife habitats exist on private land. Wetlands that produce waterfowl on the northern prairies are in this category. The preservation and improvement of such areas for ducks will require "incentives" of a special kind, including outright public acquisition.

For the waterfowl hunter it is another fact of life that, because of growing competition, the price of high-quality shooting marshes is likely to continue to increase. This applies also to other choice game lands and (under some conditions) to fishing waters. It is evident that the economic situation changes greatly from areas where wildlife is a secondary product to those where it is the primary motive in owning a property.

MEASURING ECONOMIC AND SOCIAL VALUES

It is inherent in the relationship of man to his resource base that all environmental benefits (uses) represent positive "values" regardless of units of measurement or applicable modes of expression. Dollar values are common economic terminology for commodities and may be involved in any kind of experience, useful or otherwise. However, they are not a universally satisfactory common denominator. Environmental conditions have biological and social impacts that often cannot be reliably described because of presently unmanageable complexities—they are widely variable, they tend to synergize, and, relative to human numbers, the effects are density dependent.

Thus, the value of a recreational asset or experience might be high or low, depending on the extent to which it mitigates a social need that, in itself, may be an elusive condition to measure. These technical difficulties seem to defy generalization and lead to the expression of values in terms such as "esthetic" and "spiritual," which have a subjective usefulness. The ecologist is accustomed to dealing in trends and influences that, for the moment, must be accepted with a large probable error. However, it is inevitable that biological variables will be increasingly quantified, including resource values as they apply to man. An economist accepts the situation in these terms (Machlup, 1965):

We shall have to distinguish between pecuniary and non-pecuniary advantages and disadvantages, and between judgments that rest on statistical records and others that are purely subjective evaluations without any supporting numerical data. But the point to note is that economic evaluation is not confined to the items for which price data are available. It comprises all pros and cons of the plan or activity under examination.

If these views are correct, it follows that a proper judgment of values or a choice among resource allocations must rest on a broader expertise than that of market economics. It must recognize the social and behavioral needs of man—parameters not adequately represented, for example, in the gross national product. On public lands a major part of the recreation privilege is commonly furnished free, and Pearse (1968) observed that this social value accrues entirely to the user. Even those who do not participate have an opportunity to do so. On the other hand, the easily measured dollar income from recreation belongs to the purveyors of permits, goods, and services.

The applicability of such logic may be seen in the results of a recent survey of big game hunting in British Columbia (Bowden and Pearse, 1968). In 1966, out of a total of 117,000 big game hunters in the province, 6,500 were nonresidents, principally from the United States. The nonresidents spent $3.7 million in British Columbia, of which the major items were $2.2 million for guide services, $348 thousand for licenses and fees, and $386 thousand for food, liquor, and lodging. These figures have obvious usefulness to the government, the tourist industry, and others concerned with serving the public. However, for truly evaluating the almost unique combination of big game species now available in British Columbia, a host of intangibles must be considered. The big game resource paid a 1-year dividend of 115,000 animals, most of which were taken by residents interested in meat and the remainder primarily by nonresidents interested in trophies. Many other people both inside and outside Canada can hunt big game in British Columbia, and an even greater number can enjoy *seeing* the animals in their native setting whenever they wish. There are few standards against which the last two values can be appraised, but the values unquestionably are increasing as human numbers increase.

Krutilla (1967) made a point that is almost universally applicable to unique natural features of our environment, including geologic forms, threatened biotypes, or rare ecosystems. For the indefinite future, it will be essential to keep open the scientific option of studying their natural processes or utilizing for unforeseen purposes the species thus preserved.

Traditional Assumptions

Our review of historic trends provided ample evidence that in North America we have not been much concerned with nonmarketable amenities or with our environment as such. In the early period of occupation and population buildup, there was a vast fund of natural wealth to be disposed of, and if the human habitat suffered, there were always fresh scenes to turn to. In truth, the attitudes born of our early conditions not only persist in the minds of people but also are effective in legal forms that continue to dominate important aspects of resource use. So much of our public management concerns water, and water is so universally tied into the wildlife interest, that one may turn to the complexity of water issues to illustrate many kinds of problems.

The example cited in Chapter 1 relative to the totality of traditional economic thinking on drainage laws (Haik, 1957) illustrates this situation. It is generally true that in the United States we have never stopped reclaiming the native environment for irrigation and drainage projects and for other purposes. In the large nationally subsidized undertakings of this kind, we most clearly threaten wildlife and scenic resources whose usefulness we have only begun to appraise in the modern context. On a grand scale we appear to be following old assumptions that open space is wasteland and that making such areas "productive" is inherently good, irrespective of developmental costs or the usefulness of what is being produced.

In this connection, Krutilla (1966, 1968) examined cost and benefit criteria and reviewed recent evaluations of various national water development and land reclamation projects (see Ulrich, 1953; Renshaw, 1957; Ekstein, 1958; Hufschmidt *et al.*, 1961; White, 1961; Ruttan, 1965; Breathitt, 1967; National Advisory Commission on Food and Fiber, 1967; Udall, 1967), including types concerned with hydroelectric power, common storage, and low-flow augmentation. He (1968) concluded that:

Large water resource developments . . . have been justified spuriously by grossly overestimated benefits to accompany parallel understatement of costs; the real value of the actual output in many cases will fail to cover real costs by a wide margin (as in the case of the Bridge and Marble Canyon projects) and they *should not be built in any event whether or not there would be damage to wildlife habitat or scenic values.*

The author noted, however, that "most of such developmental activities, as for example large multiple-purpose water resource projects, with finite useful lives, result in a permanent and irreversible injury to the natural environment." Elsewhere (1967) he mentioned that the cost of not changing rare natural environments may be relatively small, and that "with the continued advance in technology, more substitutes for conventional natural resources will be found."

Quantity versus Quality

Servicing the demand for continuous economic growth has been integral to many public programs, and it undoubtedly abets the drive to expand agriculture and industry into new areas. It is a widely held view that any enterprise contributes to "progress" and human well-being if it stimulates population growth and a greater volume of business. Such assumptions have critical long-range implications when applied to making decisions between alternative recreational uses. This is well illustrated by Krutilla's (1968) discussion of multipurpose reservoirs that may be constructed at the expense of choice scenic canyons, whitewater streams, and the valley ranges of big game herds (see also Chapter 3). He mentioned the characteristic attitudes of sponsors and construction agencies and noted that

. . . unlike the generous imputations of value from land and water resource development, the estimate of the value of preserving the natural environment tends to be systematically depressed. This is a result of the failure to reflect adequately the qualitatively different outdoor recreation experiences in evaluating comparative benefits and costs. One practice has been to consider the *number* of individuals who would participate in outdoor recreation in an area with and without the prospective water impoundment. By the very nature of things, this biases the valuation of recreation benefits to the flat water (reservoir) activities as these tend to be more gregarious in character (picnicking, swimming, etc.). However, the value of a day of swimming may be very much less than a day of quality trout or salmon fishing, or a day of hunting big game which may be dependent upon the prospective reservoir bottom for wintering range, etc. This would follow because of the relative abundance of alternatives available for indulging the former, and thus the low value one would place on an *additional* opportunity if alternatives were readily available; and the relative scarcity and thus high value placed on preserving the latter because of the increasing rareness of opportunities available and the absence of close substitutes. Accordingly, proposed impoundments which rely for their justification on the provision of water-based recreation, in appreciable part, should be subjected to critical economic and ecological examination so that what may be rare and valuable is not traded for what is commonplace or in surplus, and of low or negligible value at the margin.

In mediating among competing interests for resource use, public agencies often cater to the side most numerously represented, irrespective of the intensity of feeling involved. Thus, small groups of sophisticated outdoorsmen could be overwhelmed by a superficial interest of the many who might, for example, like to see development money spent in a local area.

If such cases come up for decision one at a time, all the small, specialized, and rare recreational features are likely to be eliminated. Thus, diversity in the human habitat and the options of the future will be lost.

The extent and quality of the service rendered by outdoor environments and assets (fish, game) frequently depend on the way they are used. Seining fish obviously would be a less rewarding way to use the crop than hook-and-line angling; yet seining is useful for prescribed purposes. Hunting deer with the bow and arrow provides more man-hours of sport per deer than gun hunting; yet shooting with rifle or shotgun is the usual way to obtain mass public benefits from a game resource. The management agencies attempt to provide many options and spread activities as widely as possible.

Doing things "the hard way" by methods requiring particular motivation, effort, and skill is widely regarded as one means of improving the quality of outdoor experiences. Thus, hiking or packing into wild country is likely to be more rewarding for many people than driving to the scenic destination in a car. Widespread highway development probably assures the possibilities for mass movement of citizens into many desirable areas. But in the interest of preserving diverse opportunities and a sampling of country with minimum disturbance, it may be assumed also that it is not desirable to build roads for public access into all parts of our remaining wild areas.

In an evaluation of the wildlife resources of the Tennessee Valley, Emerson (1968) stated that the enjoyment of wildlife is inversely proportional to the artificiality of the situation. He expressed a viewpoint that probably has been neglected in many public programs but which will inevitably need to be a part of realistic planning:

Quality experiences are those that increase man's perception of his environment and his relationship to it. At the same time they are satisfying, enjoyable, and nondestructive of the resources upon which they depend. To maintain quality, only limited numbers of people can be accommodated for observing wildlife in wilderness areas, waterfowl hunting, and other such uses.

It is commonly assumed that outdoor areas used by many people must offer all conveniences and that travel must be highly mechanized. In some situations, however, this is not true, and more people may, in fact, be served by keeping things simple. This was aptly illustrated by Brooks (1961) in discussing the recent buildup of visitation in the national parks:

The space available in the national parks is not big enough for all who want to use it. But the size of the park is directly related to the manner in which you see it. If you are in a canoe traveling at three miles an hour, the lake on which you are paddling is ten times as long and ten times as broad as it is to the man in a speed boat going thirty. An hour's paddle will take you as far away as an hour in a speed boat—if there are no speed boats. In other words, more people can use the same space with the same results. Every road that replaces a foot path, every outboard that replaces a canoe paddle, shrinks the area of the park.

Living Standard and Environment

The validity of the American expectation of continued population growth, unlimited resource development, and economic expansion in every part of the country is being seriously questioned. Persistence of such an expectation could have disastrous effects on the human environment and on living standards. In the face of many pressures, it is essential that public agencies apply professional expertise in identifying the most vulnerable of our resources and in taking steps to protect them. Wildlife is clearly one of these resources, since it is not immediately competitive in the context of traditional business enterprise, and there is no established socioeconomic mechanism that can assure its continued usefulness in our culture.

Usefulness, in a highly discriminating sense, without degradation will need to be the objective in managing wildlife and other aspects of our out-of-doors for this and future generations. In the following chapters, policies and methods are discussed that should be helpful in accomplishing this objective.

REFERENCES

Allen, D. L. 1962. Our wildlife legacy. Funk and Wagnalls Co., New York. 422 p.

Allen, R. P. 1952. The whooping crane. Nat. Audubon Soc. Rep. 3. 220 p.

Banko, W. E. 1960. Trumpeter swan, its history, habits, and population in United States. U.S. Bur. Sport Fish. and Wildl., N. Amer. Fauna. 63. 214 p.

Bowden, G., and P. H. Pearse. 1968. Non-resident big game hunting and the guiding industry in British Columbia: an economic survey. Brit. Columbia Dep. Recr. & Conserv. Fish and Wildl. Br., Study Rep. 2. 72 p.

Branch, E. D. 1929. The hunting of the buffalo. D. Appleton & Co., New York. 240 p.

Breathitt, E. T. 1967. The people left behind. President's National Advisory Commission on Rural Poverty. U.S. Government Printing Office, Washington, D.C.

Brooks, P. 1961. The pressure of numbers. Atlantic Monthly 207(2):54-56.

Carrier, L. 1923. The beginnings of agriculture in America. McGraw-Hill Book Co., New York. 323 p.

Day, A. M. 1959. North American waterfowl. Stackpole, Harrisburg, Pa. 363 p.

Edwards, E. E. 1940. American agriculture—the first 300 years, p. 171-276. *In* Farmers in a changing world. The yearbook of agriculture 1940. U.S. Department of Agriculture. U.S. Government Printing Office, Washington, D.C.

Ekstein, O. 1958. Water resource development. *In* The economics of project evaluation. Harvard University Press, Cambridge, Mass.

Emerson, F. B., Jr. 1968. Tennessee Valley wildlife: an outlook for the year 2000. Tennessee Valley Authority, Div. of Forest. Dev. 27 p.

Ewers, J. C. 1955. The horse in Blackfoot Indian culture. Smithsonian Inst., Bur. Amer. Ethnol. Bull. 159. 374 p.

Forbush, E. H. 1912. Game birds, wild-fowl and shore birds. Massachusetts State Board of Agriculture. 622 p.

Fuller, A. W. 1962. The biology and management of the bison of Wood Buffalo National Park. Can. Wildl. Serv. Manage. Bull. 1(16):1-52.

Graham, E. H. 1947. The land and wildlife. Oxford University Press, New York. 232 p.

Greenway, J. C., Jr. 1958. Extinct and vanishing birds of the world. Amer. Comm. Intern. Wildl. Protection Spec. Publ. 13. 518 p.

Griscom, L. 1946. The passing of the passenger pigeon. Amer. Scholar 15:212-216.

Gross, A. O. 1928. The heath hen. Boston Soc. Natur. Hist. Memoirs 6(4):491-588.

Haik, R. A. 1957. Water, habitat, and wildlife. Conserv. Volunteer 20:1-5.

Hallenbeck, C. 1940. Alvar Nunez, Cabeza de Vaca. The journey and route of the first European to cross the continent of North America, 1534-1536. Arthur H. Clark Co., Glendale, Calif. 326 p.

Hardin, G. 1968. The tragedy of the commons. Science 162:1243-1248.

Hufschmidt, M. M., J. V. Krutilla, and J. Marglin. 1961. Standards and criteria for formulating and evaluating federal resource development. Report of the Panel of Consultants to the U.S. Bureau of the Budget.

Koford, C. B. 1953. The California condor. Nat. Audubon Soc. Res. Rep. 4. 154 p.

Krutilla, J. V. 1966. Is public intervention in water resources development conducive to economic efficiency? Reprint No. 56, Jan. Natur. Resour. J. 6:60-75. Resources for the Future, Inc., Washington, D.C.

Krutilla, J. V. 1967. Conservation reconsidered. Amer. Econ. Rev. 57(4):777-786.

Krutilla, J. V. 1968. Balancing extractive industries with wildlife habitat. 33rd N. Amer. Wildl. & Natur. Resour. Conf. Trans., p. 119-129.

Linduska, J. P. 1967. Endangered species—the federal program. Western Ass. State Game & Fish Comm., 47th Annu. Conf., p. 40-48.

Lorant, S. (ed.). 1965. The new world; the first pictures of America. Duell, Sloan & Pearce, New York. 292 p.

Lyles, C. H. 1965. Fishery statistics of the United States. U.S. Fish and Wildl. Serv. Statist. Dig. 59. 756 p.

Machlup, F. 1965. Comments: economic and non-economic values, p. 155. *In* R. Dorfman (ed.), Measuring benefits of government investments. The Brookings Institution, Washington, D.C.

Martin, P. S. 1967. Pleistocene overkill. Natur. Hist. 76(10):32-38.

McMillan, I. 1968. Man and the California condor. E. P. Dutton & Co., New York. 191 p.

Miller, J. P., and B. P. Powell. 1942. Game and wild-fur production and utilization on agricultural land. U.S. Dep. Agr. Circ. 636. 58 p.

National Advisory Commission on Food and Fiber. 1967. Food and fiber for the future. U.S. Government Printing Office, Washington, D.C. 361 p.

Pearse, P. H. 1968. A new approach to the evaluation of non-priced recreational resources. Land Econ. 44(1):87-99.

Renshaw, E. F. 1957. Toward responsible government: an economic appraisal of federal investment in water resource programs. Idyia Press, Chicago.

Rockefeller, L. S. *et al.* 1962. Outdoor recreation for America. Outdoor Recr. Rev. Comm. 246 p.

Roe, F. G. 1951. The North American buffalo. University of Toronto Press, Ontario, Canada. 957 p.

Roe, F. G. 1955. The Indian and the horse. University of Oklahoma Press, Norman. 434 p.

Ruttan, V. 1965. The economic demand for irrigated acreage. Johns Hopkins Press, Baltimore.

Sauer, C. O. 1947. Early relations of man to plants. Geogr. Rev. 37(1):1-25.

Schorger, A. W. 1955. The passenger pigeon: its natural history and extinction. University of Wisconsin Press, Madison. 424 p.

Swenk, M. H. 1916. The Eskimo curlew and its disappearance, p. 325-340. *In* Smithsonian Inst. Annu. Rep. 1915.

Udall, S. L. 1967. Policy recommendations of the Department of the Interior on reservoir storage and release for flow regulation for water quality control on federal and federally supported projects. U.S. Department of the Interior, Washington, D.C.

Ulrich, R. 1953. Relative costs and benefits of land reclamation in the humid Southeast and the semi-arid West. J. Farm Econ. 35(1):62-73.

U.S. Bureau of Outdoor Recreation. 1967. A report on recreation land price escalation. U.S. Department of the Interior, Washington, D.C. 33 p.

U.S. Bureau of Sport Fisheries and Wildlife. 1966a. Rare and endangered fish and wildlife of the United States. U.S. Dep. Interior Resource Publ. 34.

U.S. Bureau of Sport Fisheries and Wildlife. 1966b. National survey of fishing and hunting, 1965. U.S. Dep. Interior Resource Publ. 27.

U.S. Bureau of Sport Fisheries and Wildlife. 1968. Fur catch in the United States, 1967. U.S. Dep. Interior Wildl. Leafl. 482.

Wharton, W. P., *et al.* 1928. Recreation resources of federal lands. Joint Committee on Recreational Survey of Federal Lands, American Forestry Association and National Parks Association. National Conference on Outdoor Recreation, Washington, D.C. 141 p.

White, G. F. (ed.). 1961. Univ. Chicago, Dep. Geogr. Res. Paper 70. 228 p.

Wissler, C. 1940. Indians of the United States: Four centuries of their culture. Doubleday & Company, Garden City, N.Y. 319 p.

CHAPTER 3

New Patterns on Land and Water

MODERNIZATION OF AGRICULTURE

A productive and efficient agriculture is one of the great strengths of the United States. Applications of new knowledge and techniques have made it possible to engage a steadily declining proportion of the population in food and fiber production and, at the same time, increase the quantity, quality, and variety of output.

The rising trend in farm production had its beginning in the late 1930's and early 1940's, as the national economy recovered from a catastrophic depression and geared for war. It has yet to show signs of slackening. In 1967, American farms turned out a volume of food and fiber that exceeded by 37 percent the volume produced in 1950.

Trend toward Large Cropping Units

This increase in production seems all the more remarkable when the circumstances are considered. From 1950 to 1967, the number of farms in the nation dropped by about two and a half million. In order to utilize the work potential of machines and offset rising costs of labor and materials, commercial farmers have increased the size of their operations. Farmers harvested 34 million fewer acres in 1967 than in 1950, and farm employment declined by 5 million persons in the 17-year period. The small subsistence farm is rapidly passing out

55

of existence as older operators die or move. A major portion of the abandoned acreage is in the eastern United States, lands once reclaimed from the primitive forest. Thus, the area is now in various stages of reversion to forest, and its wild fauna is changing accordingly.

The foregoing trends, accepted without further inquiry, sometimes lead city dwellers to the specious conclusion that our agriculture is undergoing a national decline. But it is the essence of economic and technologic progress that a nation devote progressively less of its activity to the production of basic necessities and more to endeavors that make life more stimulating and enjoyable.

The 37 percent increase in agricultural yields in 17 years represents an accomplishment strikingly different from the progress shown in our historic development. Until early in this century, farm output increased with the growth of population and with the expansion of that population westward to bring new lands under the plow. In the decade after 1870, a time when settlement of the West was in full swing, the number of farms rose by half, and production showed a similar rise. After 1880 the rate of establishment of new farms slowed somewhat as the better lands were settled. In the 40 years it took for the number of farms to reach a maximum, the acreage in crops nearly doubled. Expansion of cropland still was the principal means of increasing agricultural yield, and the volume of crops for human use also nearly doubled.

The recent major spurt in production came long after the peak of areal expansion. In fact, with this growth has come a reduction in the need for more cropland. Land so used dropped from 377 million acres in 1950 to 342 million in 1967. During that period, farmers over the nation withdrew from crops an acreage exceeding the land area of New England. On the northern plains, farmers withdrew more than 1 acre in 20, primarily in response to programs instituted to reduce grain surpluses. But the proportionate shrinkage has been sharpest in the South. There almost 1 acre in 4 has been converted from cropping to other uses.

Causes and Effects

The extensive and rapid reduction in crop acreage has been effected in several ways. In part it represents the withdrawal of whole farms from agriculture, particularly those surrounding urban areas, and many in submarginal areas. Some of the decrease can be attributed to land-rationing programs the government has sponsored since 1950. But much of it stems from the discovery by farmers that, within broad limits, it is more economical to increase yields through improved methods than to cultivate more land for the same amount of product.

In the 17-year period, crop production per acre rose nationally by nearly 50 percent and in some parts of the South by about 100 percent. Such changes have been the basis for predictions that by 1980 we can readily supply our sharply increasing domestic requirement for farm products and increase exports moderately with even further reductions in our cropland base.

The advent of the tractor and other motor-driven equipment released millions of acres of land that had been used in producing feed for horses and mules. Between 1930 and 1967, land used for this purpose was reduced from 65 million acres to 4 million acres (Economic Research Service, 1968a). Thus, an area equivalent to 80 percent of the cultivated land in the Corn Belt was added to land available for producing human food. Indirectly, availability of this acreage made it possible for managers to assign less intensive uses to marginal lands that previously had been cultivated.

The ability of agriculture to achieve striking improvements in productivity while constantly yielding part of its land to nonfarm uses suggests that the structure of the industry has been substantially changed. The change has evolved as a response to the persistent pressures that accompany national economic expansion. That it has been healthy for segments of the industry is evidenced by the increased size of the average farm. Today's "average farmer" operates a farm twice the size of the one run by his 1940 counterpart.

Expansion of farm enterprises has long been a characteristic of American agriculture. In the days when labor was a major component of farm input, farmers expanded their operations as new tools, better horse-drawn equipment, and new methods slowly improved the work capacity of labor. Although the largest gains in acreage per farm have occurred since the advent of the tractor, a national trend to larger management units was well under way by the turn of the century. The trend continued in the North and West even as the number of farms was pushed higher by the establishment of new farms. Prevalence of the sharecropper system in the South delayed by several decades the beginning of the trend in that region. But since 1940 southern farms have displayed a spectacular gain in acreage. Changes in the economic pattern have been accompanied by major changes in the ecological pattern on the land. Poorly managed "patch farming" produced excellent quail habitat and a colorful kind of hunting; unfortunately,

the larger modernized agricultural unit does not do so well for wildlife by-products.

Generally, when small farms are converted into large management
units, wildlife habitat deteriorates drastically (see Chapter 4). This
deterioration undoubtedly has occurred on a broad scale. Early tabulations from the 1964 Census of Agriculture indicate that about three
fourths of the 2.2 million loss in number of farms occurred among
units of less than 100 acres. In fact, more than half the farms that
disappeared were less than 50 acres.

Ownership and Tenancy

The American agricultural "revolution" has featured not only a major
overhauling of the land-use pattern and a shift to mechanization but
also a significant change in the tenure of farm operators. By 1959,
about 80 percent of all farms were operated by owners and part
owners, in comparison with only 57 percent in 1935. Between 1935
and 1959, the proportion of all farms worked by tenants declined
from 42 percent to less than 20 percent. In the South, the proportion
of farms operated by sharecroppers changed from 10.5 percent in 1935
to slightly more than 3 percent in 1959 (Economic Research Service,
1966).

Who owns and manages the land has important implications in the
long-term outlook for soil and water conservation as well as for other
values not associated with immediate returns. There is little incentive
for a sharecropper or tenant to invest his efforts in management for
the future or to consider a by-product such as wildlife. There is, instead, a real incentive to emphasize practices promising the greatest
income in the shortest time.

An increase in the proportion of owners and operators of farms
means generally greater attention to scientific methods. However, the
end result is likely to be a specialized, more intensive land use, and this
is largely inimical to the kind of management that benefits wildlife.
That this is not true of all types of agriculture is evident from Chapter 4.

Impacts of Change

Combined effects of the foregoing trends appear to be promoting
specialization in agricultural production. Sharp differences in cropping
systems are developing, even within long-established production areas.
To exploit their available resources, farmers are making not less than
three kinds of major organizational adjustments:

(1) Crop production is being shifted to areas of expansive, level, productive soils that lend themselves to mechanization and to intensive use of fertilizers and other chemicals. (2) Within these areas, farmers with a suitable land base are confining their attention increasingly to a few regionally adapted crops. (3) Location shifts accompanied by specialization make it possible to exploit the capacities of costly field equipment and frequently to achieve a higher degree of efficiency than is possible with a more diversified operation on less productive soils. When supplementary enterprises are reduced, it is often the livestock group that is dropped.

These reorganizations are resulting in major changes in the cropping pattern and the agricultural landscape—changes that significantly affect the potential for recreation benefits. Improved land management and greater industrial values reduce the economic position of wildlife, which, in most cases, depends in part on the presence of uncropped areas and semipermanent types of vegetation (see Chapter 4). These essentials of the wildlife habitat are being wiped out by the efficient technology that is taking over our best soils.

Trends in drainage are a case in point: Excess water is a problem on much cropland in the humid part of the country. Nationally, about 112 million acres need further artificial drainage for maximum agricultural use (U.S. Department of Agriculture, 1965). Half of this acreage lies in the Corn Belt and the lower Mississippi Valley, two major areas where the rapid shift to large-scale cropping is occurring. The alluvial and glacial soils are pocketed with sloughs, potholes, and other wet depressions, which provide excellent wildlife habitat but commonly are an agricultural liability (Chapter 5). Some of the earlier attempts at drainage left spoilbank barriers or resulted in irregularly shaped fields poorly adapted to the use of multirow equipment.

Land grading for improved drainage and the removal of surface irregularities is increasing. Artificial reshaping to a constant slope, a practice originating in the arid West as an aid to irrigation, is now used in humid areas. The Soil Conservation Service provides technical assistance in land forming and by 1966 had contributed to these practices on 13.6 million acres. Of this total, 190,000 acres was classified as drainage land grading, requiring detailed engineering survey and layout; 8.6 million acres as irrigation land leveling; and 4.9 million acres as land smoothing or rough grading to remove irregularities.

As part of the readjustments in land use, livestock operations are becoming more specialized. In the Corn Belt fewer farmers feed cattle and hogs, and the average size of such enterprises is increasing.

Poultry production (non-land-based) is being shifted to sites of low agricultural value. Cotton raising is moving (as fast as artificial restraints permit) to irrigated areas in the Southwest and California. In the three Delta states this crop is being shifted from small hill farms to the level fertile soils of the Delta proper. Even more corn is being raised in the Corn Belt; this region has increased its proportionate share of the national crop by a third since 1950. While the northern plains area is still dominant in wheat, production is increasing on the southern plains. The great advantages of mechanization and irrigation in vegetable production have caused a concentration of these crops in the California Central Valley and level lands in the southeastern states. The pasturing of livestock is declining in the Corn Belt, the Lake States, and the Northeast, and is gravitating to rangelands of the South and West. The largest percentage gains in livestock production have been in the Delta and southeastern states.

All these trends have added to agricultural efficiency and yields. The land-use picture is one of a highly technical and specialized food and fiber industry taking over almost exclusive use of the most fertile and productive lands of the continent. Correspondingly, marginal farming is on the decline, thus making way for uses more compatible with land capabilities and public demand. Where such areas are not pre-empted for human occupancy, wildlife, forests, and recreation are likely to improve their standing as social and economic benefits.

Federally financed programs dealing with soil and water conservation problems on a national scale have profoundly influenced practices and attitudes as they relate to land use. Extensive knowledge of land capabilities, collected over the past three decades, serves as a guide in determining the wisest and most profitable use for a given tract of land. In addition, there has developed a conservation consciousness in both farm and nonfarm people to a degree unknown before.

Gains and Losses in the Agricultural Base

Our uses of land have by no means adjusted fully to the agricultural potential, nor are they likely to do so. Charles E. Kellogg has estimated (unpublished data) that we have some 50 million acres of soil used for crops—or with an official cropping history that makes them eligible for crop uses—that are not suitable for farming under any known combination of practices. On the other hand, about 230 million acres of soils (leaving out temporarily idle areas, federal lands, highways, and urban sites) suitable for cropping are not so used. Most of this land has a cover of brush, trees, or grass.

Despite the striking decline of land in farms, cropland acreage, and number of farms, a substantial acreage of new land is being brought into cultivation through drainage and irrigation and in other ways. Eight states have increased their cropland harvested up to 1965: Delaware, to which vegetable production has shifted as urbanization has taken over cropland in other states; Florida, where drainage and irrigation have brought large acreages into sugarcane, citrus, melons, and tomatoes; Arkansas, which reflects the effects of drainage and clearing of Mississippi Delta alluvial land; and Montana, Idaho, Arizona, Nevada, and Washington, where irrigation developments have brought about net increases in cropland. In total, these eight states added to their cropland harvested by 1.9 million acres; the total decrease in the 48 contiguous states was about 43 million acres.

In view of the fact that major problems of American agriculture are associated with surpluses, adding new land is open to question. This is especially true since the most readily available land has been taken up, and today the reclamation of more desert, swamp, and low forest lands is a high-cost enterprise. Also, it is frequently destructive of outdoor recreational environments and wildlife. Although pressing need for human food worldwide may eventually require that more lands be brought into this type of production, there should be a more careful weighing of costs and values than in the past.

New Croplands by Irrigation

The availability of irrigation water makes cropping possible on the highly mineralized soils of the arid West, and it supplements rainfall on many areas in the humid eastern states. In rice culture, irrigation is a routine requirement for profitable yields.

Irrigated land on farms throughout the United States totaled more than 37 million acres in 1964. Seventeen western states accounted for more than 33 million acres. Nationwide, land under irrigation is now increasing at the rate of 780,000 acres annually, and in the period 1949 to 1964, western states accounted for 80 percent of the increase. The total area of irrigated land is now approximately 40 million acres.

Changes in irrigated acreage are uneven within regions and within time periods because of variations in availability of water, the amount of rainfall, and demand for products. Although irrigated acreage in the West increased by 6.5 million acres during a recent 10-year period, acreage decreased substantially in three of the states because of a shortage of surface water. In the Delta states, restrictions on rice acreage resulted in a decrease of total acreage irrigated, despite a marked increase in irrigation of cotton and soybeans.

A survey by the U.S. Department of Agriculture (1965) appraised irrigation potentials based on the limiting factors of soil suitability and the availability of water within watersheds as planning units. It appeared that 66.9 million acres of cropland and pasture (slightly more than double the 33.2 million acres estimated by the Bureau of the Census to have been irrigated in 1959) would benefit from additional water.

Although there has been a steady increase in irrigation, much of the land already was in crop production, particularly in the humid East. But much of the 9-million-acre increase in land irrigated between 1950 and 1965 in the 17 western states also comprised land previously cropped under dry-land conditions. In the most arid states—New Mexico, Arizona, Utah, and Nevada—the irrigated area increased from 2.7 to 3.0 million acres between 1950 and 1965, and most of this represents "new" cropland.

From the standpoint of wildlife relationships, it is of interest to note that 51 percent of the irrigated cropland in the West is used for the production of livestock feed. In addition, more than 5 million irrigated acres in the region are in pasture or other nonharvested crops (U.S. Department of Agriculture, 1962b).

About 56 percent of the irrigation water in the West is from streamflow, representing an annual withdrawal of some 120 million acre-feet (U.S. Department of Agriculture, 1962a). Major impoundments help provide this large volume of water, and nearly complete use is being made of streamflow in some of the older irrigation areas; yet the search for new sources continues.

The wildlife species most notably associated with western irrigated land from the latitude of Colorado northward is the ringneck pheasant (Hart et al., 1956; Yeager et al., 1956). This Asian gamebird was first naturalized in North America in the Willamette Valley of Oregon and has since shown its outstanding capabilities to survive in the presence of various types of intensive hay and grain agriculture. Without question, irrigation has been the key to pheasant productivity in many valleys of the West.

Where riparian lands are converted to intensive agriculture and settlements, the wildlife that inhabits native ranges is largely eliminated. In various western states such species might be deer, elk, pronghorns, javelina, Gambel quail, and white-winged doves. In decades to come, major changes in western fauna may be expected if extensive water developments are carried out on the scale envisioned by Senator McGee of Wyoming (1960):

Even with transpiration, evaporation, comsumption, and seepage into impervious aquifers, three-fourths of the water of our western rivers still discharges into the ocean. This means that the West has only begun to use its water. The Bureau of Reclamation, in its report to the committee [Senate Select Committee on Water Resources], states, "The amount of physically feasible water resource development remaining in the seventeen reclamation states is enormous."

Their report summarizes 1,085 reclamation projects, both public and private, upon which construction has not yet been undertaken.

The bureau estimates that 75 percent of the federal projects and 90 percent of the non-federal projects listed can be developed by the year 2000. Such a program would provide for the irrigation of 17 million acres of new land equivalent. It should pour over 4 million kilowatts of hydropower into our transmission systems. It would cost $22 billion.

Plans for these major works involve the possibilities for weather control (especially cloud seeding) and transmountain river diversions. In the face of a prospective near-total mechanization of the hydrology and, indeed, the entire human environment, the position of wildlife probably has relevance as only one of an entire spectrum of outdoor resources requiring space and a (somewhat) natural scene. Such fragile amenities will take their place in planning insofar as the total ecological picture of defined goals and human population relationships is given critical and realistic consideration. This kind of policy appears to be extremely slow in developing.

Added Acres through Drainage

In common with irrigation, drainage has been an important means of bringing more land into crop production. Compilations of the Agricultural Research Service indicate that nearly 100 million acres of agricultural land had been "reclaimed" by drainage by 1960—more than 3 times the area made available by irrigation. In the United States there are still some 172.5 million acres of level, or nearly level, land that need group drainage outlets if they are to be used efficiently for cropping (U.S. Department of Agriculture, 1965). Almost two thirds of the acreage in watershed projects that would be feasible to drain for farming is in the eastern third of the country. Currently, the greatest area of development of new cropland through drainage is on the alluvial land of the Mississippi Delta, where almost a million acres were added between 1959 and 1964. Some new areas also are being developed on the southern coastal plain.

In the humid eastern half of the United States, it has been common practice to invoke the authorities of local drainage districts to dredge the outlets of natural lakes to expose areas of organic soil for cultivation. Through the same process, marshes large and small have progressively disappeared. Extensive drainage projects helped to create some of the nation's most valuable croplands. Parts of Indiana's famous Kankakee region exemplify this, as do Michigan's lake plains and the Black Swamp area of northwestern Ohio. Often such enterprises were speculative and failed as a result of poorly understood conditions, as in the case of Wisconsin's Horicon Marsh and Georgia's Okefenokee Swamp. Both of these "failures" are now dedicated to wildlife refuges.

Drainage on lands already in cultivation must be continued for reasons of efficiency. This type of drainage is not to be judged by effects on wildlife, although frequently the benefits to one species may balance the disadvantages to another.

There is perhaps no other phase of land use where wildlife relationships are more clearly and more extensively influenced favorably or unfavorably than in drainage for the conversion of "idle" wet areas to agriculture. Nor has there been any other comparable area of disagreement between agricultural interests and the proponents of wildlife conservation. This is particularly true of government-sponsored, tax-supported drainage that in recent decades was in the anomalous position of contributing to the production of surplus, price-supported grains, while at the same time reducing a wildlife resource (especially waterfowl) for which there was unlimited demand. Historically, this process has gone ahead as though no valid reason existed for preserving lakes, marshes, swamps, and other wet sites if these could be made to support any kind of cropping enterprise. Minnesota's legal basis for drainage exemplifies such statutes as described by Haik (1957):

A typical law authorized the "County Board to establish any ditch, drain, or other water course, which ditch could in whole or part follow and consist of the bed of any stream, creek, or river, whether navigable or not, or any lake, whether meandered or not, and the Board could widen, deepen, straighten, change, lower, or drain the channel or bed of any creek, river, lake or other water course. . . ."

The authority granted by the legislature was very broad and was apparently based upon a policy that considered surface waters to be a common enemy which could be disposed of even if it meant taking property against a landowner's will in condemnation proceeding.

The validity of such laws was upheld in the courts, and in one opinion it was stated that:

As a rule, drainage proceedings are begun for the sole purpose of reclaiming wet lands, primarily for the direct benefit of the owners thereof, and incidentally for the promotion of the public welfare by increasing the productiveness and taxable value of lands having little or no value unless drained.

In drainage statistics there usually is no reliable indication of true relationships of costs to benefits, or identification of ecological effects of one kind or another. Thus, the recorded acreages are only an index of the scale on which such operations have been carried out. Commonly the scale is broad, as the Wisconsin Conservation Department found in a survey and evaluation of wetlands in 1954. Files of the State Drainage Engineer showed that from 1906 to 1940 more than 900,000 acres had been involved in organized drainage (Dahlen and Thompson, 1955).

Beginning in 1941, farm drainage was subsidized at the rate of 6 cents per cubic yard of earth moved and 40 cents per rod of tile put down. By the end of 1953, when this subsidization was withdrawn, payments had been made to one out of every four farms in the state, affecting the drainage of 1,692,750 acres. . . . Combining these figures, we arrive at a total of over *two and one-half million acres*, or 4,075 square miles.

The authors noted that these operations did not always destroy wetlands as wildlife habitat and that some projects were abandoned. However, more detailed work in Racine County indicated that only 10,000 acres of wetland remained—a loss of 87 percent of the wetlands in 50 years.

One obvious result of drainage is the loss of deep marshes, which are so important to waterfowl. With the exception of refuges and marshes along lakes or rivers, hardly an area remains in Racine County which could be called good for duck production. . . .

An advantage recently gained for wildlife interests was the revision of Chapter 88 of the Wisconsin Statutes, the Farm Drainage Law. This revision requires that the Conservation Department be notified of hearings concerning proposed drainage projects. In many instances the benefits to be derived from drainage are of less consequence than the detrimental effects of lowered ground water levels, loss of fish habitat in the outlet stream from siltation and warming, and the possible increase of flood danger due to acceleration of run-off. In cases concerning navigable waters, the Public Service Commission may be called upon to determine whether the proposed drainage is in the best interests of the public.

In the present era of agricultural abundance and declining wetland wildlife, widespread reappraisal of drainage policies and economics is needed, as well as an updated consideration of private versus public values. Obviously, most of the loss of wildlife habitat through drainage was unavoidable in the past, but recognition grows that there is a logical stopping point somewhere on the continuum of conditions represented by a vast and variable array of sites that might be, and are being, drained. That this point has been passed on numerous occasions probably is indicated by the investments of public funds now being made for the restoration of aquatic habitats for fish, waterfowl, and other wildlife. Particular phases of the wetlands problem are given more detailed treatment in Chapter 5.

Changes in Forested Lands

While various types of farming have continued to expand into areas potentially suited to modern agricultural systems, there has been a corresponding loss of cultivated acreage on the marginal fringe. A history of declining productivity and deterioration has shown that certain lands were overextended in row-crop culture; these are being gradually returned to the protective custody of trees and grass. Abandoned homesites on every 80 acres of what is now dense forest or traces of old crop rows among giant hardwoods present vivid lessons in these land-use changes. Actually, reversions of cropland have taken place in the United States throughout its history.

Forest land acreage in the United States has increased markedly since 1950. However, statistics on woodland in farms for the period 1959-1964 indicate a decrease of 18 million acres. Over 10 million acres of this change occurred in the South and most of the remainder in the Northeast. In these two regions the change in land use involving the largest acreage is from cropland to forest.

This paradox arises from a change in the census definition of a farm rather than from actual shifts in land use. Once an entire farm is converted to forest, the acreage of woodland is no longer shown as a part of "woodland in farms" but is included in the total forest land acreage.

In the lower Mississippi River Valley a major shift from forest to cropland is under way. Most of the land being cleared is for the production of soybeans. High prices and heavy demand for soybeans, accompanied by improvements in drainage, have encouraged this change (Beltz and Christopher, 1967).

Unfortunately, hundreds of thousands of acres of valuable hardwood timber are being destroyed to produce a crop for which surpluses are in prospect. Also, excellent habitat is being destroyed for deer, wild turkeys, waterfowl, raccoons, squirrels, and other wildlife. Much of the land involved is subject to periodic flooding, making it uncertain for crop production. This is an example of destruction of a forest resource in short supply and elimination of excellent wildlife habitat for immediate economic return. Here the long-term values have been given only slight consideration.

According to the 1959 Census of Agriculture, forests and woodlands occupied 614 million acres in the 48 states, indicating an increase of 13 million acres since 1930 (Bureau of the Census, 1962b). In the Northeast, Lake States, Appalachian region, Southeast, Mississippi Delta, and Pacific States, the growing of wood products is the principal use of land. In the Southeast, 63 percent of the land is in forest and woodland.

Projecting needs and resource use from 1959 to 1980, the Secretary of Agriculture (U.S. Department of Agriculture, 1962b) reported the following changes in cropland and forest:

The area of commercial forest land available for timber production was estimated at 530 million acres in 1959. The amount expected to be available by 1980 is 537 million acres. This net gain results from an expected shift of 19 million acres of cropland and 8 million acres of pasture and range to commercial forest, compared with shifts from commercial forest to other uses of about 20 million acres. However, in view of the timber demand situation and the fact that forest land will continue to be sought for other uses, no surplus of commercial forest is in prospect. A net of 5 million acres of noncommercial forest land is expected to shift to other strictly nonforest uses. Thus, the overall gain in forest land area is only about 2 million acres. It is expected that the use of 34 million acres of forest land will be limited primarily to recreation or wildlife purposes in 1980, or 7 million more acres than in 1959.

Successional stages in reversions from cropland to forest have major significance to wildlife production. Food and cover for many species are more abundant during earlier phases of succession than after the forest has formed a canopy. The nature of vegetation and duration of the transitional period from cultivated field to forest are influenced by climate, soil, seed and root stocks in the soil, and proximity of seed-trees. Even in fields that were cultivated for many years, the presence of viable seed and root stocks gives rise to a cover of forbs and grasses. Eventually the area is invaded by coniferous or hardwood forest.

In the hill country of the Southeast, where fields are relatively small, the growing season long, rainfall abundant, and tree seed plentiful, dense stands of young pines may cover an area within 5 years after cultivation ends. An invasion by hardwoods follows, and for an extended period brush growth provides excellent browse and cover for deer.

In regions where soil moisture is severely limited, or the growing season is short, early successional stages are extended. Under these conditions the forb-grass cover gives way slowly to trees. Usually there are stages during which shrubs occur as colonies and later as the dominant vegetation.

The importance of forests to wildlife and the benefits to be gained from wise management of both forests and wildlife are well described by Wingard and Heddleson (n.d.):

Forests cover over half of Pennsylvania. They are increasing slightly in area, substantially in growth and volume of wood, and greatly in value for watersheds, open space, recreation and wildlife lands. The challenge of the future will be to scientifically manage the forests of the Commonwealth to provide all these goods and services in a satisfactory combination.

These authors noted the great improvement in conditions and the increases in several important game species since the early part of this century. The wild turkey and beaver are now plentiful, and the deer herd yields a kill greater than it did in the thirties, when deer were three times more numerous than they are at present.

Projected land-use adjustments for the next 20 years indicate the conversion of 7 million acres of forest to cropland. During the same period it is estimated that 19 million acres of cropland will revert to forest (U.S. Department of Agriculture, 1962b).

Reliable data on land-use changes from forest to grassland are not available. Although changes in acreage are indicated in census statistics, differences in interpretations and definitions are probably of greater influence than actual shifts on the land. Projected land-use change from forest to grassland in the period 1959-1980 should be 11 million acres and from grassland to forest 8 million acres, resulting in a net change of 3 million acres (U.S. Department of Agriculture, 1962b).

According to the national inventory of soil and water conservation needs of 1965, the shift of land use from forest to grassland in the period 1958-1975 is expected to be 14 million acres and from grassland to forest 6 million acres, resulting in a net change of 8 million acres.

Adjustments in Grassland Area

Agricultural summaries indicate that in 1964 at least 640 million acres of grassland plus 225 million acres of woodland in the contiguous states were used for pasture or range (Economic Research Service, 1968b). Although changes occur from year to year, it is generally agreed that almost half of our land area is in permanent use for grazing livestock, and that about two thirds of this grazing land is in a grass or forb cover.

Between 1900 and 1964 there was a decline of more than 100 million acres in land used for permanent grassland pasturage. Most of this change occurred between 1900 and 1920, when extensive areas of range were converted to dryland and irrigated cropland. Following the severe drought and dust storms of the 1930's, there was a shift of 14 million acres of cultivated lands to grass. Most of this change took place in the Great Plains and the Southeast. Unfortunately, high prices and demand for wheat during World War II negated this conservative trend and resulted in even further destruction of range.

Statistics related to land use on a national scale tend to conceal significant regional changes. The issue is further complicated by wide differences in climate and the characteristics of grassland vegetation in the eastern and western halves of the nation.

Changes in the wording of questions on acreage of grassland and cropland on farms in taking the 1964 Census of Agriculture make comparison with statistics from earlier censuses difficult, if not impossible. For this reason, the following discussion of land-use changes from crops to grass is limited to the 5-year period 1959-1964 (Bureau of the Census, 1966: table 16).

There was a decrease of 8 million acres, nationwide, in cropland used only for pasture for the period 1959-1964. At the same time, there was an increase of about 24 million acres in land listed as "other pasture." The soil class "improved pasture" shows an increase of about 13 million acres for the 5-year period.

"Other pasture" areas increased by about 4 million acres in the North and by 8 million acres in the South between 1959 and 1964. Much of this land was in cultivated crops at one time. In the West, "other pasture" increased by a little more than 12 million acres. Although some of this was changed from cropland to grassland, much of it had not been cultivated.

It seems fairly certain that a substantial acreage of cropland is being shifted to grassland. This change has important implications for wildlife through habitat changes and in the extent of the land involved.

Land as Living Space

The rapid increase of population in the United States has been particularly significant in the cities. That we have become a predominantly urban nation is evident in the fact that lands used for urban purposes have increased from 10 million acres in 1919 to 29 million acres in 1964 (Economic Research Service, 1968b). Clawson (1959) stated: "It is our small cities that are the most lavish users of land; half of all the land used for urban purposes is in cities of less than 25,000, although such cities contain but one fourth of the urban population." He predicted that growth of this kind to the year 2000 would be particularly significant in the West where the 2½ million acres now used for urban purposes would become 8½ million acres. He noted that the areas taken over would include some of the most productive agricultural lands, especially irrigated valleys. He also said:

The best available evidence is that the city idles and wastes as much land as it uses. That is, twice as much land is taken out of agriculture or other use, because of city growth, as is actually put to use by the city. The rest lies idle, hopefully "ripening" for later actual urban use but often blighted by unwise subdivision, excessive taxes, and fouled-up titles.

Particular problems of this kind in the nation's most rapidly urbanizing state were described by Nelson (1961):

In California, one of our major problems is the engulfment of prime agricultural land by suburbia. Each day some 375 acres of our best soils are being taken out of production. About 140,000 acres annually are being converted to nonagricultural use. . . . It should be noted that, of California's 16,000,000 acres of land suitable for intensive agriculture, only about 6,000,000 acres are Class I and Class II soils.

Although national losses to urban development of various classes of cropland are not known in detail, Regan and Wooten (1963) stated that areas in special-purpose uses had doubled since 1920. Rural lands have been absorbed at a rate of about 2 million acres per year. "About 54 million acres of land were devoted to urban uses, transport, and other intensive uses in 1959." Cities, towns, and roadways of various kinds accounted for 90 percent of the total.

Vlasin (1963) has estimated that the 41,000 miles of interstate highways authorized by the Federal-Aid Highway Act of 1956 will eventually require about 1½ million acres of additional land. Interstate routes of this kind require 250 to 300 feet of right-of-way, and in agricultural areas most of the land must be taken from farms.

Information furnished to the Senate Public Roads Subcommittee in 1965 showed that streets and highways in the United States occupy about 22 million acres, of which all but 1 million is accounted for by rural thoroughfares. All forms of transportation were utilizing about 25 million acres by the middle of the century. Railway rights-of-way probably have passed their maximum, and further requirements for roadways and airports probably will not be significant in terms of our total land area. Projections indicate that a total of perhaps 30 million acres will be so used by the year 2000.

CHANGES IN WATERS AND WETLANDS

As was pointed out in Chapter 1, great areas of inland and coastal waters, marshes, and swamps furnished habitats for aquatic and semi-aquatic wildlife in primitive times. The progressive disappearance or modification of such environments constitutes one of the most significant changes affecting wildlife in North America. Many such areas have become valuable agricultural land after being drained. The compulsion to drain what is commonly regarded as a "mosquito breeding wasteland" has likely had its own impetus. As will be seen, also, natural processes alter the character of aquatic sites over fairly long periods.

Inland Lakes and Marshes

In the United States there are about 250 freshwater lakes with surface areas of 10 square miles or more (Bue, 1963). Alaska has about 100 such lakes, and 100 more are in Minnesota, Michigan, Wisconsin, New York, and Maine. Twenty-three states contain all the lakes of this size. There are more natural lakes in glaciated areas than elsewhere, and glacial lakes are far more plentiful than those of other origins.

No rule exists as to how large or deep a body of water must be to qualify as a lake rather than a pond. Also, lakes are found in all stages of filling up as they become bogs and marshes and, eventually, dry land. Thus, it is difficult to obtain precise figures on total numbers and acreages of lakes. However, the amount of water stored in natural lakes, exclusive of the Great Lakes, which hold an estimated 5,500 cubic miles of water, is much greater than the quantity in all our artificial reservoirs (Bue, 1963). The smaller freshwater lakes are better known as recreation sites than for their contributions to economic development.

In terms of geologic time, all lakes (including the largest), are transitory. It is their natural "life cycle" to be filled by erosion products from the land and by annual deposits of plant material; at the same time, shallow areas are sapped and desiccated by transpiration from their vegetative cover.

A counteracting natural rejuvenation process can sometimes be seen in operation. In periods of extended drought, deposits of peat that had been largely preserved from decomposition in water are laid bare and dried out. They are exposed to air, and oxidation liberates soluble nutrients that will contribute to the fertility of the waters when flooding again takes place. In dry periods an even more radical kind of renewal may occur when desiccated peat is ignited from a surface fire. The deposit may smolder for months, or even years, producing a deep cavity and ultimately open water when the weather pattern changes and rains return. In this manner an old bog or sedge meadow can be converted into a new lake that, after a period of leaching, is ready to start its life history again.

The rate of natural aging, or eutrophication, of lakes is greatly influenced by the condition of watersheds. In particular it is accelerated by agricultural or other land-use practices that may induce erosion. The artificial fertilization of waters with agricultural chemicals or with sewage and other wastes may similarly produce excessive plant growth and deplete the oxygen (see Freeman and Bennett, 1969).

Natural lakes and their bordering marshes also are being significantly reduced through direct occupancy by man. Shorelines commonly are the sites of summer cottages built on landfills at the water's edge. Practices that alter the natural character and affect the wildlife productivity of a body of water are increasingly being controlled through local or state zoning restrictions.

Stimulated by widespread evidence that wetland wildlife was facing a developing crisis, the Fish and Wildlife Service carried out a national wetland survey (Shaw and Fredine, 1956). This included sites covered with shallow, temporary, or intermittent waters (marshes, swamps, wet meadows, potholes, sloughs, and river-overflow lands) but excluded the permanent waters of streams, reservoirs, and deep lakes. It revealed that there were 74.4 million acres of wetlands in the contiguous 48 states. Of this acreage, 63.5 million acres were categorized as inland fresh water and 1.6 million acres as inland saline water, the remainder being coastal water and wetland areas. It is estimated that, originally, the natural wetlands of the 48 contiguous states totaled 127 million acres. In historic times, more than 40 million acres have been converted to cropland or other dry-land uses by drainage and flood protection.

A discussion of particularly critical wetland problems that affect wildlife is reserved for Chapter 5.

Coastal Lowlands and Estuaries

Shaw and Fredine (1956) estimated that once about 4 million acres were coastal freshwater areas and about 5.3 million acres were coastal saline wetlands. An estuary has been defined as a semienclosed coastal body of water having a free connection with the open sea and within which the seawater is measurably diluted with fresh water from land drainage (Cameron and Pritchard, 1963). The estuary is an ecotone, or transition zone, whose boundaries merge gradually with the ocean, the freshwater environment, and the land. The edge relationships are dynamic and commonly in a state of change.

The peculiar biological values of the estuarine zone were recognized by the President's Science Advisory Committee (1965). Salt marshes such as the Sapelo Marshes of Georgia have been found to produce nearly seven times as much organic matter per unit area as the water of the continental shelf, 20 times as much as the deep sea, and 6 times as much as average wheatland. The same report stated that over 90 percent of the harvest of sea foods from waters surrounding the United States is from the continental shelf, and nearly two thirds of that amount consists of species that depend for their existence on the estuarine zone or must pass through the zone on the way to spawning grounds.

Waterfowl and other types of water and marsh-dwelling birds are abundant in the estuarine zone, as are fur animals and other species. The Bureau of Sport Fisheries and Wildlife (1967), in an interim report on its estuarine programs, mentions that 78 of the 312 units in the National Wildlife Refuge system are coastal installations, of which 42 contain significant estuarine areas.

In a review of the role of man in estuarine processes, Cronin (1967) states that prior to 1950 the effect of human activity probably was unimportant and limited largely to silt from agricultural areas and disposal of human wastes. In the past 20 years, however, destruction of estuarine areas has been accelerated. During this period at least 570,000 acres of estuarine habitat have been lost by dredging and filling. Although the data are scattered, they show clearly that the problem warrants attention. Between 1954 and 1963, an estimated 45,000 acres of tidal wetlands from Maine to Delaware were lost; 20 square miles of Tampa Bay, Florida, have been filled and converted into residential areas. Of a former 435 square miles in San Francisco Bay, 17 square miles have been reclaimed and 240 square miles are in danger of being reclaimed. Of the original 300 square miles of marsh area surrounding the Bay, 240 square miles have beeñ eliminated. Cronin (1967) stated:

> Vulnerability to human influence is a characteristic of estuaries. They lie in proximity to man's terrestrial habitat, produce large quantities of his food supply, and are doorways between the oceans and the land masses. Each receives the impact of many human activities throughout an entire watershed and many are subjected to the most intensive levels of use applied to any marine water areas.

Siltation of estuaries is increased by deforestation, flash runoff, and poor agricultural practices. In the Patuxent River, Maryland, for example, deposits of sediment have accumulated to depths of 40 feet over recent (not fossilized) oyster beds. The Mississippi River carries into the Gulf of Mexico each year enough silt to form 38,000 acres, 3 feet deep. Narrow canalization of the river between high levees increases velocity and silt transport so that much of the load is deposited directly in the Gulf rather than in the basin by overflow. Weighing total economic benefits for the present system against deterioration of the estuarine ecosystem poses a difficult problem.

About one third of the population of the United States resides within a 50-mile coastal border. Most of these people, and many others who live far inland, use recreation facilities along the nation's seashores. The Outdoor Recreation Resources Review Commission (1962), using information from the U.S. Coast and Geodetic Survey, reported that the shoreline along the Atlantic and Pacific Oceans and the Gulf of Mexico totals 53,677 statute miles. In addition, Alaska has 33,904 miles of coastline and Hawaii 1,902 miles. Of the marine coasts of the contiguous 48 states, 17,455 miles were considered by the Commission to be recreation shores, but only 753 statute miles were open to the public. This mileage has been increased as a result of the establishment of national seashores and other recreation areas, but public access to much of the coast, whether for hunting, fishing, or other outdoor pursuits, continues to be severely limited.

Rivers and Floodplains

Natural drainageways characterize the topography and land-use potential of every part of North America. Flowing water is endlessly useful, uniquely beautiful, and vulnerable in many ways to degradation. Using information of the Geological Survey, Leopold (1962) gave a summary description of the nation's riverways:

The three million miles of stream channels in the United States vary widely in size and occur in a wide variety of topographic and geologic circumstances. Included in this figure of total length are those high mountain streams epitomizing wilderness beauty, the dirty and trash-filled channels too often coursing through our cities, and the majestic but turbid large rivers flowing in wide valleys of central United States and the flat expanses of the coastal plain.

Human interference with the natural dynamics of rivers has been the rule rather than the exception, with far-reaching effects from the height of land to the coastal delta. Peak flows may be reduced by many upstream practices. Land treatments such as contour farming, terracing, reforestation, managed grazing, and other water-conserving practices reduce runoff. Diversions of river water for human consumption and industrial use and for irrigation of agricultural land are especially important in reducing river flow. On the other hand, rapid runoff from denuded slopes or from paved urban and highway surfaces increases flooding below the watershed and augments the transport and deposit of silt.

In addition to providing habitat for many forms of life, rivers carry the excess of precipitation over evapotranspiration losses from the continents back to sea along with great quantities of sediment, debris, and dissolved materials. Leopold states that slightly more than half of all the materials carried by river water from continent to ocean is dissolved load. The nature of such dissolved materials, the amount of sediment, water temperature, depth, velocity, and other factors determine, to a great extent, the kinds and numbers of organisms the water will support.

Although some of these streams and rivers run through canyons with few or no flood plains, Wooten *et al.* (1962) state that from 109 to 125 million acres, or between 6 and 7 percent of the land area of the United States, lie in the floodplains of rivers and streams.

From earliest times, these overflow lands of river basins have been favored agricultural sites. The sedimentary soils are fertile, except where covered with sand or coarse outwash, but their use has been subject to the acknowledged hazard of flooding. Since rivers and river junctions were commonly the choice sites for early settlement, the buildup of floodplains in cities followed, with recurring damage during times of heavy runoff. The extent of flooding in various sites ranges from high to low, and similarly there is wide variability in the possibilities and costs of controlling or mitigating floods.

Flood control on some of our major river systems has been a matter of public concern for over a century. Greenshields (1964) describes the history of such work in the Mississippi system dating back more than

150 years. The best-known feature is the construction of some 3,500 miles of levees on the Mississippi and its tributaries. Included also are a growing number of reservoirs on the tributary streams to hold back floodwaters, cutoffs to speed flow down the river, revetment of flood control structures, bank stabilization, dikes, pumping plants, siphons, floodgates, and floodwalls. The magnitude of past and future works on the Mississippi system may be envisioned by the fact that it drains 1,246,605 square miles in 31 states and in 2 provinces of Canada.

Since the beginning of this century, flood losses have averaged about $200 million annually, with great variability. Despite the spending of billions of dollars on structural measures since passage of the Flood Control Act of 1936, the yearly cost of destruction by floods has continued to increase (Holmes, 1961).

White *et al.* (1958) studied the flood problems of 17 representative urban sites. They estimated that at least 40 percent of the potential annual flood losses of the nation are occurring in the built-up flood-plains of towns and cities. Summarizing estimates of various types of damage costs as a "rough measure of trends,"

we arrive at the tentative conclusion that at present the damage potential in urban flood plains in the United States is increasing at the rate of about 2.7 per cent per year. When allowance is made for protection works which are reducing all losses at the rate of about 3 per cent per year, the net decrease is about .3 per cent per year. That is, every $6 of potential flood damage reduced each year by new flood protection measures is offset by at least $5 of additional flood damage resulting from growth in the number and value of new residential, commercial, transportational, and industrial structures placed on the flood plains.

Inasmuch as structural measures such as retention reservoirs, channel improvements, and levees have failed to halt the rise in flood damages, the use of nonstructural methods should be more fully explored. Before these measures can be used to their greatest advantage, procedures must be developed for determining the optimum combination of measures to apply in a given floodplain and the level of protection each should provide.

The use of river overflow lands for agriculture, for example, bears on other uses of such areas and raises pertinent questions: When should a bottomland farmer have high-cost public protection against flood damage, and to what extent is this a personal-risk business? Under what conditions can we afford to control floods on floodplains? What future problems are involved in fostering a buildup on bottomlands that will no longer be protected when the reservoirs are silted in?

Would forestry, wildlife, and recreation constitute an adequate return from many of these bottomlands without large public investments for flood control?

Such questions are the subject of increasing study as the total costs of flood damage and mitigation of flood loss mount. After an appraisal of various methods of regulating the use of floodplains, Murphy (1958) concluded that:

Results of the extensive field investigation of past and present uses made of channel-encroachment laws, flood-plain zoning provisions, subdivision regulations, building codes, and other methods of flood-plain regulation indicate conclusively that as now applied they do not halt the continued increase of flood losses. The framework of enactment and environment of operation are insufficient to fulfill their publicized and appropriate role in the family of flood-damage-prevention methods.

A critical factor in the continued unrealistic and uneconomic management of flood plains is the type of justification being used by the Corps of Engineers for flood control works. This logic counts the savings gained through the protection of anticipated *future* developments on the floodplain that will be stimulated by the proposed construction. This situation has been described by Krutilla (1966):

For example, of 59 Corps of Engineers projects authorized by the 1965 Act that were 'justified' wholly or in part by flood control benefits, from 3 to 85% of the total flood control benefits were accounted for by the expected future invasion of the flood plain. For half of all the projects, the proportion of benefits represented by anticipated future development in the flood plain amounted to over 40%. Approximately half of the single-purpose flood control projects would not have been 'justified,' save for the anticipated more intensive use of the flood plain (enhancement benefits) stimulated by the flood control projects.

In some measure, the acceptance of this kind of rationale appears to constitute an economic feedback for the automatic justification of many "flood control" projects.

The continuing growth of floodplain problems was recognized by the Federal Council for Science and Technology Committee on Water Resources, which in 1966 recommended a fivefold increase in research on nonstructural alternatives to flood control. Also, a report by the Task Force on Federal Flood Control Policy outlines some of the problems involved and makes recommendations for action. The related Executive Order 11296 states:

The heads of the executive agencies shall provide leadership in encouraging a broad and unified effort to prevent uneconomic uses and the development of the Nation's flood plains and, in particular, to lessen the risk of flood losses in connection with Federal lands and installations and federally financed or supported improvements.

It is evident that in most communities the natural dynamics of streams and rivers are poorly understood and largely ignored in planning the course of urban development. Further studies and pilot experiments in this field are urgently needed, with such extensive uses as parks, forestry, and recreation offering alternatives to the vulnerable, high-cost, commercial buildup that creates major problems to be solved at public expense.

Relatively few of our rivers have remained in an unpolluted, undeveloped, wild state. A growing body of public opinion recognizes that the damming of every stream for power or flood control is not desirable. It is being increasingly recognized that there are many reasons for preserving diversity in the human environment. As part of this thesis, the "wild river" idea has merit.

Man-made waters

For 200 years, the widespread trend in water management was the reduction of surface waters and the desiccation of moist sites. However, largely within the present century, and with the rapid development of engineering technology, there has been a contrary trend. The desirability of holding runoff for many uses, and in a variety of situations, has gained recognition. In many regions an aerial view reveals the popularity and significance of water impoundment in systems of land use.

Tanks, Ponds, and Small Impoundments

Small storage reservoirs, an acre or so in extent and built by private landowners, constitute one of our most important and useful types of water management. Largely in the past 25 years, farmers and ranchers of the United States have built more than 2 million tanks and ponds having a combined surface area approaching that of Lake Ontario (Gambell, 1966). About 60,000 a year are constructed, of which about 10,000 are in authorized flood prevention watersheds and Public Law 566 (Chapter 5) watershed projects. Various government credit and assistance programs encourage the building of ponds with technical and direct financial aid. Edminster (1964) predicted that the number of ponds in the nation would rise by another 1.3 million by 1980. Under the stimulus of the Soil Conservation Service, larger ponds are being

built, with management emphasis on fish production and recreation.
Reports on ponds in the South that are stocked with fish indicate that
the percentage ranges from about 60 in Texas to nearly 100 in Alabama, Florida, Georgia, and South Carolina.

In the upper Great Plains region, ponds, tanks, and dugouts are
becoming increasingly important in maintaining waterfowl production
in spite of the loss of habitat occasioned by drainage in the prairie pothole country (Chapter 5). In land of irregular topography, and near the
headwaters of streams, farm ponds and other small impoundments
have many practical and esthetic benefits. They furnish water for livestock, help distribute grazing pressure, store water for household use
and irrigation, and offer some protection from floods and fire. A well-
managed, landscaped pond adds beauty and value to the farmstead. It
utilizes runoff from the farmed watershed and acts as a settling basin
for silt. It delays the escape of water from the property, permitting the
growing of a fish crop. Farm ponds add significantly to recreational
possibilities in the rural scene. Headwater impoundments on streams
can be important backstops to larger reservoirs, and they store water
to maintain streamflow through dry summers.

Relationships between wildlife and small artificial waters are discussed further in Chapter 5.

Large Reservoirs

A compilation by the U.S. Geological Survey (Martin and Hanson,
1966) revealed that the surface area of 1,562 reservoirs (having at least
5,000 acre-feet of usable storage each), including eight in Hawaii, was
14,831,000 acres. The total storage capacity of these large impoundments was more than 359 million acre-feet. Half of the states have no
natural lakes as large as 10 square miles in area, but more than three
fourths have reservoirs of that size or larger, and all have some impoundments. The surface area of all our artificial reservoirs—more than
23,000 square miles—is nearly double that of the large natural lakes exclusive of the Great Lakes.

California, Texas, and Colorado have the most reservoirs. On the
basis of surface area, Minnesota, Florida, and Texas have the most
water acreage of this type. As in the case of natural lakes, these reservoirs vary widely in depth and in stages of silting. The water level of
most is subject to relatively large seasonal changes.

Although reservoirs may have the outward appearance of natural
lakes, they are so constructed that most of the water is above the
lowest outlet and can be released, whereas almost all the water of un-

regulated natural lakes is dead storage, or below the level of the outlet.

Because of these features, most reservoirs serve several purposes, such as water supply, irrigation, flood control, and power generation. They are becoming increasingly important for recreation, providing a great deal of fishing and boating, and many are resting areas for waterfowl. On the shores of the larger reservoirs, such as those of the Tennessee Valley Authority, are state, county, and city parks; commercial fishing camps; resorts and boat docks; private clubs; camps for Boy and Girl Scouts, YMCA and YWCA, church, and educational groups; and lakefront lots for vacation homes.

From the standpoint of fish and wildlife, reservoir construction has resulted in drastically changed habitat conditions. Wild rivers have been tamed to the benefit of some species of fish and the detriment of others, and bottomlands that once were important winter ranges for big game are now covered with water. Water from the reservoirs, when used for irrigation, has converted semidesert country into farm land, which inevitably eliminates some wildlife forms and enables others to multiply.

In the case of reservoirs constructed in connection with large-scale multipurpose river basin development, we may note here that, while the purposes to be served will have a terminal economic life, either because the storage reservoirs will silt up or because of the likelihood of eventual technological obsolescence, the damage done to the natural environment through the construction of permanent works is likely to be lasting.

Other socioeconomic aspects of reservoir construction and irrigation projects are discussed in Chapter 5.

PROBLEMS OF REMNANT ECOSYSTEMS

As might be expected, the extensive changes that have taken place in North American habitats since the time of settlement were largely the result of single-purpose enterprise. They took little account of what was being destroyed, with the result that today only vestiges of certain primitive habitats remain. The near-extinction of many animal species in this century is in most cases the result of eliminating the environment on which such species depended. The pressure for land reclamation for human habitation and for agriculture is so great that certain endangered animals and ecosystems could easily be lost entirely unless strong measures are taken.

The Disappearing Grasslands

On this continent, as in other parts of the world, semiarid grasslands have been particularly vulnerable to deterioration under regimes of heavy grazing or grain cropping. Darling (1956) has pointed out that truly nomadic peoples, such as the "Reindeer Lapps and western Asiatic tribes," have used their extensive pasturelands in a manner similar to naturally adjusted herds of wild ungulates. In comparison, the more intensive exploitation of sedentary cultures has not been ecologically attuned and handled within the limits set by climatic extremes. In North America we probably have no grassland of any appreciable size that is exactly as it was in primitive times. At the least, it has been invaded by numerous species of exotic plants.

According to that epochal work *The Western Range* (Forest Service, 1936), the tall grass of the prairie has decreased more than any other range vegetation. Originally this subclimax grassland extended as the "prairie peninsula" eastward into Indiana with outliers to central Ohio. In all, it covered some 252 million acres. Westward, conditions became steadily drier, and in eastern Nebraska the mid-grasses of the true prairie became dominant; these, in turn, gave way largely to short grasses on the high plains.

Today some of the most fertile farms of North America occupy the tall grass country. A suggestion of what this rich flora was like may still be seen in old cemeteries and along railway rights-of-way in the Midwest. Native prairies, as modified by heavy grazing, still exist in blocks of some thousands of acres in the Nebraska Sandhills and the Flint Hills of eastern Kansas. These soils are obviously unsuited for cultivation.

Large marshes of the northern prairies once were nesting grounds for the whooping crane, greater sandhill crane, and trumpeter swan. Prairie chickens occupied nearly all the tall and mixed grasslands, habitats that were lost progressively as the native sod was broken. The heath hen of the east coast barrens had disappeared from most of the mainland a century ago and became extinct in the early 1930's. Other prairie chickens now are greatly reduced and on the endangered list. Probably the tall grass prairies were optimum range, at least for the greater prairie chicken, but today the bulk of remaining habitat is in the mixed grass region, where the land is too sandy or hilly to farm.

Other components of the grassland fauna have been decimated. The bison and wolf are gone, and the pronghorn is largely restricted to intermountain grasslands and brushlands. The huge flights of eskimo curlews that migrated northward in spring across the prairies disappeared late in the nineteenth century as a result of unrestricted shooting, and the species may well be extinct. Extensive control operations and the breaking up of grasslands led to widespread decline of the black-tailed prairie dog and also its most dependent predator, the never abundant black-footed ferret. Efforts are being made by the National Park Service, the Bureau of Sport Fisheries and Wildlife, and others to preserve the ferret and its prey as part of the quasiprimitive ecosystem in parks and natural areas.

The Gulf coastal prairie, including the part in Texas that supports remaining populations of the endemic and endangered Attwater prairie chicken, is undergoing extensive conversion to agriculture (especially grain sorghum and cotton) and grazing.

Lehmann's (1941) early surveys of the Attwater prairie chicken indicated that the area it occupied in Texas in 1937 totaled less than half a million acres, as compared with an original range of some 6 million acres of coastal bluestem (*Andropogon*) prairie. He also considered the encroachment of mesquite, live oak, various acacias, and other kinds of brush (held in check by prairie fires in earlier times) to be an important factor in degrading habitat. He believed that overgrazing, especially during drought years, speeded the transformation of grassland into brush jungles. By 1936 more than 2 million acres of former prairie chicken range were in cultivation, and thousands of acres of sod were being plowed annually, especially to extend rice farming. Pasture mowing, oil development, drainage, overhunting, and uncontrolled pasture burning were other factors listed as detrimental.

The Attwater prairie chicken once was common from southwestern Louisiana southward to the Nueces River in Texas. It had disappeared from Louisiana by about 1919 (Lehmann, 1968), and the total remaining population numbered about 8,700 birds in 1939. Another survey by Lehmann in 1967 revealed that in 30 years the regularly occupied habitat had shrunk to less than a quarter of a million acres, and the population had declined to about 1,070 birds.

Lehmann pointed out, however, that conditions are not hopeless for this species, and efforts on its behalf exemplify the possibilities in cooperation among agencies. Texas still has a "seed stock" and more than a million acres that can support more of these birds. Public interest in restoration is high. On Ellington Air Force Base a population of more than 100 chickens represents a hazard to air traffic; the Texas Parks and Wildlife Department and the Bureau of Sport Fisheries and Wildlife are transplanting these to vacant ranges. The World Wildlife Fund purchased 3,400 acres in the heart of the important prairie chicken range in Colorado County in 1965. In 1967, by a gift of Mr. and Mrs. J. M. Tatton of Corpus Christi, 7,000 acres were added to the Aransas National Wildlife Refuge. With technical guidance available, some landowners are willing to manage these birds at their own expense. To this end, renewed research efforts are now under way.

The Attwater prairie chicken program illustrates the kind of organized effort that will be necessary if other endangered habitats and wildlife are to be salvaged on at least a token basis.

Tall Brush of the Rio Grande

In the valley of the Rio Grande River a subtropical ecosystem unique in the United States has been reduced through clearing and cultivation to less than a thousand acres. This semiarid type, characterized by a mixture of tall shrubs, harbors no species of wildlife threatened with extinction, but it supports within our borders a peripheral community of Mexican species that is well on the way to being lost. Included among these are the northern chachalaca, northern white-fronted dove, northern groove-billed ani, Merrill's pauraque, northeastern elegant trogon, northeastern rose-throated becard, northern green jay, northern white-collared seedeater, and perhaps a dozen other birds. Mammals ranging northward from Mexico into this part of Texas include the jaguar, jaguarundi, coatimundi, ocelot, and margay.

It may be said of most such remnant ecosystems that relatively few people see them and they will contribute little in the way of mass public benefits. This usually is true also of alternative uses for the land they occupy—in this case, more fields of vegetables and citrus groves. It probably is public business if a sample of primitive biota anywhere is to be preserved for long-term casual use. Such historic and biological landmarks help to maintain the character of a locality. More broadly, their service to science and intellectually curious minorities probably helps to assure the integrity of our heterogeneous society. In a degree these are abstract and sophisticated viewpoints, but such terms of reference must be considered admissible if our resource management context is not to be completely utilitarian.

Florida Everglades

The everglades are a tropical wetland extending over southern Florida from Lake Okeechobee to the tip of the peninsula. Congress recognized the unique character of this biologically rich combination of ecosystems in 1947 by establishing Everglades National Park. It is our third largest (1.4 million acres) national park and is visited by more than a million people a year.

This vast and variable wilderness of estuaries, lagoons and sloughs, coastal prairies, sawgrass glades, hammocks, cypress islands, mangrove swamps, and pine forests harbors many rare and vanishing species of birds and other wildlife. Nearly extinct birds include the everglades kite, Cape Sable sparrow, great white heron, roseate spoonbill, reddish egret, wood ibis, pink ibis, and southern bald eagle. Rare mammals include the manatee, Florida water rat, and everglades mink. A few American crocodiles still are found there, and the glades are one of the principal remaining habitats of the alligator.

As a major and irreplaceable wilderness, the Florida everglades probably present the most serious and urgent preservation problem facing the nation. The prime question is one of water supply and progressive changes in the hydrology of central and southern Florida over the past century. If it is to survive in approximately the natural state that justified its establishment as a national park, the conditions that brought about this finely adjusted ecosystem must be maintained. A National Park Service research plan (Robertson *et al.*, 1966) describes the situation well:

For centuries the sheet of fresh water moving southward over the Everglades from Lake Okeechobee, flowed through sawgrass areas of the Park and entered the Gulf of Mexico through a labyrinth of mangrove-lined rivers and creeks. Where fresh water flowing out of the Everglades merged with salt water of the Gulf, a shifting zone of brackish water up to 12 miles wide has developed. The width of the brackish zone is dependent on the quantity of fresh water flowing seaward from the land, and hence is greatest in wet years and very restricted during drouth.

The estuarine zone referred to is well known as a rich nursery ground for many important marine fishes, including the menhaden, black mullet, spotted sea trout, snook, tarpon, and pompano. The same is true of the pink shrimp, the most important commercial fishery of the state. The Institute of Marine Science has carried out studies showing that great reductions of fish, mollusks, and other aquatic organisms occur with the reduction of freshwater flow and the buildup of salinity.

Such changes have occurred with increasing frequency and in greater degree in recent years. Long-term flood control and agricultural reclamation operations, including diversion canals to carry water directly to the sea, have steadily changed the character of the region north of the park and altered natural water relationships. A 5-year drought from 1961 to 1965 brought desiccation and near destruction to the glades. In 1966 it was estimated that the surviving alligator population was not more than 5 percent of that present before 1960. Bird rookeries failed; freshwater fish survived only in deep holes; cypress domes and bayheads were destroyed; and other plant types were jeopardized. The fact that the park received no water through the gates in the Tamiami Trail accentuated the natural shortage and produced the greatest emergency of this kind in history (Craighead, 1966).

The drought was broken by rains in May and June 1965, and in 1966 a June hurricane brought water levels up to capacity. The recovery of aquatic food organisms and the creatures dependent on them was slow, with signs of permanent changes in evidence.

With the buildup of human populations and the competing uses for water, the biota of the park has become critically vulnerable to drought, and it may likewise suffer damage through the rapid release of water in times of flood. Problems have multiplied since the creation by Congress of the Central and South Florida Flood Control District in 1948. This agency, the Corps of Engineers, and the National Park Service are now coordinating studies of water control and allocation problems in the hope that adequate provision can be made for the everglades, in which a nationwide public interest has become manifest. Except for this interest, the march of "progress" in southern Florida would quickly overwhelm and obliterate an area that easily qualifies as one of the biological wonders of the New World.

Preservation of Natural Areas

Although many values may be claimed for setting aside undisturbed areas, a single overriding purpose probably would be sufficient justification for establishing a carefully guarded national system of this kind. The study of biotic communities is being steadily refined. Natural relationships of living things represent the most elaborate and orderly systems of the universe, and for the foreseeable future much is to be learned from them. It would be poor resource and science strategy to destroy the remaining check areas and controls against which our land-use enterprises can be measured and judged.

In conformity with this concept, and also to help implement the participation of the United States in the International Biological Program, a Committee on Research Natural Areas has been established in the federal government. It includes representation from the Forest Service, National Park Service, Bureau of Land Management, and Bureau of Sport Fisheries and Wildlife. The committee will prepare a directory to protected research reserves on federal lands and will encourage the establishment of new areas needed for research and education. Among the lands and waters administered by the agencies mentioned, a wide variety of natural or near-natural ecosystems occur and can be preserved. It is recognized that these have value as pools of genetic material in its primitive forms.

It is encouraging that the American public is becoming increasingly aware of the need to identify, establish, and protect natural areas wherever they may still be found. Contributions to this end are being made by public agencies, private organizations, and informed individuals.

In March 1966, Assistant Secretary Stanley A. Cain of the Department of the Interior established an *ad hoc* Natural Areas Committee in that department. Agencies of other departments administering federally owned land were invited to attend the committee meetings. One of the results was publication in 1967 by the Department of the Interior and the Department of Agriculture of a federal directory of natural areas. If of national significance, such areas qualify for registration under the Natural Landmarks Program of the National Park Service.

The most important step in this field was made in 1964 with passage by the Congress of the Wilderness Act. This act established a national system for protecting the primitive features of qualifying areas of the national forests, parks, and wildlife refuges. Under other legislation, parts of the public domain may be considered for wilderness classification. With certain exceptions, units of the wilderness system are 5,000 acres or more in size. The Wilderness Act provided for a lengthy and somewhat unwieldy review process for adding new units. It also sanctioned the continuation of grazing and other established nonconforming uses on wilderness areas. Improvements in the system may well be in order as a result of the work of the Public Land Law Review Commission.

In 1967, the various states purchased 201,000 acres of land and water with assistance from the federal Land and Water Conservation Fund. They acquired an estimated 153,000 acres under the federal aid to wildlife and fisheries acts, the Open Space Program of the Department of Housing and Urban Development, and the Greenspan Program of the Department of Agriculture. Most of these tracts would not qualify as natural areas in the primitive sense, but some are of high quality and will steadily improve through natural processes if left undisturbed. Their preservation for public conservation and recreation purposes helps to protect them from the encroachment of urban development, highways, airports, and similar uses.

Private organizations such as the Nature Conservancy, the National Audubon Society, the Natural Area Council, and World Wildlife Fund are playing a highly significant role in saving endangered remnants of our primitive ecosystems. They are able to take options and make other moves quickly as may be required by circumstances in which government action is often too little and too late. Areas privately acquired often are conveyed in due course to units of local, state, or federal government for long-term administration. As an outstanding example of the cooperative effort being made in this field, the Nature Conservancy has a $6-million line of credit from the Ford Foundation for immediate use in making critical land purchases for the executive branch of the federal government. This is one answer to the problem of escalating land prices in public projects.

PUBLIC LANDS FOR PUBLIC PURPOSES

A great ideal of the first settlers of North America was to build homes on land that was their own. They knew well the conditions in Europe where the Crown and a privileged nobility held great tracts and commoners little or nothing. The right of the individual to own land was, from the first, one of the primary reasons for risking one's future in the New World.

As a natural consequence of this viewpoint, soon after the colonies were united as a nation, the government embarked on a program to give away or sell all of its public lands. It was an unprecedented program. Between 1781 and 1963, the United States Government disposed of 1,143,800,000 acres (Orell, 1965). Small wonder that the expression "doing a land office business" was coined to describe booming activity.

Mass disposal of land in the public domain to private citizens, corporations, and states resulted in rapid settlement and development across the nation. Sale of public land brought some financial support to the young federal government but less than had been anticipated by the Congress. Rushes of land-hungry settlers onto tracts ceded by tribes of Indians, and range wars over possession and use of vast areas of grazing lands in the West, made colorful pages in our history.

Notwithstanding the general policy of public land disposal, it became clear early in our history that certain areas of land and water would sometimes need to be kept in public ownership to serve common needs of the citizens. By 1817, Congress had empowered the President to withdraw areas from entry for *ad hoc* purposes, such as roads, military posts, and lighthouses. An act of 1832 authorized reservations having extraordinary natural features, and later the authority was broadened to include other objectives (Orell, 1965). Following the rise of the conservation movement led by Theodore Roosevelt and his chief forester, Gifford Pinchot, the Congress was encouraged to permit the reacquisition of lands by purchase or gift from private and corporate owners. Since 1900 numerous acts have resulted in extensive land acquisition by the federal government and by state and local governments for many uses. By 1964 some 916 million acres were owned as public property or held in trust—about 39 percent of the total land area in the 50 states. The federal government owned 770 million acres (34 percent of the total land area) and held 50 million acres (2 percent) in trust for Indians; state governments owned 78 million acres (3 percent); and local governments owned 18 million acres (less than 1 percent).

Undoubtedly, some land will continue to be acquired by public agencies both for new projects and to block out areas now owned. However, compared with existing acreage, the additions will not be substantial. Many of the lands now administered by federal agencies have been transfers from the public domain. For the future, it is likely that most acquisitions will be in the East, and those in the West will be more than offset by the transfer of lands now under the jurisdiction of the Bureau of Land Management to state and private ownership.

The extent to which the 480 million acres of the public domain will remain in federal ownership or be transferred to the states or other interests may depend upon recommendations to the Congress by the Public Land Law Review Commission. This commission studied existing statutes and regulations as well as policies and practices of administrative agencies relative to the retention, management, and disposition of federal lands. In addition, data were compiled as necessary to determine and understand the present and future demands on areas in public ownership.

Wildlife as a public resource is likely to be most intensively managed and made most easily available on public lands of various categories: federal, state, county, and city.

The largest area of public land is the remainder of the public domain administered by the Bureau of Land Management. For the most part, this is low-value grazing land that can, in many areas, be made more useful to the public by managing it for recreation. All land-holding agencies of the federal government are giving recognition to this kind of public demand, and a similar trend is growing in state and local governments. As a basic recreational resource, wildlife is featured as a by-product of forestry and grazing, and it is a primary objective in certain lands set aside as parks or managed refuges. The developing technology by which uses are integrated for maximum benefits is examined in the next chapter.

REFERENCES

Beltz, R. C., and J. F. Christopher. 1967. Land clearing in the delta region of Mississippi, 1957-67 (research note S0-69). U.S. Forest Service, Washington, D.C.

Bue, C. D. 1963. Principal lakes of the United States. U.S. Geol. Surv. Circ. 476. 22 p.

Bureau of Sport Fisheries and Wildlife. 1967. Estuarine programs—interim report. U.S. Department of the Interior, Washington, D.C. 29 p.

Bureau of the Census. 1962b. Graphic summary of land utilization (ch. 1, part 6). *In* U.S. census of agriculture, 1959: Special reports. Vol. 5. U.S. Department of Commerce, Washington, D.C.

Bureau of the Census, 1966. Farms and land in farms (ch. 1). *In* U.S. census of agriculture, 1964. Vol. 2. U.S. Department of Commerce, Washington, D.C.

Cameron, W. M., and D. W. Pritchard. 1963. Estuaries, p. 306-324, Vol. 2. *In* M. N. Hill (ed.), The sea. John Wiley & Sons, New York.

Clawson, M. 1959. Changing patterns of land use in the West, p. 217-228. *In* F. S. Pollak (ed.), Resources development: frontiers for research. University of Colorado Press, Boulder.

Craighead, F. C. 1966. Further observations on the effects of the closure of the culverts along the Flamingo Highway on plants and wildlife. National Park Service, U.S. Department of the Interior, Washington, D.C.

Cronin, L. E. 1967. The role of man in estuarine processes, p. 667-689. *In* G. H. Lauff (ed.), Estuaries (AAAS Publ. 83). American Association for the Advancement of Science, Washington, D.C.

Dahlen, J. H., and D. R. Thompson. 1955. Wisconsin wetlands and their importance. Wis. Conserv. Bull. 20(1):9-12.

Darling, F. F. 1956. Man's ecological dominance through domesticated animals on wild lands, p. 778-787. *In* W. L. Thomas (ed.), Man's role in changing the face of the earth. University of Chicago Press, Chicago.

Economic Research Service. 1966. The balance sheet of agriculture, 1966. Agr. Inf. Bull. 314. U.S. Department of Agriculture, Washington, D.C.

Economic Research Service. 1968a. Farm costs and returns, commercial farms, by type, size, and location. Agr. Inf. Bull. 230. U.S. Department of Agriculture, Washington, D.C.

Economic Research Service. 1968b. Major uses of land and water in United States with special reference to agriculture, summary for 1964. Agr. Econ. Rep. 149.

U.S. Department of Agriculture. U.S. Government Printing Office, Washington, D.C.

Edminster, F. C. 1964. Farms, ponds and waterfowl, p. 399-407. *In* Waterfowl tomorrow. Bureau of Sport Fisheries and Wildlife, U.S. Department of the Interior, Washington, D.C.

Forest Service, U.S. Department of Agriculture. 1936. The western range. Senate Doc. 199, 74th Cong., 2d Sess. U.S. Government Printing Office. Washington, D.C.

Freeman, O. L., and I. L. Bennett, Jr. 1969. Control of agriculture-related pollution. Report to the President by the Secretary of Agriculture and Director, Office of Science and Technology. 102 p.

Gambell, E. L. 1966. Two million farm ponds backstop America's streams, p. 48-55. *In* Soil Conserv. Soc. Amer., Proc. 21st Annu. Meeting.

Greenshields, E. L. 1964. Water has a key role, p. 72-96. *In* Farmer's world. The yearbook of agriculture 1964. U.S. Department of Agriculture. U.S. Government Printing Office, Washington, D.C.

Haik, R. A. 1957. Water, habitat, and wildlife. Conserv. Volunteer 20:1-5.

Hart, C. M., B. Glading, and H. T. Harper. 1956. The pheasant in California. *In* D. L. Allen (ed.), Pheasants in North America. Wildlife Management Institute, Washington, D.C.

Holmes, R. C. 1961. Composition and size of flood losses, p. 7-20. *In* G. F. White (ed.), Papers on flood problems. University of Chicago Press, Chicago.

Krutilla, J. V. 1966. Is public intervention in water resources development conducive to economic efficiency? Reprint 56, Jan. Nat. Resour. J. 6:60-75. Resources for the Future, Inc., Washington, D.C.

Lehmann, V. W. 1941. Attwater's prairie chicken, its life history and management. U.S. Fish and Wildl. Serv., N. Amer. Fauna 57. 65 p.

Lehmann, V. W. 1968. The Attwater prairie chicken, current status and restoration opportunities, p. 398-407. *In* 33d N. Amer. Wildl. and Natur. Resour. Conf. Trans.

Leopold, L. B. 1962. Rivers. Amer. Sci. 50(4):511-537.

McGee, G. W. 1960. Water resources developments: key to tomorrow. Western Resources Conf. paper. University of Colorado Press, Boulder.

Martin, R. O. R., and R. L. Hanson. 1966. Reservoirs in the United States. U.S. Geol. Surv. Water-Supply Paper 1838. 115 p.

Murphy, F. C. 1958. Regulating flood-plain development. University of Chicago Press, Chicago. 204 p.

Nelson, D. 1961. Resource and metropolitan sprawl, p. 77-89. *In* H. L. Amoss and R. K. McNickle (ed.), Land and water: planning for economic growth. University of Colorado Press, Boulder. 219 p.

Orell, B. L. 1965. Government land acquisition. American Forest Products Industry, Washington, D.C.

Outdoor Recreation Resources Review Commission. 1962. Shoreline recreation resources of the United States. ORRRC Study, Rep. 4. U.S. Government Printing Office, Washington, D.C.

President's Science Advisory Committee, Environmental Pollution Panel. 1965. Restoring the quality of our environment. U.S. Government Printing Office, Washington, D.C. 317 p.

Regan, M. M., and H. M. Wooten. 1963. Land use trends and urbanization, p. 59-63. *In* A place to live. The yearbook of agriculture 1963. U.S. Department of Agriculture. U.S. Government Printing Office, Washington, D.C.

Robertson, W. B., Jr., G. Sprugel, Jr., and L. Sumner. 1966. Everglades National Park natural sciences research plan. National Park Service, U.S. Department of the Interior, Washington, D.C.

Shaw, S. P., and C. G. Fredine. 1956. Wetlands of the United States. U.S. Fish and Wildl. Circ. 39. 67 p.

U.S. Department of Agriculture. 1962a. Basic statistics of the national inventory of soil and water conservation needs. Statist. Bull. 317. Washington, D.C.

U.S. Department of Agriculture. 1962b. Land and water resources, a policy guide. U.S. Government Printing Office, Washington, D.C. 73 p.

U.S. Department of Agriculture. 1965. Soil and water conservation needs, a national inventory. Misc. Publ. 971. Washington, D.C. 94 p.

Vlasin, R. D. 1963. Highways and adjustments in farms, p. 479-488. *In* A place to live. The yearbook of agriculture 1963. U.S. Department of Agriculture. U.S. Government Printing Office, Washington, D.C.

White, G. F., W. C. Calef, J. W. Hudson, H. M. Mayer, J. R. Sheaffer, and D. J. Volk. 1958. Changes in urban occupance of flood plains in the United States. University of Chicago Press, Chicago. 235 p.

Wingard, R. G., and M. R. Heddleson. (n.d.) Conservation—living in harmony with land. Pennsylvania State University, University Park.

Wooten, H. H., K. Gertel, and W. C. Pendleton. 1962. Major uses of land and water in the United States, summary for 1959. Agr. Econ. Rep. 13. U.S. Government Printing Office, Washington, D.C.

Yeager, L. E., J. B. Low, and H. J. Figge. 1956. Pheasants in the arid Southwest, p. 159-203. *In* D. L. Allen (ed.), Pheasants in North America. Wildlife Management Institute, Washington, D.C.

CHAPTER 4 *Influence of Land Management on Wildlife*

Historical attitudes toward the land and its products were discussed in Chapter 1. Over the past century, the elaboration of land-use concepts and the development of policy guidelines have accompanied the intensification of management. The growing expectation that every area can yield more products and services through applied technology than through single-purpose exploitation has raised issues with which land managers were not earlier concerned. It became evident that benefits of several kinds might be obtained through a recognition of the diverse values that any particular land type might provide for various segments of the population. That the general public has an interest and a responsibility in effecting and perpetuating sound management policies for all natural resources has been inherent in the conservation idea from its beginning.

MULTIPLE USE

A significant and commonly accepted policy relating to land husbandry is that of "multiple use." Logically it developed first as a guide to operations on certain public properties, especially the national forests, although its applicability to other types and ownerships is becoming progressively evident. Since wildlife is a public resource, commonly of secondary value in land-use economics, its status and utilization as a land and water product generally depend on effective multiple-use policies. How such policies vary and how they are implemented in different economic situations must be understood in determining relative investments for, and expected returns from, the wildlife resource.

Policies on Public Lands

In 1960, after many years of multiple-purpose operations by the U.S. Forest Service, Congress authorized and directed the Secretary of Agriculture to develop and administer the renewable surface resources of the national forests for multiple use and sustained yield (PL86-517; 16 USCA 528-531; 74 Stat 215). In this act a definition was included:

"Multiple use" means: The management of all the various renewable surface resources of the national forests so that they are utilized in the combination that will best meet the needs of the American people; making the most judicious use of the land for some or all of those resources or related services over areas large enough to provide sufficient latitude for periodic adjustments in use to conform to changing needs and conditions; that some land will be used for less than all of the resources; and harmonious and coordinated management of the various resources, each with the other, without impairment of the productivity of the land, with consideration being given to the relative values of the various resources, and not necessarily the combination of uses that will give the greatest dollar return or the greatest unit output.

This definition is remarkably similar to the 1905 directive of the Secretary of Agriculture to the Forester concerning the national forests—" . . . when conflicting interests must be reconciled the question will always be decided from the standpoint of the greatest good of the greatest number in the long run."* Both imply the satisfaction of minority interests as well as those of a simple majority.

In 1964, the Congress instructed the Secretary of the Interior to develop and administer for multiple use and sustained yield those public lands under the administration of the Bureau of Land Management consistent with and supplemental to the Taylor Grazing Act (48 Stat 1269; 43USC 315). The definition of multiple use in this act (PL 88-607; 43USCA 1415 (b); 78 Stat 987) is nearly identical with that applying to national forests except that the 1964 act includes also nonrenewable and subsurface resources. Wildlife and outdoor recreation are recognized resources under both acts.

Thus the Congress has established a national policy of multiple use,

---

*In a letter of February 1, 1905, from James Wilson, Secretary of Agriculture, to Gifford Pinchot, Forester, upon transfer of the Forest Reserves (now national forests) to the Department of Agriculture.

including wildlife resources, in the administration of national forests
(186 million acres), and on lands temporarily under the administration
of the Bureau of Land Management (459 million acres) pending their
classification for retention in federal ownership or disposal to private
ownership.*

The administrator of federal lands is subject to competitive demands
from different segments of the public, not all of whom are likely to be
fully satisfied. Pressures also arise from specialized staff personnel
within the agency, and the desire of each of several specialists to produce the maximum output from "his" resource. Under multiple-purpose
management, a given use seldom can attain its *maximum* production;
rather, the objective is *optimum* benefits from all or several uses in
combination. Ridd (1965) stated:

Multiple use management of the land may be accomplished by any one of the following three options, or by combination of the three: (1) concurrent and continuous use of the several resources obtainable on a given land unit; (2) alternating
or rotational use of the various resources or resource combinations on the unit, so
that multiple use is achieved on a time basis; or (3) geographical separation of uses
or use combinations so that multiple use is accomplished across a mosaic of units.
All of these are legitimate multiple use practices and should be applied in the most
suitable combination on lands under public administration.

It is here that a form of zoning is essential—zoning, not for a single
use, but in terms of a dominant value. For specific areas within a large
planning unit, one use may be given precedence, with others permitted
to the extent that they do not materially conflict with it.

Many federal lands other than the national forests and lands administered by the Bureau of Land Management are managed for several
uses. Military lands, for example, are being developed for wildlife
habitat, hunting, and fishing, when compatible with military objectives.
On some wildlife refuges, timber operations, hay cutting, or livestock
grazing are beneficial habitat improvement practices. Many state-owned
areas are managed similarly.

On certain public lands little, if any, management is directed toward
marketable products. Thus a primary motive in establishing national
parks and wilderness areas has been to reserve some lands from such
disturbance factors as mining, cultivation, livestock grazing, forest
cutting, and hunting; here the premium is on natural conditions. The
Wilderness Act, as passed, did not conform fully to this objective.

*The Bureau of Land Management multiple-use authorization expired June 30, 1970.

Under congressional definitions of multiple use, hunting, fishing, and wildlife habitat development are not *required* in all places and at all times on the national forests and public domain lands. However, these are acceptable practices on most public lands, and the wildlife resource has generally benefited from them.

Applications on Private Lands

The American Society of Range Management (Huss, 1964) defines multiple use as:

Harmonious use of range for more than one of the following purposes: Grazing of livestock, wildlife production, recreation, watershed, and timber production. Not necessarily the combination of uses that will yield the highest economic return or greatest unit output.

The Society of American Foresters (1964) considers multiple use to be:

The practice of forestry which combines two or more objectives, such as production of wood or wood-derivative products, forage and browse for domestic livestock, proper environmental conditions for wildlife, landscape effects, protection against floods and erosion, recreation, production and protection of water supplies, and national defense.

Orell (1964) describes multiple use from the standpoint of the timber industry as:

. . . the accommodation of a maximum of other compatible uses with the highest single use of the land. On private commercial forest land the highest primary use is the production of successive timber crops. The maximum use of every forest land acre is the objective of every forester.

Still another description of multiple use is that of American Forest Products Industries (Sayers, 1966).

Continuous growing and harvesting of crops of trees is the primary objective of Tree Farm management. Other multiple-use benefits, including the protection of watersheds, maintenance of desirable wildlife populations, and recreational opportunities are the natural results of well managed forest lands. Multiple use is encouraged on Tree Farms consistent with the primary objectives of the owners.

It is evident that the intensive management of one resource often is not good management for another. The growing of fully stocked pure stands of conifers over extensive areas may preclude game production;

it might well comply with the primary timber objective of the landowner but would fail in maintaining wildlife populations satisfactory
to the hunter. In the coordinated management of timber and wildlife a
moderate reduction of timber yield may permit a more than moderate
increase in wildlife production. Yet the incidental improvement of
wildlife habitat, or even just the granting of permission to hunt, con-
forms with most definitions of multiple use. Hence there is need to
analyze the objectives, procedures, and actual results on any unit of
land to ascertain the prevailing direction and extent of the application
of multiple-use concepts.

The fact that multiple use is a desirable policy in the management of
most public lands does not mean that it is applicable in equal degree to
private lands. Motivations in public land management derive from legislation (including appropriations) as a response to public demands; on
private lands the motivation is primarily in terms of dollar returns.
Subject to ecological limitations, certain governmental controls, and
occasional zoning restrictions, the landowner will determine the uses
to which his land will be devoted. Wildlife production and utilization
may or may not be a management objective, and it is commonly true
that the landowner has little economic incentive to develop wildlife
habitat or to encourage its utilization.

Multiple use can mean different things to different people. Under
various definitions and practices the wildlife resource may be benefited
greatly or not at all, according to the nature of land and water, the
economics of competitive land and water uses, and the mores of various
social groups.

FOREST AND WOODLAND MANAGEMENT

Within the 50 states, 759 million acres support forests and woodlands.*
Two thirds (509 million acres) of this area is classified as commercial
forest land, suitable for growing continuous crops of sawlogs or other
industrial timber products. One third (250 million acres) is classified as
noncommercial either because of low productivity for timber growing
(234 million acres), or because of legal reservation (16 million acres)
for parks, wilderness, or other nontimber uses (U.S. Forest Service,
1965).

---

*Woodland includes both small forested areas, such as farm woodlots, and larger areas of
mainly noncommercial species. Many acres classed as forest and woodland are grazed by
domestic livestock; hence there is an overlap of areas (244 million acres) in *forests and woodlands* and *range and pasture*.

Of the commercial forest land, 142 million acres are in public owner-ship, of which four fifths is federally owned; 67 million acres are owned by forest industries; 151 million acres are in farms; and 149 million acres are under miscellaneous private ownership. Of the noncommercial (low productivity) forest land, over three fourths is federally owned and situated largely in Alaska and other western states.

Covering one-third of the land area of the United States, forest land supports a wide variety of wildlife. Much of the big game, many upland small game species, and some waterfowl are hunted in the forest environ-ment, and nongame species are numerous. Many fishing waters are in, or have their sources in, forested areas. Significantly, from the stand-point of the management of wildlife for public recreation, nearly half of the forested area of the country is under public ownership.

Wildlife Habitat Objectives

From latitudes 20°N in Hawaii to 60°N in Alaska, at elevations from sea level to 12,000 feet, and showing many different successional stages within the several life zones, forest lands of the United States vary greatly in the composition of their plant and animal communities. For the contiguous 48 states, Küchler (1964) recognizes 69 potential na-tural types of forest and grassland-forest combinations. The Society of American Foresters recognizes 156 timber types that vary widely with respect to age, species composition, soils, and other conditions. Within this broad spectrum of environmental conditions lie forest-wildlife management opportunities for directing management toward compat-ible objectives. It is here that wildlife managers seek to identify and lessen the adverse effects of such limiting factors as food, cover, water, or space and to attain a range of habitat types favorable to the species of wildlife concerned.

Interspersion of Types

Aside from seasonal migrations, the ranges of individual animals of dif-ferent species may vary from a few acres or less (cottontail rabbits) to a square mile (deer) to 36 square miles or more (wide-ranging carni-vores). Each individual needs ready access to habitat that meets all of its requirements, and the more home ranges there are in a forest hold-ing the larger the wildlife population is likely to be.

Many species of wildlife—deer, rabbits, turkeys, grouse—are "edge" creatures, requiring variety in their ranges. They make extensive use of openings and early forest successions and are benefited by an intimate mixture of vegetative, topographic, and moisture conditions. The need for "interspersion" in the habitat is an accepted principle among wild-life managers, and to meet this need is a basic objective in developing productive environments in forested areas.

Thus extensive stands of a single tree species do not support high populations of wildlife; small farm woodlots, closely associated with croplands and pastures, are more productive. On extensive forest areas the manager frequently has a clearly defined wildlife habitat objective, in terms of variety and edge, that he can approximate in harmony with timber management priorities.

Water Conditions

Runoff waters from forested watersheds provide the basic resource for a fishery, and for some mammals and birds as well. The physical, chemical, and biological factors that constitute fish habitat are affected by the forest and the activities therein. The temperature of streams and degree of siltation relate to condition of the watershed. The stability of streambanks and the presence or absence of bank cover and shade greatly affect the fishes and their food supplies. Aquatic fish-food organisms depend closely, in species and abundance, on the type of stream bottom; particularly in mountain trout streams, fish food production in clean rubble stream bottoms exceeds that in silted stream-beds (Chapman, 1962). To an appreciable extent, the amount of runoff and the time and degree of peak flows are influenced by the species of trees and their distribution (Hoover, 1962).

To some degree, nearly all actions (or their absence) on the forest watershed affect the suitability of the aquatic habitat for wildlife. Thus the decisions of the forester can result in habitat improvement or deterioriation, depending upon the objectives of management and the ways in which objectives are fulfilled. Through well-coordinated management for timber *and* wildlife, habitat conditions can be fostered; without coordination they may be damaged. Public clamor for fish hatcheries has often obscured the fact that effective fishery management starts with land management on the watershed.

Timber Management Practices

A virgin forest seldom supports an abundance of wildlife—either in number of animals or number of species. Increases in game animals often followed early exploitation of our forests. Today the saw and axe, controlled fire, and chemicals can be employed to improve wild-life habitat without destructive effects. Forest management provides many opportunities for improving wildlife habitat.

Incidental wildlife benefits are likely to accompany most modern types of timber harvest and thinning operations. Greater and more predictable benefits result where forest managers plan their operations to favor wildlife habitat as one of the multiple uses of the forest. On the managed national and state forests, and on managed private lands where there is an incentive to do so, wildlife biologists working with timber managers can develop plans that will increase the more useful species of both animals and trees. On unmanaged "preserves" such as the New York State Forest Preserve and some national and state parks, the opportunities are limited or lacking.

In recent decades there has appeared to be some division of public opinion relative to forestry; in particular, growing numbers of people generally have opposed harvesting timber crops. Presumably this attitude goes considerably beyond the acknowledged need for setting aside certain areas as undisturbed wilderness. It has earned for such individuals the somewhat anomalous designation of "preservationist," as opposed to the "conservationist," who believes in preservation plus use.

Perhaps the opposition to harvesting timber crops is a reaction to the early history of "cut-out and get-out" logging in this country and to appreciable areas of recent clear-cutting of large blocks.* It may be fostered also by instances of erosion, scenic defacement, and slash burning—not all condoned by either lay conservationists or professional foresters (Twiss, 1969). Although some logging operations do not provide adequately for watershed protection and esthetics, many do; timber industries in general are recognizing the public's interest in forests. Perhaps the distinction between conservationists and preservationists relates to varying degrees of tolerance of such things as the disturbance of natural conditions by logging—some of which may be unavoidable if forest managment is to be practiced at all. With respect to wildlife, the distinction becomes real to the extent that the saw and axe are tools without which habitat management would be extremely limited.

Few question the need for both commodity production areas and natural areas; the difficult questions concern where and how much land shall be devoted to each, and to what extent both needs can be met through multiple use. On federal lands designated for multiple-use management the success of administrators in satisfying diverse interests may determine the duration of delegated authority, which the Congress can retract at any time.

---

*Clear-cutting of blocks of moderate size is an accepted silvicultural practice in several forest types. The distinction between large and small blocks will necessarily vary, and size is unlikely to be determined solely with consideration for wildlife; but, in a multiple-use forest, it need not be a matter of logging economics alone.

Rotations and Cutting Cycles

With the decrease of virgin timber stands—in the 1960's less than 8 percent of commercial forests—and the increase of managed forests, the problems and opportunities of wildlife managers are changing. In many cases the old-growth trees are replaced naturally or artificially by species of lower successional stages, and wildlife communities change. Wildlife management objectives and techniques must be modified to fit the managed forests and, in turn, may influence timber management practices. The development of markets for small trees and more efficient equipment for logging and road-building have shortened both the time required to produce merchantable timber (the rotation) and the frequency of practical cuttings (the cutting cycles).

To meet anticipated sawtimber demands, more frequent and more extensive cultural cuttings can be expected. Substantial acreages, especially in the Rocky Mountains, support far too many trees per acre for acceptable timber growth. In western Washington and Oregon, for example, 5 million acres are supporting young stands in which commercial thinning would increase the log harvest. In the South, extensive stand improvement on at least 150 million acres would be needed to reduce the excessive stocking of culls and undesirable trees. Without thinnings, stand densities in many northern forests are expected to increase to the extent of serious overstocking (U.S. Forest Service, 1965). Whether timber cultural operations are favorable or unfavorable to wildlife depends upon the objectives of forest management and the degree of coordination between foresters and wildlife managers. Each cutting provides opportunities for wildlife habitat manipulation.

For example, on the Allegheny National Forest in Pennsylvania, coordination between timber management and wildlife management is a part of the multiple-use program. Here, in a predominantly northern hardwood forest, black cherry is the favored timber crop; game species include deer, bear, squirrel, snowshoe hare, cottontail rabbit, ruffed grouse, turkey, and woodcock. Both stumpage values and recreational demands are high. Jordan (J. S. Jordan, U.S. Forest Service, unpublished data) described the program:

Under unit area management, the Forest is divided into approximately 1200 compartments, each averaging about 350 acres in size. Timber management objectives, as they concern wildlife, are: (1) to produce high quality hardwoods consisting of 50 percent black cherry, 40 percent in a variety of other commercial hardwoods, 10 percent in coniferous species; (2) maintain 5 percent of the area in coniferous types; (3) make 3,000 acres of regeneration clearcuttings annually in areas 2 to 20 acres in size.

Several habitat objectives for the forest have been established: (1) brush stage—about 5 percent of the total area in units of 3 to 5 acres spaced 30 to 40 chains apart; (2) open herbaceous areas—2 to 3 percent in units not less than 0.2 acre in size; (3) coniferous cover—about 8 percent of the area in units ½ to 2 acres, spaced about 10 chains apart (can be overstory or understory); (4) water sources spaced not less than 40 chains apart.

Clearcutting for regeneration will generally be made in mature and over-mature stands; but where brush stage is needed to satisfy habitat needs, regeneration cuttings will also be made in immature stands. This will aid in achieving a better balance in age classes, now skewed strongly to poletimber stands—a common wildlife problem in northeastern forests. In addition to the rotation age of 100 years, 10 years is allowed in the forest regulation period to obtain natural regeneration. This time is provided for wildlife utilization following clearcutting.

Pre-commercial thinnings in immature stands will be light to moderate release. Where required to meet wildlife needs, heavy release will be made in 10-acre blocks spaced about 30 chains apart; all stems except the future crop trees are winter-felled to provide browse for deer in the tops and later from the stumps, and to create much-needed cover for small game. Studies have shown that this practice yields a tenfold increase in browse production in the first year.

Wherever possible, cutting blocks are located in relation to other habitat components to obtain optimum use of the browse and cover created.

Under unit area management, each compartment should eventually contain a balance of 10-year age classes, each averaging 35 acres in size and suitability distributed for habitat needs. There is sufficient similarity between compartment size—or multiples of it—and game species home range so that timber management operations will approximately satisfy general habitat needs. Supplementary practices to satisfy other habitat needs are incorporated in the planning.

Each compartment is examined at least every 10 years and treatments are prescribed which include minimum habitat requirements according to prescribed objectives. A continuous inventory of all vegetation is maintained by sampling 10 percent of the compartments annually. Condition and trend in understory vegetation of the Forest is determined from permanent transects measured at 5-year intervals.

Reforestation and Afforestation

The popular idea that for every tree cut another should be planted overlooks the fact that in many situations forests are regenerated both naturally and through planned silvicultural operations. Also overlooked is the fact that if planting is necessary, the number of trees planted should exceed the number cut—the excess providing for mortality and to insure quality in the ultimate crop trees. If only one tree were planted to replace a tree cut, there would be less concern by wildlife managers.

The U.S. Forest Service (1965) reports that nationally in recent years tree planting has covered about 1.3 million acres annually, but more than 100 million acres of commercial forest land is either nonstocked (36 million acres) or poorly stocked (76 million acres) with trees of acceptable quality or species.

While forest plantings on many sites are not inimical to wildlife (and sometimes are beneficial), extensive solid plantations of a single tree species, especially conifers, leave little favorable habitat. Conifers create cover but soon reduce or eliminate shrubs that yield browse and fruit and herbaceous plants that supply food, ground nesting sites, and a source of insects for young birds (Bailey and Alexander, 1960).

Since most hardwood forest types are more productive of wildlife than are the conifers, conversions from the former to the latter generally result in lower wildlife populations. The unfavorable effects can be offset, as in pine plantations on scrub oak sites in Florida, where, on the Apalachicola National Forest, planting is done in strips, with alternate strips left for browse and herbage. Within the brush strips dominant oaks are released from competition to increase mast production.

Large areas of cutover pine lands in the North have been invaded by such pioneer associations as the aspen-birch. These early successional stages are favored habitat for grouse. Because they are potentially productive pine sites, plantings have been fairly extensive and there has been a loss of grouse habitat. To maintain the multiple uses by providing an interspersion of pine and open land, some large blocks of public lands have been left unplanted and others have been only partly planted.

In the West, deep snow at high elevations forces deer and elk to winter ranges in the foothills. Early logging and fires changed many of the lower south-facing slopes from timber stands to the brush types that are essential for browse forage. Conversion of these critical winter ranges to tree cover by planting conifers would in time practically eliminate the game. Planting north slopes, where snow accumulates, may be desirable in places where escape cover is needed.

Where wildlife habitat is one of the recognized uses, coordination between timber and wildlife managers is essential, both for enhancing wild animal values and for protecting forest regeneration from excessive animal damage.

An example of afforestation (the establishment of a forest on an area not previously forested) is the Nebraska National Forest in the sandhills of that state. Since 1903, 30,000 acres of natural grasslands have been planted with primarily coniferous trees. Deer were indigenous, but increased greatly in the plantation areas, to the extent that hunting was permitted in 1945—the first legal hunting of deer in that state since 1907 (Mohler *et al.*, 1951). Favorable habitat in plantations was one of several factors to which deer responded. Records of ornithologists show marked increases in the number of bird species (principally nongame) as the planted areas expanded. Wildlife habitat development was not the reason for afforestation, but it was an incidental benefit for some species.

Prescribed Burning

In recent decades great progress has been made in controlling wildfire in forests. From a total of 17.6 million acres burned in 1950 (2 percent of the total forest area), losses were progressively reduced to 4.1 million acres (about 0.5 percent of the total forest area) in 1962. The average area burned from 1962 through 1967 was 4.5 million acres, or 0.4 percent of the total forest area.* Concurrently, much has been learned about the planned use of fire—prescribed burning—as a tool of forest management to reduce wildfire hazard, control disease, and prepare sites for regeneration. Under some conditions, controlled burning can be used beneficially without the catastrophic results of wildfire. Wildlife has benefited incidentally from many of the burns prescribed for timber management, but little has been done experimentally toward burning for wildlife habitat improvement itself (Komarek, 1966). Stoddard (1931) pioneered in the controlled burning of southern pine lands for quail habitat; Biswell *et al.* (1952) and Biswell (1959, 1961) have improved brush range for deer in California; and Lay (1956, 1957) improved forage quality by burning pine land in Texas. Following are brief excerpts from Komarek's (1966) paper:

In general, the basic condition of the wildlife landscape is variety: forest, brush, grass, weeds, lakes, ponds, creeks. Abundant historical records indicate that during primitive times, it was largely a fire landscape. It depended upon this agent as a source of disturbance to rejuvenate the quality and the distribution of its vegetative composition to which wildlife increase responded, sometimes spectacularly.... How to produce the favorable wildlife response so frequently produced by wildfire, without the associated destruction of scenic and forest values should be a major concern of wildlife management. . . .

While the techniques developed by forestry and range management may well be useful in the management of the wildlife landscape, the needs of wildlife differ

*Figures are from U.S. Forest Service, Fire Statistics, and are compiled in relation to 1,172 million acres *needing protection*—an area about 50 percent greater than the 759 million acres shown on page 96 as the total area of forest and woodland in the United States; hence some of the acreage burned was probably brush and grassland intermingled with, or managed in conjunction with, forest or woodland.

and experimentation in developing other techniques can be visualized. The forester seeks clean burns and complete coverage; wildlife burning may be less intensive with incomplete coverage to provide sufficient cover until new growth appears. Season of burning, frequency of burning, purpose and size of burn for wildlife purposes do not necessarily coincide with needs of other land uses and, accordingly, will vary with species, habitat and region. Much of the controlled burning for wildlife may well follow more closely the practice of the south Florida cattleman than that of the forester. The cattleman was concerned with providing new growth of grass over longer periods and accordingly his burning was staggered to "stretch out" winter grazing. Protection and distribution of cover, development and maintenance of scenic vistas, the production of berries, mast, seeds and other food plants are not the primary concern of the forester or range manager but are of essential importance to the wildlife manager. Restricted use of controlled burning, such as the "spot" burning of Stoddard, which is entirely different from the spot burning of the forester, may have special application, and the exercise of ingenuity should produce new techniques. . . .

. . . The forest has been promoted so long with wildlife as an associate and the past history of forest destruction has been repeated so many times that forest preservation has automatically meant wildlife preservation. To preserve forest was to preserve wildlife. But in most cases the reverse has been true. Browse has grown out of reach of big game animals and herbaceous plants have been smothered out by competing vegetation. Trees have marched into the open areas upon which wildlife in reasonable abundance once depended and many wildlife landscapes have become solid, sometimes monotonous, forest landscapes.

One example of prescribed burning involves the habitat of a rare bird, the Kirtland's warbler, which has an estimated total population of less than 1,000; it winters in the Bahamas and has been found nesting in only 12 counties in Michigan. It nests on the ground under relatively open stands of jack pine in the 8- to 20-year age classes. To perpetuate the exacting stand requirements of this rare bird, the Audubon Society, the Michigan Conservation Department, and the U.S. Forest Service, with cooperation of the timber industry, have set up management areas in three state forests and the Huron National Forest. Prescribed burning is a major tool; approximately square-mile blocks of mature timber are to be burned on a 5-year cycle to provide a perpetual supply of young jack pines. Selective planting will be used where natural regeneration fails (Line, 1964).

There are other examples of the use of fire in forest-wildlife habitat management, but the opportunities probably are far greater than have been explored. However, with growing public concern over air pollution, studies of the effects of prescribed burning should not be overlooked.

Logging

Harvesting timber is an essential periodic operation on commercial forest lands. Unavoidably, it disturbs the environment to a degree ranging from moderate to profound. Similarly, the effects may be of short or long duration. In contrast with early logging by man and animal power, modern equipment has brought about great changes, some creating more disturbance, some less. Much of the opposition to commercial timber operations is motivated by esthetics—a situation deserving industry consideration. From the standpoint of wildlife management logging may be favorable or unfavorable.

Moderate disturbance of the forest floor, along with opening of the forest canopy, may promote herbaceous and shrubby vegetation where little or none was present. Where seeding is practiced to stabilize exposed soils, natural plant succession may be artificially improved upon and recovery hastened. Where slopes are steep or soils unstable, fishery values may be severely damaged. In clear-cutting operations, large blocks are less favorable to wildlife than small clearings that provide better interspersion of habitat types. Logging slash in small amounts may furnish desirable cover for small game, but extensive areas of nearly impenetrable accumulations are a detriment.

Logging road systems, if properly planned, can provide access for wildlife harvest and management operations. On the other hand, improperly located, constructed, and maintained roads may bring about nearly irreparable damage to streams and render them useless for recreational purposes. Choking of stream channels with slash and debris, invasion of streambeds by roads or road fills, channel changes, sediment from poor road drainage, and culverts that impede spawning runs are particularly harmful. Studies in the northern Rocky Mountains have indicated that roads were the source of the greatest logging damage to trout streams (Chapman, 1962).

Efficient road-building equipment cuts road costs; improved markets encourage shorter cutting cycles; intensive forest management calls for intermediate cuttings; economics dictates fast movement of logs from woods to mill; woods crews live in town rather than in the woods— all these point to the need for better and more permanent road systems.

RANGE AND PASTURE LANDS

Approximately 1 billion acres, or over 40 percent of the land area of the 50 states, are grazed by domestic livestock. This acreage includes

645 million acres of pasture and range land,* 244 million acres of forest and woodlands, and 66 million acres of cropland used for pasture only. It excludes an undetermined acreage of hay and cropland pastured after crop removal (U.S. Department of Agriculture, 1962).

Of the federal lands grazed (243 million acres), nearly three fourths are administered by the Bureau of Land Management and most of the rest by the Forest Service. The nonfederal grazed lands are largely in private ownership but include some state and other government areas. Livestock includes primarily cattle, sheep, horses, and goats, totalling approximately 200 million animals. Grazing may be seasonal or year-long and usually continues year after year. Nearly a third of our total area of forest and woodland is so used. Big game animals forage extensively on many types of grazed lands.

Country-wide, and even locally, native range sites vary greatly in forage productivity. Grazing capacity, in terms of animal-unit-month,† may vary from half an acre on wet meadows in good condition to 30 or more on semi-arid or depleted ranges. The capacity of some grazed lands may be sufficient only to keep the animals alive during a part of the year. A relatively small proportion of the lands grazed by livestock is highly productive range, whereas forage production on extensive areas is low.

Forage production on native ranges may vary greatly from year to year—by as much as 300 percent for perennial forage and 1,000 percent for annual vegetation (Stoddart and Smith, 1955). Differences largely result from varying precipitation. However, stocking rates tend to remain relatively stable except during periods of extended drought.‡

Range is defined by the American Society of Range Management (Huss, 1964) as "all land producing native forage for [wild or domestic] animal consumption, . . ." The acreages shown as grazed by domestic livestock exclude those grazed by game alone. Ranges are further described as *suitable* and *unsuitable*, the former being "range which is accessible to livestock or game which can be grazed on a sustained yield basis without damage to other resources." Because of evident damage in some places to forest, wildlife, and watershed values, the acreage shown as grazed by livestock is known to include some lands unsuitable for grazing. While no accurate figures are available for croplands grazed after harvest, such usage is important as it may reduce wildlife cover in fields or eliminate travel lanes by which wildlife seeks safe passage from one part of its habitat to another, as along fencerows and irrigation ditches.

†One animal-unit-month (AUM) is the amount of feed or forage equivalent to that required by a mature cow with calf for 1 month. Use of AUM as a factor for converting range carrying capacity for one animal species to another is scientifically untenable because it is well established that each animal species has its own food preferences, and that between animals the plant species grazed may overlap much, little, or not at all.

‡Skeete (1966), answering the question of whether ranchers can adjust to fluctuating forage production, described a ranch operation on the Edwards Plateau of west Texas. The 60-year average annual rainfall was 19.5 inches, with 15 years of less than 13.5 inches. In 3 consecu-

Reasons include the desire for stability of livestock operations and, perhaps optimistically, the "calculated risk" that permitted use has been set sufficiently low to allow for variations in forage production without permanent damage to the range. Optimism in this respect could relate to the present low production of many ranges compared to their potential, and the need for correction of overgrazing on so much range and pasture land. Atkins (1956), stockman and past president of the American Society of Range Management, said: ". . . overgrazing of ranges has been the besetting sin of stockmen since Biblical times. . . ."

A study by the U.S. Department of Agriculture (1965) showed that pasture and range lands are producing forage at no more than half their potential.

For the past half century or more, continued overuse has seriously depleted forage resources. Brush, weeds, and other unwanted vegetation have encroached upon millions of acres that once were good grazing land; tons of topsoil are being eroded from them to pollute streams, fill reservoirs, and damage domestic, agricultural, and industrial water supplies.

Concerning overgrazing on nonfederal lands, the inventory report shows:

Overgrazing is the most widespread hazard to established pastures and ranges. Of the nearly 185 million acres needing only protection of plant cover, 163.2 million acres or 88 percent needs protection from overgrazing. In addition, the 72 million acres needing establishment of new cover and the 107 million acres needing improvement of existing cover will require protection from overgrazing to make these treatments successful. Altogether, then, about 343 million acres or 68 percent of non-federal pasture and range needs additional protection from overgrazing.

Much of the federal range needs similar treatment and protection (Clawson *et al.*, 1960). The Bureau of Land Management (U.S. Department of the Interior, 1960), optimistically in the light of trends on other lands,* set a range management objective to increase forage

---

tive years forage production was 1,361, 980, and 371 pounds per acre. Carrying capacity of the range had declined from 125 animal units per section in 1900 to 100 in 1916, and 32 in 1948. Through moderate stocking and a rotation-deferred system, the capacity was raised to 35-40 animal units per section. Stocking was adjusted as necessary through sale of stock from the base herds of cattle and sheep according to spring precipitation.

*Permitted livestock use of the national forests rose from 1.0 million cattle and 5.7 million sheep in 1906 to a World War I peak in 1918 of 2.2 million cattle and 8.5 million sheep, and has since declined to 1.4 million cattle and 2.1 million sheep in 1965 (U.S. Bureau of the Census, 1960 and 1965). Livestock AUM's were reduced about 60 percent from 1918 to 1965. Big game AUM's have increased substantially.

production on the public lands from 17 million AUM's in 1959 to 46 million AUM's by the year 2012—"an increase in livestock and big game of approximately 300 percent."

If this nation should need greater livestock production, with the alternatives of grazing more land or improving production from lands now being grazed, the latter appears to offer substantial possibilities.

Effects of Livestock on Wildlife Habitat

Because of wide variations in range types, species of livestock and wild animals, grazing seasons and management practices, and other factors, it is not possible to generalize concerning livestock-wildlife relationships. Some effects of grazing are direct and obvious; others are indirect and inconspicuous. However, with more than 40 percent of our land grazed by livestock, and many waters affected by sources on range lands, grazing probably is the greatest single year-after-year agricultural influence on wildlife.

Vegetation Changes

Progressive alteration of the composition, stocking, and vigor of the range plant community results from continued livestock use. Taylor and Buechner (1943) described for the Edwards Plateau of Texas six recognizable stages between the climax and bare ground, and indicated the suitability of each stage for game and the suggested livestock management practices. The stages are: climax, perennial tall grass, perennial short grass, weed grass range, unpalatable weed stage, and bare ground. Similar descriptions have been made for other range types. The authors note that perennial grass, and not the climax, may be the most productive stage for livestock. Lower stages usually are undesirable in terms of both grazing and soil stability. Soil Conservation Service methods for determining range sites and conditions are widely used on private lands (Renner and Allred, 1962).

Range condition and trend standards have been developed for many range types by federal and state agencies. Parker (1954) lists the more reliable criteria for classifying the condition of vegetation as (1) density index of plant or forage cover, (2) composition of vegetation as to species, grouped in accordance with their reaction to grazing use, and (3) vigor of the desirable forage species. He lists the more important soil condition factors as (1) amount of litter coverage, (2) current erosion, and (3) stability as indicated by amount of living and dead (plant) cover. These are ecological factors with which the wildlife manager is equally concerned.

With respect to game animals, seldom will the livestock and wildlife objectives differ as to soil stability standards. In rating vegetation, however, interests may diverge. A given stage in plant succession can seldom provide maximum per-acre production for each of two species of livestock, or for two or more species of game. However, with coordinated planning, a single successional stage may provide optimum production for one species of livestock together with one or more species of game. The ecological approach to livestock range management does not imply that climax conditions are the ultimate objective, for climax types often are low in livestock and game production.

Some wildlife managers have missed opportunities by not working more closely with range managers in developing livestock range condition ratings. While many range managers are aware of the winter range requirements of deer and elk, they may not fully appreciate the relationship between vegetation bordering streams and the fish life in them; the effects of grazing intensity on the success of duck, grouse, or quail nesting; or the dependence of beavers on sustained growths of willow and aspen. Some have considered all herbage as forage, with insufficient regard for vigor of range plants, wildlife cover, or the maintenance of soil conditions. Costello (1956) is an exception; he points out that

Any system of judging range, which does not include consideration of all products of the land, is incomplete. We must include measurement or evaluation of factors which affect stream flow, siltation, water yield, wildlife production, and recreation values.

Modification of the Fauna

The effects of livestock grazing on wildlife may be competitive, beneficial, or neutral, depending upon many variables. Such factors as vegetation types, kinds and combinations of livestock, topography, soils, and availability of water are involved.

Competition between livestock and game may be direct where both feed on much the same forage species, as do sheep and deer. Where grass seeds are important (as for wild turkeys), grazing may reduce or eliminate that source of food; hogs in hardwood forests may be similarly competitive for mast. In many cases, however, big game and livestock in moderate numbers do not graze the same areas or the same species. Through intensive studies such as those of Julander and Julander *et al.* (1950, 1951, 1955, 1958, 1961, 1962, 1964), also Robinette *et al.* (1952), and Smith and Julander (1953) in the intermountain region, the degree of conflict can be measured; generalities are of little help in solving problems in specific areas.

At the risk of oversimplification, the extent of direct competition

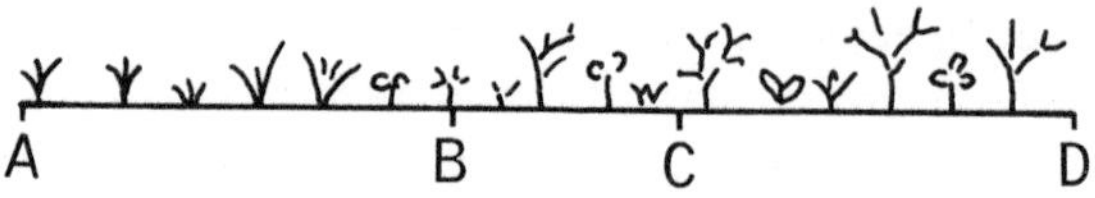

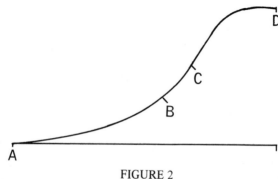

FIGURE 1

for forage between cattle and deer at moderate stocking can be illustrated diagrammatically (Figure 1), where on a given range area, A–D is the total range of forage species. If cattle eat only species A–C, and deer eat only species B–D, the competition is limited to species B–C. Obviously, where stocking rates are more than moderate or forage plant composition is dissimilar, or where different species of livestock or wildlife are involved, the degree of competition would likely change materially.

Again somewhat oversimplified, Figure 2 diagrammatically illustrates a topographic profile of a range terrain. With moderate stocking, cattle may use only slope A–C, and deer only B–D, and the area of competition would be limited to B–C. In this instance, or others, A could represent proximity to livestock water, and D proximity to deer cover, with somewhat similar expectancy of area competition.

Indirect effects are numerous although often not clearly evident. Grazing has affected duck nesting favorably in some places and unfavorably in others, depending to a large extent upon degrees of stocking and range conditions. Prairie grouse have been affected by habitat changes caused by livestock grazing. The development of a livestock industry on brown bear range on Kodiak Island in Alaska has resulted, as might have been anticipated, in bear damage to livestock, and the current solution is control of the native animal (Erickson, 1965).

The longer term effects of grazing in changing plant successional stages may be unappreciated until extreme conditions are evident. The

FIGURE 2

increase of cheat grass, a short-lived introduced annual, on many western ranges has resulted in rapidly spreading range fires that have killed browse plants on deer wintering ranges.

Many publications on the interrelationships of livestock grazing and wildlife omit information needed by rangeland managers if uses are to be better coordinated. Often lands are described merely as grazed (or overgrazed) and ungrazed; stocking rate, system of grazing, and range condition classification frequently are not given; few relate quantitatively the response of wildlife to conditions under study. The need is great for research that will determine for each range type the degree and method of grazing that may be beneficial, or least harmful, for the habitat of each desirable wildlife species.

Soil and Water Changes

Livestock grazing tends to compact soils, with resulting increase in soil density, reduction in pore space, reduction in water infiltration capacity, and slowed water movement through the soil; surface runoff may occur more frequently, increase in volume, and result in erosion (Lull, 1959). Infiltration rates decline with lowered range conditions (Leithead, 1950) and heavier rates of stocking (Rhoades *et al.*, 1964). Concerning the effect of grazing farm woodland on watershed values in the southern Appalachian Mountains, Johnson (1952) observed that

Measurements made over the 9 years of observation show that accumulative effects of browsing and trampling are beginning to influence the quantity, timing, and quality of water that comes off the drainage area in storm periods. . . . During storms the stream comes up faster and reaches higher flood peaks.

These factors, as they may affect streams and lakes, undoubtedly influence the quality of fish habitat. Research directly relating livestock grazing and range conditions to fish production is lacking.

Read (1957) reported that

according to a survey made in 1954 by the Rocky Mountain Forest and Range Experiment Station, 30 percent of the shelterbelts planted in the Great Plains region between 1935 and 1942 have been seriously damaged by their use as 'stomp and shade lots' for livestock.

He reported soil conditions for heavily used and protected shelterbelts, respectively—bulk density, 1.22 and 1.01 grams/cc, total pore space 51.7 and 57.3 percent, and large pore space 7.6 and 14.1 percent.

Describing the causes of million-dollar-damage mud-rock floods of 1923 and 1930 in the Farmington-Centerville area of Utah, Bailey *et al.* (1947) said:

... The great bulk of the flood waters originated on areas near the mountain top where the plant and litter cover had been destroyed or reduced and the soil eroded and compacted ... depleted and eroded barren areas covered less than 10 percent of the total area of the several catchment basins. ... The inadequate capacity of the flood-source areas to restrain runoff was unnatural. It was due to a change in the character of the soil. This was brought about by long-continued overgrazing by domestic livestock, and unwise burning.

The grazing of livestock along streambanks frequently results in loss of riparian vegetation such as willow, alder, and birch that serves to protect streambanks, shade the streams, and develop overhanging banks where fish may hide. Boussu's (1954) study of the ecological effects of presence and absence of streambank cover on a Montana trout stream, while only simulating commonly observed range and pasture conditions, measured such effects on trout populations. With the removal of natural willow cover overhanging 13 percent of the surface area of the stream, the total fish population was reduced 41 percent by weight, and the 7-inch and larger fish were reduced 58 percent. With the application of comparable brush cover on 5½ percent of the area of the stream totally lacking cover, the fish population increased 258 percent, and the larger fish 533 percent. With the removal of natural overhanging (undercut) banks from less than 2 percent of the stream surface, the total fish population decreased 33 percent, and the number of larger fish 64 percent. Streambanks within cattle ranges are particularly subject to damage because of the preference of cows for the more level lands near water and the greater production there of succulent vegetation.* In some places stream bottoms have been fenced out, and the cost may be justified where necessary to protect fishing values. Muddying of waters by wading livestock and increased water temperatures resulting from destruction of shading vegetation also are common adverse situations on ranges and pastures.

Management of Livestock Grazing

Grazing practices vary widely—for example, from daily barn-to-pasture for dairy cattle to year-long grazing on some ranges; and from single species of livestock to two or more concurrently (termed "common use"). Different practices may affect wildlife in different ways and degrees; general and unqualified statements as to the effects of livestock grazing on wildlife mean little.

*Such key areas for fish habitat are often treated by range managers as " 'sacrifice areas' ... intentionally overgrazed to obtain efficient overall use of the management area" (Huss, 1964).

The basic grazing management systems recognized by the American Society of Range Management (Huss, 1964) and further described by Driscoll (1967) are: continuous, rotation (or alternate), deferred, deferred-rotation, and rest-rotation. With respect to wildlife food and cover, each of these systems and modifications within them can be expected to result in variations in wildlife habitat conditions. Much of the reported wildlife research refers only to lands as grazed or ungrazed. Until researchers recognize the various systems of management being practiced, and the standards for range condition classes, sound bases for grazing and wildlife coordination are lacking; merely comparing "grazed" and "ungrazed" is not enough.

Fencing is a major tool of range and pasture management, and often a benefit to wildlife habitat if range condition improves as a result; it can also protect key areas for wildlife. Some types of fencing create wildlife problems. One critical problem in the West is the fencing of ranges used by both antelope and domestic sheep, which may prevent the antelope from reaching water or sheltered areas in times of stress. The scarcity of capable sheep herders and other economic factors have resulted in a substantial increase in sheep range fencing, but a fence that will hold sheep and pass antelope has not yet been developed. Similar problems may occur where fences are so high as to be difficult for deer, elk, and moose to jump; many deer hang up on top wires, and elk and moose occasionally tear the fences down. Satisfactory wire-spacing standards have been developed to alleviate such problems but they are not always followed.

The tendency of cattle, in particular, to graze waterside areas as long as food is available usually results in loss of key wildlife habitat. To alleviate the problem, the fencing of springs, streams, and portions of stockponds is often recommended and sometimes practiced. Stock water developments, if properly planned and constructed, can provide good wildlife habitat. Day (1966) described how waters of the Crescent Lake and Valentine National Wildlife Refuges in northern Nebraska were originally fenced against grazing. Shoreline vegetation became so lush and dense that use by breeding waterfowl was impaired, predators were favored, and fire hazards were created. Restoration of controlled grazing brought about more favorable conditions and an increased production of ducks. Bue and his associates (1964), discussing stockponds in North Dakota, noted that

Shallow, completely protected shorelines grow up to tall emergent plants, such as cattail and bulrush, and are not suitable for dabbling ducks, although occasionally diving ducks use this emergent vegetation. The greatest use is had when the range is grazed within its carrying capacity. Good range management is also good waterfowl management.

This is an example of how light to moderate grazing pressure serves to thin out a vegetation type that is too dense for optimum wildlife production.

Trucking livestock (particularly sheep) to mountain ranges can sometimes be practical to avoid damage from the use year after year of established driveways. Related to this, and sometimes a problem in the mountains, is the erosion caused by stockmen, hunters, and fishermen driving motorized vehicles on steep slopes, unstable soils, or boggy areas.

Prescribed burning for range improvement is used, particularly in the South. As discussed in the section on forest and woodland, there is need for experimentation in the use of controlled fire for wildlife habitat improvement. Referring to a test showing significant weight gains on cattle on burned range, Komarek (1966) concludes, "It is reasonable to assume that a similar favorable response might be obtained on control burned range occupied by native wild ungulates."

Damage to range and livestock by wild animals is discussed in Chapter 6. The interrelationship of predator and prey, the methods of animal-damage control and their direct and indirect effects on other wild animals, and the determination of cause and effect of range condition are complicated and require specific study.

In summary, the attitudes of rangeland owners toward wildlife, recreation seekers, and particularly toward sportsmen who seek areas to hunt and fish; the economic and social balance between wildlife benefits and costs; the owners' knowledge of causes and effects and their discernment of the difference between the two are all matters that directly or indirectly affect wildlife management on private range and pasture lands. How, where, when, and if wildlife fits into the multiple use of their lands is primarily their own decision.

We may conclude that overgrazing by livestock is generally detrimental to nearly all species of wildlife using or influenced by grazed lands. Moderate grazing has been reported as beneficial, neutral, or harmful, depending upon species and other variables. From evidence that much of the domestic livestock range and pasture is overgrazed and yielding considerably less than its potential, one may infer that better livestock management would frequently result in better wildlife habitat. The potential for benefits to both land uses appears to be great. Although the history of the grazing industry is not conducive to optimism, recent progress has been encouraging.

Brush Country Problems

The West has more than 250 million acres of brushland, most of it used jointly by livestock and wildlife. The brushlands may be either mixtures of several woody species or relatively pure stands. Some of the major types include mesquite and shinnery oak ranges in the Southwest, pinyon-juniper and scrub oak in the southern Rockies, sagebrush in the intermountain region, and chamise ranges in California. The mixed shrub types of California and the Southwest are often called chaparral, while mixed brushlands of the Rockies are often just called mountain shrub types.

In the early 1950's there were many "brush eradication" programs. However, it soon became apparent that a more appropriate term for these efforts would be "brush control." Further consideration of the ecological factors involved, including wildlife, prompted a shift of emphasis toward the concept of "brushland management." The following discussion deals with brushlands as related to wildlife in the context of brushland management.

Mesquite

There are an estimated 55 million acres of mesquite in Texas and Oklahoma, 9 million acres in southern Arizona, and 6 million acres in southern New Mexico (Allred, 1949; Parker and Martin, 1952). Records of early travelers across Texas indicate that the mesquite and prairie grasses on uplands formed a savanna. However, settlement of the Southwest, with control of fires and introduction of livestock, brought increased densities of the trees and a spread into adjoining grasslands. Livestock operators have been faced with loss of forage and problems of handling animals in the dense thickets. The effect of increased density of mesquite may be partial reduction of the understory grasses as noted in a Texas study (Workman et al., 1965), or almost complete reduction of understory grasses as found in southern Arizona (Parker and Martin, 1952). Foliage of the mature mesquite tree furnishes little forage to livestock or game, although the beans are taken by livestock and deer. Box and Powell (1965) found that the utilization of regrowth following mowing was 60 times greater than for the mature foliage, by both deer and cattle.

Management of mesquite ranges has emphasized reducing the tree stand to favor understory herbage. Widespread acreages were sprayed with herbicides or otherwise treated during the 50's and 60's in Texas. Herbicide treatments have resulted in only temporary control but provided economical increases in range forage (Workman et al., 1965).

Joint evaluations by state and federal agencies in Texas determined that planned brush control benefited deer. Planning provided for leaving brush on rough areas, along watercourses, and on ridge tops. In studies of mixed brush (which included mesquite) in south Texas, Box and Powell (1965) recommended:

If a rancher chose to raise wildlife as well as livestock, he could treat approximately one-fourth of his land each year by mowing or roller chopping. By arranging his treated areas in long strips throughout the ranch, he could be assured of adequate cover for his wildlife, an increase in edge effect, and adequate forage for his animals.

Box and Powell's recommendations are based upon the strong sprouting characteristics of the brush species. Only 60 percent control of the brush was achieved, and this was short-lived, but retreatment of the brush provided a management system favoring both deer and livestock. The economics of mowing or roller chopping was not determined. These techniques may not be applicable generally throughout the mesquite areas of the Southwest, but the management system suggested appears to have merit where deer or other wildlife species need consideration.

Juniper

Juniper is often mixed with pinyon, and, either alone or mixed, it occupies about 75 million acres in the Southwest. Two thirds of the juniper acreage is on federal lands. Under long-continued heavy grazing, juniper stands have thickened and spread, with resulting decreases in forage, increased erosion, and added difficulty in handling livestock. To reverse this trend, more than 1.2 million acres have been treated in Arizona alone (10 percent of the juniper acreage in the state) at a cost of about $4 million. Cotner (1963) indicated that the acreage treated annually is decreasing because the remaining lands have less potential for improvement.

Juniper woodlands may be important winter ranges for deer and, in some localities, for elk. They also provide habitat for wild turkeys, rabbits, and doves.

Juniper has been removed by cabling, chaining, burning, or bulldozing, and grasses have often been seeded immediately thereafter. Results have been variable: in many cases the increases in grazing capacity have been economically significant; in others the gain in grasses and shrubs has been insignificant. Unfortunately, the extensive action program in juniper control was preceded by a minimum of research, and adequate information for successful control and range improvement is still lacking. Predictions on costs, however, are available (Cotner, 1963).

There is a similar dearth of facts about the effect of juniper control on game populations. Tentative guidelines have been adopted by the U.S. Forest Service to protect wildlife resources in pinyon-juniper areas where control is planned. These guidelines include: (1) retention of dead woody plant material over at least 15 percent of the area; (2) restriction of treatment areas to less than 120-acre blocks; and (3) preservation of 10- to 15-acre patches of live juniper trees, these patches comprising at least 5 percent of the total area.

In Nevada, Utah, and Colorado, pinyon-juniper stands are being improved specifically for the benefit of wildlife. The trees are removed by mechanical means and the areas then seeded to a mixture of grasses, forbs, and browse. The objective is to convert closed stands of trees to grass-forb-browse vegetation for use by deer in late winter and spring and by cattle in the spring. Additional benefits are noted for other big game animals, upland game birds, and songbirds, and for erosion control. In the conversions, pinyon-juniper stands are left for cover in areas normally favored by deer for shelter.

Sagebrush

Sagebrush ranges occupy some 95 million acres in the intermountain region of the West. Much of this range had become depleted prior to World War II, with "closed communities" of sagebrush that contained but little understory of desirable grasses and forbs. Several methods of sagebrush removal became available after the war, and by the late 1950's large acreages were being treated on both federal and private lands. Many studies reported increases of 200 to 300 percent or more in grazing capacity through mechanical or chemical control of sagebrush, or by burning (Pechanec *et al.*, 1944, 1954; Hyder and Sneva, 1958; Hervey, 1961; Hyatt, 1966). The immense success of improving sagebrush ranges for livestock and the resulting expansion of control programs aroused the concern of hunters and game managers.

As well as constituting a conspicuous feature of the environment of several game species and, presumably, supplying some of their cover needs, big sagebrush and other species of *Artemisia* contribute significantly throughout the West to the diets of antelope (Einarsen, 1948; Ferrel and Leach, 1950; Cole, 1957; Hoover *et al.*, 1959), sage grouse (Patterson, 1952; Leach and Hensley, 1954; Rogers, 1964), and mule deer (Dixon, 1934; Longhurst *et al.*, 1952; Hill, 1956; Morris and Schwartz, 1957). Elk seem to have little direct dependence on sagebrush, but they use the range type extensively in winter and, in their competition with livestock for forage, are of more direct economic concern to ranchers (Pickford and Reid, 1943; Murie, 1951; Smith, 1961; Stevens, 1966).

The concern of individuals, conservation groups, and land management agencies for resources other than livestock forage has engendered a mounting controversy over sagebrush control. Carson (1962) called it to general public attention in her best-selling book, *Silent Spring*. It was publicized nationally in a news release of the National Wildlife Federation (Johns, 1965). The Western Association of State Game and Fish Commissioners, meeting in Anchorage in July, 1965, passed a resolution urging federal agencies responsible for public land management and for technical and financial assistance on private lands to give adequate consideration to wildlife habitat requirements in planning and executing sagebrush control projects.

Other authors ascribe to sagebrush control possible improvements in game habitat. Alley (1965) refers to a decrease in sage grouse numbers in Wyoming during years when sagebrush density was increasing and an increase after sagebrush control programs were under way. Wilbert (1963) found that elk, in spring after the snow had left, made more use of two 25-acre sprayed areas than they did of adjacent unsprayed areas. It must be concluded, however, that the influences of sagebrush control on wildlife habitat are still largely speculative.

Since sage grouse occur primarily in sage, with occasional seasonal use of adjacent vegetation types, there is little question that the continued existence of these birds depends upon the persistence of sagebrush in proper amounts and patterns. The dependence on sagebrush itself is less critical for deer and elk; they exist equally well on shrub ranges lacking it. Smith (1950) considered sagebrush to be the most important winter deer forage in much of the West, but he learned (1959) in pen feeding that among several browse species fed singly it was taken in the least amounts. Yet, while Utah juniper, Gambel oak, bitterbrush, curlleaf and birchleaf mahogany, chokecherry, and cliffrose were obviously more palatable, sagebrush was consistently taken when offered in combination with these feeds.

Despite the apparent conflict of interest in sagebrush control, little research has been done under field conditions to resolve the problem. However, the grazing habits of livestock and game animals are sufficiently well known to suggest certain systems of management of sagebrush ranges to allow improvement for both livestock and big game animals. These systems require an ecological approach to control programs rather than the massive area approach. For example, ridges required for deer winter range should be left in sagebrush, and adjoining swales that may be covered with snow in the winter can be converted to grass for increased use by deer in the spring and by livestock in the summer.

Information available on the movement and grazing habits of livestock and wildlife is being used by federal agencies in planning sagebrush management. State game managers are consulted, and if areas of deer winter range are involved, plans may be adjusted to leave these areas in sagebrush. Likewise, where sage grouse habitat is desired, strips ¼ or ½ mile wide are left adjacent to meadows, booming grounds, and brood sites. On other areas, alternate strips of sagebrush 100 feet or more wide are left.

The foregoing methods of management apply to federal lands, but private landowners are not under similar constraints. Thus there is no assurance under present policies that wildlife habitat needs will be considered in sagebrush control on privately owned lands. There is need for more research on the effect of sagebrush control on wildlife, and for incentives to encourage private landowners to utilize practices known to benefit wildlife.

California Chaparral

"Chaparral" denotes any dense thicket of stiff or thorny shrubs or dwarf trees. In California there are two major types—"true" chaparral and timber chaparral. True chaparral occupies about 11 million acres on dry slopes at elevations between 1,000 and 4,000 feet west of the Sierra Nevada summit and the Mojave Desert. Chamise (*Adenostoma fasciculatum*) ist the most characteristic and widely distributed species of this type. Sampson and Jesperson (1963) report that foothill chaparral occurs in two characteristic situations—as pioneer plants in habitats where the soil mantle is in early stages of development, and in secondary successions on disturbed areas.

The timber-chaparral community covers extensive areas above the upper limits of the foothill chaparral. It is found on soils too shallow for timber growth and as a stage of secondary succession on disturbed timber areas. Shrub species include manzanita and ceanothus. Dense chaparral stands impede animal movements and many of the mature plants are low in nutritional value. The aim of the wildlife manager is to break up areas of mature brush and provide open stands of young plants. Land management efforts to accomplish the objectives fall into three major classes:

1. Complete conversion of chaparral to grass: A typical treatment of this sort consists of burning the brush (often preceded by crushing), seeding to grass, and following up with spray treatments to kill brush

seedlings or sprouts that become established after the seeding. The opening up of dense chaparral and establishment of grass benefits deer, quail, and doves (Biswell *et al.*, 1952).

Nearly all brush-to-grass coversions are multipurpose projects aimed at improving range and watershed conditions and reducing fire hazards. Value to game depends upon the size of the converted unit, large areas being generally less valuable to game than small. Where acreages are large, some brush is left standing to provide cover and browse between the areas of grass. Brushpiles are sometimes left in a converted area to provide cover for quail and songbirds. The U.S. Forest Service and the Bureau of Land Management consult with the California Department of Fish and Game during the planning stage prior to field operations.

The greatest effort in California in converting brushlands to grass has been by private landowners. From 1956 to 1965 over a million acres were burned under permits issued by the California Division of Forestry for private lands—740,000 acres in 1965 alone. Approximately 28.5 percent of the total acreage was seeded following burning. Federal agencies also play an important role. The Forest Service changed 37,371 acres of chaparral to grass from 1956 to 1965—about 10,000 acres in 1965. The Bureau of Land Management treated 66,000 acres of chaparral from 1956 to 1965.

The "fuel-break" program is a specialized form of brushland management. In most brush areas of California the fire hazard is high. Fire fighters find it difficult and sometimes impossible to control fires that rage through extensive stands. The establishment of grass strips along ridge tops breaks up large brushy areas into controllable units. These strips—known as fuel-breaks—permit more rapid movement of fire fighters and equipment and an opportunity to backfire. Fuel-breaks also create excellent interspersion for wildlife. From 1956 to 1965, 13,800 acres of fuel-breaks were constructed. The acreage figures are somewhat misleading in terms of game benefits. Through the creation of desirable edge and forage interspersion, one acre of fuel-break improves habitat for many surrounding acres.

2. Encouragement of chaparral sprout growth through cutting, crushing, and burning, or burning alone: This treatment differs from conversion to grass in that it is aimed specifically at improving browse for deer and cattle. The Forest Service, in most cases cooperatively with the California Department of Fish and Game, burned more than 17,000 acres from 1956 to 1965 in an effort to provide palatable and nutritious feed. Included in this total acreage are many miles of "browseways." Browseways are narrow strips constructed through dense stands of chaparral that have the specific objective of benefiting large and

small game. The strips not only provide much more edge and interspersion than do large block treatments, but also improve access for hunters.
3. Conversion of chaparral growing on forest soils back to trees: A common method of replacing chaparral with trees is to bulldoze off the brush in strips and then to plant tree seedlings. This practice improves habitat for both game and nongame wildlife species, although in many areas there is depredation of planted trees by deer. From 1956 to 1965, the Forest Service alone undertook to replace brush with trees on 45,000 acres in California.

Other Brushlands

Chaparral of northern Arizona, shrub mixtures of the Rocky Mountains, shinnery oak of Oklahoma and Texas, sand sagebrush of the southern Great Plains, and mixed brush of south Texas are also being managed for re-establishment of a better grass-to-browse ratio to favor livestock or wildlife, or both. Control methods are not so well developed for the Arizona chaparral, Gambel oak, or mixed brush of south Texas as for big sagebrush. However, herbicidal treatments have been developed for sand sagebrush and shinnery oak. On most of these brushlands there has been little research on the effects of management on wildlife. The emphasis has been to determine the value of control for livestock enterprises.

In the Southeast, brush control is practiced on the palmetto of Florida and scrub oak in the South Carolina and Georgia sandhills. There are over 9 million acres of palmetto in central and south Florida. Control methods employing roller choppers or herbicides reduce the palmetto and permit natural increase of native grasses and broadleafed herbs. Biologists often recommend leaving palmetto around sloughs and sand ponds, along drainage ways, and around hammocks to provide cover and feed for deer, turkey, quail, doves, songbirds, and raccoons. Control of scrub oak in the Southeast favors production of wildlife, as indicated by the great increase in doves in cleared areas where pokeberry has replaced the oak. Likewise, deer and bobwhite populations have increased where scrub oak has been cleared and pine planted. Research is needed to fully evaluate techniques for brush control in both the palmetto and scrub oak areas to provide optimum benefits for wildlife and livestock or forestry.

Range Seeding

Range seeding was stimulated by improved technology and various agricultural support programs after World War II. The major objective was production of livestock forage on previously cropped land or depleted ranges. Consequently, most workers evaluated seeding results in terms of benefits to livestock and did not measure the effects upon wildlife. However, useful observations have been made, such as those by Griffith (1962) in discussing antelope management:

... antelope have shown response when old cultivated hayfields, and abandoned fields are a part of their present habitat. They have shown intensified use of areas where dominant sagebrush and rabbitbrush have been eradicated and reseeding done of grasses and legumes.

Yoakum (1962) made similar observations:

Here appears our first clue on what and how to increase antelope numbers—we gained knowledge that changing an acre from a predominant sagebrush type to a vegetative cover containing a good mixture of grass, forbs, and low-growing browse species can increase population numbers.

Other work indicates that deer favor such introduced species as crested wheatgrass and intermediate wheatgrass early in the spring when new growth starts, which is from 2 to 4 weeks earlier than many of the native grasses. In fact, ranchers are commonly concerned about the protection of newly seeded stands from excessive use by deer. They are also concerned about early spring usage by deer of established grasses intended for later feed for livestock.

Preponderant evidence shows that range seedings have benefited both wildlife and livestock, provided that sufficient shrub-forage is available to carry browse-dependent animals through critical winter periods. However, since seedings for livestock often involve only grasses, interest has developed among those concerned with wildlife habitat in the inclusion of browse and legumes in seed mixtures. Hubbard (1962) reviewed the progress in browse-seeding research, and concluded that successful bitterbrush seeding was possible, and that under proper conditions it should provide forage for 0.8 to 2.4 deer-months per acre in California.

Seeding is an integral part of type conversions. For example, most of the 20,000 acres of juniper-pinyon so treated in Utah and Nevada in 1965 included a mixture of grasses, forbs, and browse. Several million acres of the juniper-pinyon type in the intermountain region have a potential for similar improvement through tree removal and seeding. One area in Utah so treated increased deer use twentyfold (Plummer *et al.*, 1965). These areas are managed primarily for deer use in winter and early spring, with some cattle use in the late fall and spring. Dual use by cattle and deer appears to help maintain a desirable ratio of browse and herbaceous plants. Other big game animals, upland game birds, and songbirds appear to benefit from the conversion of dense stands of juniper-pinyon to grass-forb-browse mixtures.

A few studies have been made of the effects upon wildlife of grass seedings on land placed in the "conservation reserve" under terms of the Soil Bank Act. However, in view of the fact that over 18.5 million acres were converted to grass cover under the conservation reserve program, there should be much more research on wildlife relationships.

WILDLIFE ON CROPLANDS

Farms and croplands have long been recognized as a major habitat of economically important wildlife (Miller and Powell, 1942). One evident reason is the great extent of such land uses. The U.S. Department of Agriculture (1962) summarized this situation for the year 1959:

A fifth of the land in the United States is used as cropland. Somewhat over one-fourth is grassland pasture and range. One-third is in forest. If grassland and forest land used for grazing are included, about 60 percent of all land in the United States is in crop and livestock production.

Even a secondary value may be expected to have economic and social importance on such a large area. The nature of wildlife habitats is largely determined by the major land-use industry—as noted in the foregoing sections on forest and grazing ranges. This is equally true of extensive croplands, and also of diversified farms where all three of these uses combine to form a mosaic of vegetation types. As mentioned previously, the widely varied habitat pattern on lands of irregular topography has its own peculiar characteristics favorable to certain birds and mammals commonly known as farm wildlife. Typical of such species are the cottontail rabbits, fox squirrels, doves, bobwhite quail, and pheasant. Featuring game animals in this connection does not in any sense discount the importance of songbirds and other nonhunted creatures. Nearly all farm lands are privately owned, and this vitally affects public use of the wildlife resource, which by law and precedent is public property.

Cropped land has important qualities influencing its capacity to support living things of all kinds. This is a man-made habitat, largely a design of artificially managed monocultures, that may be highly productive of wild creatures under some conditions. The extent to which it does produce depends on how well it fulfills the year-round life requirements of the most closely adapted species. This means, of course, the degree to which it simulates the functioning of a natural ecosystem.

Agricultural soils are basically favorable to living organisms in that usually they are fertile and have reasonably good moisture relationships. Cultivated lands commonly abound in weed-seed and grain-residue foods (Baumgras, 1943; Allen, 1949) that support, at once, the often undesirable rodents and the usually desirable game birds. In an ecological sense, the agricultural habitat is a disturbance community, sometimes an extensive single vegetation type, at other times a complex of conditions—bare soil, row crops, annual forbs and grasses, meadowlands, perennial herb and brush stages, and other early phases of forest or grassland succession. Such types and the terms used to describe them overlap broadly.

Graham, a long-time student of wildlife and land-use relationships, described succinctly the logical and necessary emphasis that must be employed in nearly any cropping program for human benefits. He recognized initially (1944, p. 11) that:

> ... the capacity of the land to produce varies not only from region to region, but within small areas, in accordance with soil conditions, vegetation, slope, exposure, degree of accelerated erosion, and other physical characteristics. Consequently, ... in a very general way it may be said that farm land comparatively level may best be devoted to corn, cotton, and cultivated crops; gentle slopes to pasture; steep slopes to trees; and odd corners, and infertile and eroded spots to the production of useful wild plants and animals.

This general statement of land-use capability applies alike to regions, farms, and fields. We may assume that primary uses—such as cash crops on level fertile soils—may have additional worth in their contribution to wildlife by-products. In the extensive corn lands of midwest prairies, for example, or in wheat-and-fallow areas farther west, the secondary values are likely to be minor. On the other hand, where an appreciable portion of the farm is unsuited to tillage, wildlife can be much more important as an accessory product. Policies affecting wildlife and the recreational benefits deriving from it cannot be the same for all agricultural areas.

Intensively Managed Farms

The growing trend toward large intensively managed cropping units has been described (Chapter 3). This trend accompanies increasing mechanization, the operation of farms with big-business efficiency, a higher degree of crop specialization, the employment of less labor, and frequently absentee ownership. Continuous blocks of relatively level and productive lands are best adapted to such use, with resulting extensive monotypes (e.g., corn, beans, wheat, cotton, sorghum) on what once were prairies, or specialty crops occupying irrigated or drained flats.

On these areas, intensive culture is the rule, and the total acreage has high value for this primary purpose. There is little economic basis for giving consideration to wildlife, and there are few sites where it is feasible to favor its production. As noted by Allen (1952)

In some areas agricultural lands are so well adapted to intensive farming that almost every square foot will yield cash income. Little, if any, wildlife management is practicable in these situations; in truck crop areas such animals as pheasants and rabbits may be more of a nuisance than anything else.

The land-use association that Bennitt (1939) reported for Missouri prairie chickens has general significance. He found none of these birds on the best prairie soils, since such areas had been totally converted to the cultivation of corn, sorghum, and other crops. "There was almost none. . . on the next best. . . . Nearly all the birds were found on the medium to low-grade prairie soils." In the poorest areas cultivation was not extensive and hay meadows and pastures were increasing. There is little reason to doubt that in primitive times the most fertile prairies of Missouri supported the highest populations of these grassland grouse, but such areas had ceased to be "chicken" habitat.

Over a period of 14 years, Swanson and Yocum (1958) observed the degradation of habitat and the decline of pheasants and Hungarian partridges as the intensity of land use increased in wheat lands of the Washington palouse region.

This increased intensity of farming effort has resulted in larger farms, consolidation of fields, more machinery, fewer fence rows, less edge effect, subsidized drainage, elimination of brushy draws, and aerial spraying of insects and weeds. In summary, except for the planting of sweet clover, all factors mentioned have had a tendency to decrease the amount of food and cover in this area.

On prairies from Indiana to Iowa are found some of the most productive agricultural soils in the world. They exemplify the situation of intensively used land as a wildlife habitat. There is, literally, no "waste" space on such farms, except for roadsides and the banks of waterways— ditches that must be accessible to cleaning with a dragline at intervals, and streams in various stages of conversion to ditches. The stabilization of banks with grass and legumes or shrubs is an essential part of land management, and such areas receive heavy use by nesting pheasants, as well as songbirds and rabbits.

On intensively used farms an exceptional interest by the landowner can improve wildlife habitat, even at some expense to cropfield space. Windbreaks (Ferber, 1958) of Russian olive, multiflora rose, or other shrubs provide an agricultural incentive, according to local conditions, and they also introduce durable coverts into blocks of cropland where none is likely to exist otherwise (Wandell, 1948). The response of songbirds (Dambach, 1945), nesting mourning doves, and wintering pheasants to such developments may be impressive. Especially on former tallgrass prairie lands, the tolerant, rapid-growing, and easily handled multiflora rose can be used with little concern for its tendency to spread (Scott, 1965). Where the bulk of the land is in short rotations, pioneering by the shrub is automatically controlled.

That some of these practices are finding at least limited acceptance among farmers is indicated by records of Soil Conservation Districts showing the building of 1,500 miles of windbreaks and 3,700 miles of hedges annually (Anderson and Compton, 1958; see also Fox, 1942). Nelson (1953) described a cooperative program for South Dakota in which windbreaks averaging 7 acres were established at 3-mile intervals with the particular objective of protecting pheasants during winter blizzards. Planting costs were about $42 per acre.

While regionally specialized practices may be developed for multiple purposes, it is not realistic to expect measures that will favor wildlife on a large scale. For evident economic reasons major areas of class I land (see Nunns, 1958) will continue to offer the least opportunity for managing this recreational by-product. In effect, this is a natural zoning that commonly allocates the most productive soil to a single efficient use—the antithesis of multiple use.

Diversified Farms

The land-use capability classification of the Soil Conservation Service designates classes I through IV as suitable for cultivated crops, with progressively increasing limitations and need for conservation practices. Classes V through VIII are generally unsuited to cultivation but can be allocated to pasturing, forestry, and wildlife management (Nunns, 1958). Wildlife is the one product to which, in some measure, all of the associated land types contribute. For agricultural purposes a "general," or diversified, farm will be valuable in proportion to the high quality cropland it includes. Its usefulness as a wildlife habitat will usually depend on areas of land in classes V to VIII, especially if these are interspersed with fertile cropfields. If this trend of decreasing productivity is projected to areas submarginal for agriculture, the capacity to support farm wildlife diminishes and the proportion of forest-dwelling species increases. Diversified farming has developed frequently on formerly forested lands that are rolling to hilly in topography.

Habitat Objectives

Leopold (1933), pioneer in wildlife management, recognized "carrying capacity" as a universal characteristic of habitat (see also Errington, 1945). This is to say that for a given species a particular range has definite limitations in the number of animals it will support at a given time. A population could theoretically expand indefinitely if habitat resources were infinite. In reality, every population is held in check by the operation of density-dependent environmental or behavioral factors (see Lack, 1954; Dasmann, 1964: 153 *et seq.*). Logically, in any habitat a single condition of some kind or other is likely to be more effectively limiting than all others and for management purposes may be designated conveniently as the "critical" factor (see Taylor, 1934; Allen, 1954: 46 *et seq.*).

As would be expected, critical factors may be quite different from one species to another, even in the same habitat; from one region to another they may vary for an individual species. On a year-to-year basis, weather is a universally influential variable for nearly all birds and mammals (see especially Lehmann, 1953, and Jackson, 1962), yet its effects are conditioned by the kinds and pattern of vegetation. Wildlife biologists are learning to recognize the basic environmental requirements of many species, especially in terms of seasonal combinations of vegetation types that serve as food and cover. The word "combination" is not to be passed over lightly, since it is the close association of life essentials that permits an animal to satisfy its requirement with a minimum of movement and thus a maximum of security. The more various cover types are broken up and mixed together—creating the characteristic condition known as edge effect or interspersion (Leopold, 1933)—the more individual "home ranges" (Burt, 1940) there will be where animals can survive. In other words, the higher will be the habitat carrying capacity.

Contour Agriculture

In the contiguous 48 states, many farms were laid out originally to conform with section lines, producing a pattern of quadrangular fields, sometimes with little reference to surface features.* Under these conditions, cropping laid bare large continuous blocks of land at one

---

*The rectangular system of surveying land, initiated in 1785, applies generally in the states west of the Ohio and Mississippi Rivers and in Alabama, Florida, and Mississippi.

time. According to Soil Conservation Service estimates, some 61 percent of cultivated land in the United States is sufficiently rolling to erode when not protected by vegetation (Kell, 1938). The system of contour agriculture, which received great impetus during the thirties, was aimed particularly at stabilizing the soil and promoting the infiltration of water where it falls. It commonly results in fields of irregular shape, with sloping croplands laid out in narrow alternating strips of cultivated ground and close-growing grain or hay. The map of a farm planned on the basis of soil capability typically shows a markedly increased interspersion of cover types and resulting edge (Graham, 1941a; Hedge and Klingebiel, 1957).

The conversion of an agricultural area from rectangular fields to a completely revised farm plan often results in the removal of old brushy fencerows and borders and an initial degradation of wildlife habitat. However, establishment of the new system will feature permanent vegetation in critical sites and develop a pattern of coverts that may be as good as the old, or better.

On a series of selected Ohio farms, the changeover to modern land-use plans made by the Soil Conservation Service was appraised for its effects on breeding bird populations (Good and Dambach, 1943). Limiting their observations to areas in crops, pastures, and woodland (i.e., no specific wildlife management measures), the authors concluded that soil-conserving practices had increased bird populations on two areas by approximately 38 and 45 percent, respectively, and that the most influential factors in bringing about this change were:

1. Fewer acres clean-tilled and in small grains (which support small populations of breeding birds) and a corresponding increase in the acreage with permanent vegetation.

2. More acres in meadow, which support higher populations of breeding birds.

3. Breaking large crop fields into narrow, alternative strips of different crops, resulting in an increase in the number of acceptable territories for field-nesting birds.

4. Increased acreage of managed pastures which support higher populations of breeding birds than poor pastures.

5. Material increase in acreage of protected woodlands, which support about twice as many birds as grazed woods.

Cultural Practices

While the basic agricultural design is of vital importance to wildlife, so also are the methods of tillage and crop management. The mowing machine is a particularly well known threat to nesting birds and other wildlife—one that has grown steadily in importance since the advent of the first horse-drawn mechanical mower.

In Wood County, Ohio, the destruction of pheasants in hay mowing increased about 60 percent from 1938 to 1946 as a result of the growing use of high-speed power mowers (Leedy and Dustman, 1947). Night mowing of alfalfa for dehydrating mills was especially destructive to pheasants. In a sample of 590 acres cut for mills in 1946, the kill of pheasants was 106 hens and 74 juveniles. Other vertebrates killed totaled 193, including 37 cottontails.

In many states during the past 30 years, wildlife workers have experimented with various types of "flushing bars," with some measure of success. However, the encouragement vanishes as mowers become more efficient. No easily used device seems to have been perfected for avoiding the cutter bar problem. Where the time of mowing can be controlled, late mowing results in diminished mortality for some species. Leedy (1949) found that first cuttings of alfalfa in Ohio had six times as many pheasant nests per unit area as second cuttings. The productivity of nests in stands of small grain was considerably better than in alfalfa, because of the later mowing (Leedy, 1940). The development of early-maturing grasses and legumes will be an increasing liability to such species as the pheasant.

That there are situations in which an awareness of the mowing problem can be used to advantage is evident in a news release of the Iowa State Game Commission dated July 1, 1967. The chairman of the Iowa Agricultural Stabilization and Conservation Committee gave full support to the Game Commission's request that farmers raise their mower blades 8 to 10 inches in clipping "government" acres.

Intensified land use commonly involves more frequent tillage and more thorough weed control. On prairie wheat fields the spring burning of stubble has long been practiced—to the disadvantage of both soil fertility and wildlife. To avoid this result, subsidy payments were used in eastern Washington to encourage farmers to disc their stubblefields in the fall. However, this procedure and summer fallowing for weed control contributed to the total area of bare soil and the reduction of wildlife cover (Swanson and Yocum, 1958). In Colorado, Sandfort (1952) recommended that fallow discing in wheat stubble be delayed until the second week in June to avoid destroying pheasant nests. Combine harvesting of grain leaves tall stubble that is relatively good bird cover as long as it stands. Clipping reduces this value, as well as the weed-seed foods produced in such fields.

Anderson (1949, 1965) classified as favorable or unfavorable various farming practices that affect wildlife on lands primarily used for crops, pasture, and woods. Among beneficial farming methods in tilled fields are rotations that include grass-legume meadow, liming and fertilizing, strip cropping, cover crops, stubble mulching, leaving unharvested grain or spreading manure near winter cover, and delayed mowing of roadsides, watercourses, and headlands.

Similarly, pasture improvement, through fertilization and reseeding, and grazing within carrying capacity, are considered to be in keeping with good wildlife management (Anderson, 1949, 1965). Burning, overgrazing, and early clean mowing have the opposite effect. Woodlots function best as wildlife habitat when protected from fire and grazing, when selectively cut (in the case of hardwoods), when brush cuttings are piled and left unburned, and when den trees, mast trees, and hollow logs are preserved.

It is evident that nearly all of the practices desirable for the production of wild creatures are either necessary for good land management or at least are not inimical to it. It is clear also that improvements in the engineering of agricultural implements are a part of increased efficiency on the farm. This is true not only of faster mowers, but of harvesters that leave less grain residue and less cover on the ground. These trends indicate a future need for effective alternatives in favoring the wildlife crop.

Problem Sites and Wildlife Plantings

A modern land-use plan for a farm in a region of forest climax may include a wide variety of soils and sites ranging from the most level and fertile crop fields on the one hand to the "problem" topography that must be allocated to woodlot on the other. The map of site capabilities will show many locations where an informed landowner can provide for wildlife coverts. In terms of space, such coverts typically cost little or nothing; the cost of establishing and maintaining them will hinge on the problem of developing "practical" techniques and achieving worthwhile results. These aspects vary greatly. The Biology Division of the Soil Conservation Service was concerned with problems and opportunities of this kind as early as the 1930's, and experimentation with methods has gone forward on a broad scale since then (Dambach, 1940, 1945, 1948a; Edminster, 1941; Graham, 1941a, 1947; Van Dersal and Graham, 1946; Allen, 1949; Edminister and May, 1951; Anderson and Compton, 1958; Anderson, 1949, 1965).

Improvements made specifically for wildlife usually feature the establishment of relatively permanent vegetation on areas where the common purpose of erosion control and wildlife management will be served. Some of the sites used to advantage and appropriate cover types are: (1) grassed terraces and waterways, (2) contour hedges and windbreaks—especially in strip-cropped fields, (3) field borders along woodlots, where soil is sapped of moisture and fertility by the tree roots, (4) plantings of perennial legumes, shrubs, and trees around old gullies and on critical slopes and "odd areas." Living fences of multiflora rose have shown great promise; however, limited use of this species is now recommended to avoid its spreading into pastures and idle areas.

Originally, many planting materials were recognized as potentially useful in wildlife management (McAtee, 1941), and extensive trials have been made to screen out those regionally adapted to specific purposes (Davison, 1941, 1945; Graham, 1941b, 1942; Dambach, 1948a; Edminster and May, 1951; Borell, 1962). To have general value in such a program, a plant species needs to serve important needs for wildlife (either as cover or food or both) and to have a broad tolerance of climatic, soil, and moisture conditions. It should survive under indifferent handling and have good soil-binding qualities.

The vast majority of plant species tried have proven to have important deficiencies of one kind or another. Among those sufficiently promising to receive widespread use are multiflora rose, autumn olive, bicolor lespedeza, sericea lespedeza, and several species of viburnum, honeysuckle, and dogwood. All of these have fleshy fruits except the lespedezas; autumn olive is particularly tolerant of dry conditions. Pines and other conifers are popular with landowners for ease of handling and landscaping value. In early years of growth they form good ground cover.

The lespedezas merit particular mention, since they have been featured in many wildlife programs in the eastern United States south of the Great Lakes region (Davison, 1945). As a plant easily seeded, site tolerant, and with superior erosion control and wildlife cover characteristics, sericea lespedeza (*Lespedeza cuneata*) is outstanding. Well-distributed winter cover is a primary need of the cottontail, and this perennial legume serves the purpose in many situations.

Other lespedezas are more useful in quail management, which is an important wildlife interest of landowners in the central and southern states. Introduced annual lespedezas, especially Korean (*L. stipulacea*), reseed extensively as rederals and frequently provide abundant food for the bobwhite. The greatest effort to this end, however, has been made with "bicolor" lespedeza (*L. bicolor*). The seed of this plant has high palatability. The plant forms the open type of cover favored by the bobwhite. Over the past 20 years, seed and plants of this species have been extensively distributed by southeastern states as part of their farm wildlife management programs. The planting of food strips on private shooting preserves has become standard practice. It has long been evident that quail make much use of "bicolor patches," and it has been widely assumed that such a program produced more birds.

Management Appraisal

Rosene (1956) reported on a 7-year study covering nine hunting preserves in Alabama and South Carolina where more than half a million plants of bicolor lespedeza had been used for quail management. The work involved paired experimental and control tracts (with and without bicolor); information was obtained on 1,924 coveys. Rosene found that on each of the experimental areas bicolor formed not less than 32 percent of the food used by quail. In hunting season the coveys were most commonly to be found in the food strips, which made shooting easier—a desirable feature on quail preserves, where the kill is under control. As to the critical question—whether bicolor plantings produce more quail—the increase was less than one covey of quail per 1,000 acres on the developed areas, not a statistically significant difference. Evidently bicolor has value in producing excellent hunting (the dogs go from one planting to another), but it cannot be depended upon to produce more quail on areas where there is sufficient food of other kinds. On the areas studied, food was not a critical limiting factor.

As a measure of the success of more general farm game habitat programs, Marshall (1953) made a field reconnaissance of 15 states and carried out a qualitative appraisal of wildlife management practices— primarily plantings in small plots. In order of importance, the plants used were shrub lespedeza, multiflora rose, several other deciduous shrubs, conifers, sericea lespedeza, and various annuals such as Korean lespedeza and partridge pea (*Chamaecrista fasciculata*).

Marshall found that several factors militated against the effectiveness of such developments. Natural plant successions tended to invade the artificial plantings and alter their character. The actual need for small food and cover plantings by wildlife varied greatly from one area to another, and benefits frequently were uncertain. Incentives for a landowner to invest time and effort in careful establishment and maintenance of plantings were largely lacking. Planting failures and inferior stands were common. No reliable research appraisal was made to determine what had been accomplished.

Such results do not constitute a disavowal of the effectiveness of habitat management; they probably do indicate that "blanket" specifications and large-scale programs are likely to become indiscriminate and ineffective. There is no question that the numbers of a desirable wildlife species can be increased by food and cover manipulations on an area where site and climate are favorable but where the vegetation pattern is deficient. Outstanding examples can be cited where this has been done with the bobwhite and California quails (Hawbecker and Bond, 1942; Rosene, 1950; Steen, 1950; Burger and Linduska, 1967). In each of these management operations, the basis was a soil conservation plan into which quail food and cover types were fitted, especially on edges and unused areas. The striking results of such developments at Remington Farms on Maryland's Eastern Shore (Burger and Linduska, 1967) were achieved in 8 years. Quail coveys increased from 5 to 38 in this period on a 3,000-acre management area, and a substantial buildup of rabbits accompanied the program. The principal practices utilized were:

(1) creation and seeding of waterways and diversion terraces, (2) retirement and seeding under federal programs of headlands and borders of cropfields, and (3) establishment of plantings designed to improve farm-game habitat. Through 1964, these practices included seeding 49.4 acres to grass and 8.5 miles of 30-ft strips to sericea lespedeza (*Lespedeza cuneata*), and planting 7.1 miles of multiflora rose (*Rosa multiflora*) hedges and 14 acres of food-producing shrubs. Land-use changes dictated by practical farming considerations, primarily fallowing odd areas and reducing grazing intensity, also improved quail habitat.

Any reviewer of literature on habitat improvement will conclude that projects carried out with ecological realism are very often successful, and that those contrived in other contexts are likely to fail. Such expedients as large-scale artificial feeding, game stocking, and predator control were among the first putative cure-alls questioned and largely discredited by the biologist as a means of managing wildlife *on a public basis* (we do not question bird feeding as a private recreational use of the wildlife resource). Now the biologist must remind the professional manager that solving wildlife problems on the land is commonly a technical business and that a diagnosis of ecological ills should precede the cure. A reality to be faced is that "game is a thin crop." Where a fair-to-good population of a species already is present, the installation of a few plantings is not likely to produce an increase that can be measured. But under extreme conditions of habitat degradation, an intensive management program may have unmistakable good effects.

In the latter category are changes that can be seen in semiarid lands when a water deficiency is alleviated. An underground tank, the "gallinaceous guzzler," has been used extensively on California ranches to provide water for valley quail during the summer rearing season (Glading, 1943). The installation of a single water source has made possible the support of 200 birds in ranges where previously there were none (True and Glading, 1946).

Natural Successions

Nearly all wildlife managers recognize the alternative to planting clumps and strips of selected exotic (or native) vegetation specifically for wildlife. In a region of forest climate, an area retired from cultivation will be taken over naturally by successive stages of herbs, brush, and trees. In fact, the vigorous invasion of such species is one of the difficulties with artificial plantings, requiring the cutting out of invaders to preserve desirable features of the original stand. In the case of bicolor lespedeza, periodic mowing of the entire planting followed by discing and fertilizing are necessary to maintain the vigor of the legume and eliminate competition (Rosene, 1952).

In the eastern United States the early woody invaders of undisturbed sites typically are species whose fleshy fruits are borne by birds—various brambles (*Rubus*), vines (*Vitis, Rhus, Celastrus, Solanum*), and numerous shrubs. The low-growing woody species are used as perches by birds whose droppings quickly seed such pioneer tree species as cherry, sassafras, and hackberry. This habit also assures the rapid spreading of woody plants in brushpiles placed as wildlife cover around old gullies and odd areas. The adequacy of natural distribution mechanics for early shrub and tree stages of succession is evident in late summer when the droppings of omnivorous mammals (especially the fox, raccoon, and opossum) are filled with the seeds or stones of pokeberry, cherry, persimmon, grape, dogwood, rose, and other woody plants. Other trees appearing in unused sites are brought in via wind-borne seeds (elm, ash, maple) or fruits (oak, hickory, walnut) carried by squirrels and other nut-eaters.

Over the major portion of the United States there are woody species that will seed naturally into areas set aside and merely left alone. This is true of native shrubs even on central and northern grasslands (notably *Prunus, Rosa, Eleagnus, Symphoricarpos, Shepherdia*). Thus, sites where the soil can be stabilized with undisturbed seedings of grass and legumes will eventually come to support their natural complement of native woody plants to serve as wildlife cover. This approach is no doubt the "easy way" and the one that will be taken by landowners whose interest in wildlife and landscaping does not lead them into specific investments. The policy for a farmer to follow in this situation is merely to leave woody vegetation alone where it is not in the way.

One problem of managing ground cover for wildlife is that it will eventually be invaded and shaded out by trees. This effect is true for both plantings and natural coverts, and calls for periodic maintenance on the small areas where it is impractical to allow a woodlot to develop. The over-topping trees must be killed with chemicals, cut out, or hacked into and broken over—a method that contributes to sprout growth (Allen, 1949). The ecological realities of the "disturbance" agricultural community are that no stage except the climax will maintain itself indefinitely without attention.

Sponsored Government Programs

It appears to be inherent in most efforts toward the conservation of soil and water that some wildlife benefits also accrue. This is especially true where land use is reduced in intensity; it is frequently not the case where such measures as reclamation drainage bring about a greater intensity of cropping, even though the prevention of erosion may be a major issue.

The longstanding Agricultural Conservation Program (ACP) has included a variety of practices, the most useful to wildlife being those involving the planting of trees and shrubs, the establishment of other kinds of vegetative cover, and the development of water sources (see U.S. Department of Agriculture, 1967).

Payments for practices involving shrub and weed control and the improvement of woodlands are likely to vary widely, depending on local interpretation and the particular interests of the operators. In some cases, wildlife is not taken into account because biological activities in the Department of Agriculture have been thinly spread, and general specifications or policies may get a largely nonprofessional interpretation at field level. A greater participation by state wildlife agencies in adapting generally approved practices to local conditions can help this situation, and in some states the necessary relationships between state and federal personnel are well established. Some 23 states now have trained wildlife management extension specialists—a type of service for which there is great need.

The increasing orientation of many agricultural programs toward wildlife benefits is evident, and there are far-reaching possibilities. The

Appalachian land stabilization and conservation program, initiated in 1966, offers cost sharing for many practices similar to those of ACP. As another example, in 1966 approximately 47 million acres of cropland were diverted under the feed grain, wheat, and cotton programs. Such areas are converted to vegetation that often provides nesting cover for game birds or otherwise contributes usefully to the wildlife habitat. A notably beneficial requirement is that whenever mowing is undertaken for weed control it be done after the peak of nesting, or otherwise in the manner least damaging to wildlife. Another feature of the Agricultural Stabilization and Conservation Service program is a provision that can make surplus grain owned by the Commodity Credit Corporation available for feeding migratory birds or resident species. Feeding wild species is not a routine practice in state or federal management programs, but it may be useful for limited periods on waterfowl refuges or in connection with crop depredation problems.

The introduced pheasant (*Phasianus c. torquatus*) is well known for its outstanding ability to survive and reproduce on fertile, intensively farmed lands (Allen, 1956: 431). However, even this tolerant species is vulnerable to extreme reductions of both nesting and winter cover. On a test area of 12 square miles in east-central Wisconsin, 4.3 percent of the cropland was retired from production under the Department of Agriculture Feed Grain Program from 1961 to 1964. About half the retired acreage became suitable nesting cover, and studies by Gates and Ostrom (1966) indicated that an average of 17 percent of the pheasant nesting in the area was in this undisturbed acreage. An increase of approximately 10 percent in the pheasant population was attributed to the Feed Grain Program.

That retired acres can be beneficial to the prairie chicken and sharptailed grouse is indicated in Kirsch's (1964) account of the situation on North Dakota's "drift prairie" in the spring of 1964. He writes that:

Prairie grouse have probably responded to soil bank habitat [grassed areas] wherever remnant populations remained when the Soil Bank Program was begun. Most of the soil bank in this study is scheduled for return to agricultural use in 1968 and 1969. All soil bank lands will be back in such use by 1971. This leaves a few years for development of a program to save some of the prairie grouse using soil bank habitat. . . . If new grasslands are developed now, they will be suitable for prairie chicken when much of the soil bank is returned to agricultural use.

In the Food and Agriculture Act of 1965, the Congress authorized for the first time cropland acreage diversion agreements with farmers "for the preservation of open spaces, natural beauty, the development of wildlife or recreational facilities, or the prevention of air or water pollution. . . ."

For furthering this Greenspan program, the Secretary of Agriculture may transfer Cropland Adjustment Program (CAP) funds to federal, state, or local agencies for land acquisition or to share the cost of conservation practices. Significantly, the act included a provision relating to public access:

The rate or rates of annual adjustment payments as determined hereunder may be increased by an amount determined by the Secretary to be appropriate in relation to the benefit to the general public of the use of the designated acreage if the producer further agrees to permit without other compensation, access to such acreage by the general public during the agreement period, for hunting, trapping, fishing, and hiking, subject to applicable State and Federal regulations. . . .

Gambel (1967) stated that by the above authority, under the 1966 CAP, about 5,500 farmers in 30 states placed more than 480 thousand acres of their cropland under these free public access agreements. This has been a significant effort by the government to meet the incentive needs of land holders in promoting public use of outdoor resources largely at the local level. A reality to be reckoned with is that such programs are temporary, and the good they do may be undone at any time. The population outlook implies strongly that in large measure either the public will be required to own and manage lands and waters for recreation, or a stable long-term formula must be discovered to make public use of private facilities profitable and desirable for the owners.

WILDLIFE OF URBAN AREAS

Songbirds, squirrels, and other wild creatures have long been accepted as part of the "landscaping" of city and suburban dooryards and parkways. However, it is largely in recent years, with the recognition of "natural beauty" as a feature of our environment worth managing, that particular public attention has been given to the wildlife of metropolitan areas. Conditions frequently found in the urban scene may support a wide variety of birds and mammals—particularly in the vicinity of water areas, wooded stream bottoms, and parks. These habitats commonly support a seasonal migration of marsh and shore birds and serve as feeding areas for such larger species as herons and gulls. With proper encouragement, wood ducks, owls, and flying squirrels may nest in hollows or nest boxes on city lots. Raccoons, opossums, rabbits, chipmunks, and woodchucks are common where some open space remains; woodchucks may even become a nuisance in flower beds and vegetable gardens.

Where cities have had the vision to preserve natural waters or wetlands, the waterfowl visitation of spring and fall becomes a popular bird-watching feature for the residents. These areas, even in the midst of a populous and built-up environment, attract wildlife because they are closed to shooting and very often someone will practice artificial feeding. Even rare species may be helped in an important way, as was the case when Hanson (1965) "rediscovered" the giant Canada goose (*Branta canadensis maxima*) and found one of its wintering strongholds to be Silver Lake at Rochester, Minnesota. He stated that:

An attempt to establish nesting Canada geese at Silver Lake was made as early as 1936, when six geese were purchased. However, limited success was achieved until 1947, when a flock of 12 large geese from Nebraska was willed to the city by a former patient of the Mayo Clinic who had enjoyed watching the geese at Silver Lake. This pinioned flock was presumably responsible for decoying wild birds to the lake in autumn. The protection this flock subsequently received permitted its rapid buildup.

It is of interest that the geese concentrate in an area of the lake kept free of ice as a result of water being used by the city power plant for cooling purposes and then returned, heated, to the lake.

Many of the artificial lakes increasingly common in residential developments were at first a part of storm drainage systems. However, in recent years there has been growing recognition of the advantages of scenic water areas in terms of increased environmental amenity and salability of properties.

As has been pointed out by Burby (1967), in studies in North Carolina, lakes in residential subdivisions are not an unmixed blessing. Questions of safety, ownership, and liability arise, as well as questions of water quality and the related public interest in watershed use. Burby pointed out that since every urban area has a finite number of potential sites for impoundments, the expropriation of these sites for private purposes raises questions of the public's interest in the developments. Although, as he indicated, they have a high scenic and recreation value for the residents of the community, in no case were the lakes investigated in the study open to "public" use. Burby said, "Whether the public should be adequately compensated for the use of a diminishing resource is a moot question."

Burby mentioned, further, that many lake-oriented subdivisions are designed around pre-existing lakes initially intended for agricultural purposes and that, in most cases, the dams that create these lakes were not designed to withstand the pressure of surrounding urban development. As a result of more rapid and increased runoff—over that existing in more pastoral periods—as the watershed is developed, there is a constant danger of washout and flooding of downstream areas.

At present, according to available information, no public agency in North Carolina has the responsibility for supervising the construction of dams for lakes in residential areas or for converting agricultural lakes to urban use, although various public agencies may be involved or concerned in relation to highways, mosquito control, and water quality (Burby, 1967). Adequate control or solution of problems of this kind probably will require coordinated action of federal, state, and local officials.

Urban lakes can provide fishing and boating opportunities, although hunting is, in general, a nonconforming use and must be prohibited within city limits. However, the hunting season may have its effects in such localities. It is well known that, where pheasants are plentiful in adjacent agricultural lands, they will react to shooting by flying into the outskirts of towns and suburbs. There, in shrubbery and weedy lots, they will be protected from the gun but increasingly exposed to cats and dogs.

Beyond the suburban fringe changes are commonly taking place that, at least temporarily, favor small game and other wildlife. Especially where soils are not of the highest quality, such lands tend to be broken up into many small residential farms. As noted by George (1966), management is not intensive, pastures are maintained as "vista" open spaces or for riding horses, erosion scars are repaired, gullies are planted to woody vegetation or used for ponds, and conditions generally favorable to wild creatures are maintained. Often these conditions develop without any real consideration being given to the effect on wildlife. Farming, as such, is subordinated or abandoned entirely, fields being converted to grassland reserve and often allowed to grow up to brush and trees.

Although many species of wildlife have been able to survive in human population centers, the disturbing and limiting influences are many. In these areas, the chief mortality factor for some animals (especially squirrels and rabbits) is often the street traffic. In addition to the concrete, asphalt, walls, and fences that supplant the natural cover of open lands, wildlife must contend with such obstacles as buildings, panes of glass, and television towers, which produce large numbers of casualties yearly. In the suburbs, homeowners habitually use many kinds of pesticides liberally; in industrial areas, air and water pollution are likely to be local hazards.

Airports now constitute a special problem, since danger to human life is directly involved. As Drury observed (1966), many of these spacious, well-grassed areas are so attractive to certain kinds of birds one might think they were designed to be refuges. He remarked:

Consider Logan International Airport [Boston]. It was built on many square miles of onetime mudflats and gravel bars, bare at low tide, once a major gathering place for migrating shore birds, and the wintering ground of more than 5 thousand black ducks. Large mussel beds around it are a magnet for herring gulls.

Raised runways were built, but between the runways, to hold costs down and help drainage, low areas were left; they are now filled with freshwater. Before 1960, (when a crash of an airplane after colliding with a flock of starlings killed 61 people) the edges of these ponds and most of the low places on the airport were heavily grown up with tall reeds; beyond them on the edges of the runways, were bushes including bayberry and sumac.

As Drury pointed out, the area provided a maximum amount and variety of habitat and edge highly attractive to birds and other forms of wildlife. Starlings roosted in the reeds at the edge of the ponds, and gulls were attracted to the garbage that frequently is to be found on or near airports. When the reeds were kept cut, the starlings no longer returned in large numbers, but cleaning up the garbage and waste in Boston and other metropolitan areas is more difficult.

With respect to problems caused by birds at airports and in connection with the images or "angels" on radar screens, which resemble images created by small fighter aircraft, Drury (1966: 889) concluded:

Let me repeat: The problems created by birds at airports and on radar do not seem insurmountable. They would be quite simple were it not for financial or political limitations and motives. We know or can find the biological or political and physical factors and take reasonable steps to remove the basic causes. That is, when we are sensible about where we dump our filth and substitute long-range planning for short-term financial gain.

Opportunities for managing wildlife in and around cities and towns are excellent. With a program of grain feeding and a few tame mallards on water areas as decoys, nearly any community can create an outstanding wild bird spectacle during the fall and spring migrations.

Resident species of wildlife can be encouraged by such simple measures as the seasonal control of weed burning, of mowing, and of in-

discriminate use of herbicides. Open spaces can often be handled satisfactorily and can serve as study areas for school groups and outdoor
enthusiasts by allowing the native flora and fauna to develop undisturbed. As stated by Stearns (1967):

Within the boundaries of most urban units, whether small cities or vast megaloptic
[*sic*] complexes, it is still possible to find land with good potential as habitat for
wild birds and animals. Such urban wildlife habitat would bring to the city dweller
some appreciation of the realities of nature. He could learn about ecological concepts such as carrying capacity, territoriality, adaptability, competition, and the
interdependence of wildlife and its environment.

Davey (1967) noted that the Land and Water Conservation Fund
administered by the Bureau of Outdoor Recreation can be used for
wildlife-related recreational projects within urban areas and that the
Open Space Land Program administered by the Department of Housing
and Urban Development has no restriction against incorporating wildlife aspects.

It is particularly important in metropolitan districts that construction site standards receive attention as a means of preventing unnecessary erosion, with resulting siltation and degradation of water areas. In
recognition of this problem, as it is associated with road construction,
an amendment to the Federal Aid Highway Act of 1966 directs the
Secretary of Transportation to consult with the Secretary of Agriculture in formulating guidelines to minimize soil erosion. Engineers of
the Soil Conservation Service and the Bureau of Public Roads have
developed specifications to be followed by state agencies in projects
utilizing federal funds. As another provision of the act, advice from
wildlife agencies must be sought in developing road construction plans.
This should help to minimize the harmful effects of road building on
wildlife and, in some cases, result in improved wildlife habitat.

A Department of the Interior news release of February 5, 1968, reflected a growing optimism concerning the prospects of preserving and
managing the open lands and green spaces of the built-up portions of
the country:

The year 1967 marked another victory for the American people in the continuing
effort to preserve undeveloped lands and waters for public conservation and
recreation purposes against the encroachment of urban expansion, highways, airports, and similar developments, Secretary of the Interior Stewart L. Udall said
today.
    Citing statistics gathered by the Bureau of Outdoor Recreation, Secretary Udall
revealed that during 1967 some 1,715,000 acres of land and water were acquired

for permanent public use in forest, park, open space, fish and game, and multi-purpose reservoir areas, compared with about 750,000 acres converted to urban and highway development.

This marks the third successive year, Secretary Udall noted, that despite rising land prices, the Nation has set aside more undeveloped acres for conservation than for urban and other development.

PROSPECT

Discussions in this chapter should be considered to deal with a sampling of the broad array of land-use problems that must be faced if we are to preserve and make available for public benefits the wildlife of North America. In most situations, from city to wilderness, management is feasible if enough biological and economic understanding can be brought to bear. The research effort in support of land-use management is well established in public agencies and educational institutions. A reasonable level of support will enable this research effort to furnish information essential to continued progress as populations build and the scene on this continent changes.

REFERENCES

Allen, D. L. 1949. The farmer and wildlife. Wildl. Manage. Inst. Bull. 84 p.

Allen, D. L. 1952. Wildlife and the business of farming. J. Soil Water Conserv. 7(5):223-226, 245.

Allen, D. L. 1954. Our wildlife legacy. Funk & Wagnalls, New York. 422 p.

Allen, D. L. 1956. The management outlook, p. 431-466. In D. L. Allen (ed.), Pheasants in North America. The Stackpole Co., Harrisburg, Pa., and Wildlife Management Institute, Washington, D.C.

Alley, H. P. 1965. Big sagebrush control. Wyo. Agr. Exp. Sta. Bull. 354R.

Allred, B. W. 1949. Distribution and control of several woody plants in Texas and Oklahoma. J. Range Manage. 2:17-29.

Anderson, W. L. 1949. Agronomic practices in relation to wildlife. J. Soil Water Conserv. 4:107-116, 128.

Anderson, W. L. 1965. Making land produce useful wildlife. (rev.) U.S. Dep. Agr. Farmers' Bull. 2035. 30 p.

Anderson, L., and V. Compton. 1958. More wildlife through soil and water conservation. Soil Conservation Service, Agr. Inform. Bull. 175.

Atkins, A. P. 1956. Report of the president, 1955. J. Range Manage. 9:63-64.

Bailey, J. A., and M. M. Alexander. 1960. Use of closed conifer plantations by wildlife, N.Y. Fish & Game J. 7:130-148.

Bailey, R. W., G. W. Craddock, and A. R. Croft, 1947. Watershed management for summer flood control in Utah. U.S. Forest Service, Misc. Publ. No. 639.

Baumgras, P. 1943. Winter food productivity of agricultural land for seed-eating birds and mammals. J. Wildl. Manage. 7(1):13-18.

Bennitt, R. 1939. Some agricultural characteristics of the Missouri prairie chicken range. 4th N. Amer. Wildl. Conf. Trans. p. 491-500.

Biswell, H. H. 1959. Prescribed burning and other methods of deer range improvement in ponderosa pine in California. Proc. Soc. Amer. Foresters, p. 102-105.

Biswell, H. H. 1961. Manipulation of chamise brush for deer range improvement. Calif. Fish & Game 47:125-144.

Biswell, H. H., R. D. Taber, D. W. Hedricks, and A. M. Schultz. 1952. Management of chamise brushlands for game in the north coast region of California. Calif. Fish & Game 38:453-484.

Borell, A. E. 1962. Russian-olive (*Elaeagnus angustifolia*) for wildlife and other conservation uses. U.S. Dep. Agr. Leafl. 517. 8 p.

Boussu, M. F. 1954. Relationships between trout population and cover on a small stream. J. Wildl. Manage. 18:229-239.

Box, T. W., and J. Powell. 1965. Brush management techniques for improved forage values in south Texas. Tex. Tech. Coll. Range Manage. Rep. 651. 21 p.

Bue, I. G., H. G. Uhlig, and J. D. Smith. 1964. Stock ponds and dugouts, p. 391-398. In J. P. Linduska and A. L. Nelson (ed.), Waterfowl tomorrow. U.S. Bureau of Sport Fisheries and Wildlife, Washington, D.C.

Burby, R. J., III. 1967. Lake-oriented subdivisions in North Carolina: decision factors and policy implications for urban growth patterns. Part I. Developer decisions. Univ. N.C. Rep. No. 9. Water Resources Research Institute. 177 p.

Burger, G. V., and J. P. Linduska. 1967. Habitat management related to bobwhite populations at Remington Farms. J. Wildl. Manage. 31(1):1-12.

Burt, W. H. 1940. Territorial behaviour and populations of small mammals in southern Michigan. Univ. Mich. Mus. Zool. Misc. Publ. 45. 58 p.

Carson, R. 1962. Silent spring. Houghton Mifflin Co., New York.

Chapman, D. W. 1962. Effects of logging upon fish resources of the West Coast. J. Forest. 60:533-537.

Clawson, M., R. B. Held, and C. H. Stoddard. 1960. Land for the future. Johns Hopkins Press, Baltimore, Md. 570 p.

Cole, G. F. 1957. A preliminary report on antelope-range relationships in central Montana. 10th Annu. Meeting Amer. Soc. Range Manage. Proc. 10 p.

Costello, D. F. 1956. Factors to consider in the evaluation of vegetation condition. J. Range Manage. 9:73-74.

Cotner, M. L. 1963. Controlling pinyon-juniper on Southwestern rangelands. Ariz. Agr. Exp. Sta. Rep. 210. 28 p.

Dambach, C. A. 1945. Some biologic and economic aspects of field border management. 10th N. Amer. Wildl. Conf. Trans. p. 169-184.

Dambach, C. A. 1948a. The relative importance of hunting restrictions and land use in maintaining wildlife populations in Ohio. Ohio J. Sci. 48(6):209-229.

Dambach, C. A. 1948b. New lessons from old plantings. J. Soil Water Conserv. 3(4):165-169.

Dasmann, R. F. 1964. Wildlife biology. John Wiley & Sons, New York. 231 p.

Davey, S. P. 1967. The role of wildlife in an urban environment. 32d N. Amer. Wildl. & Natur. Resour. Conf. Trans. p. 50-60.

Davison, V. E. 1941. Shrubs for wildlife on farms in the southeast. U.S. Dep. Agr. Leafl. No. 200. 8 p.

Davison, V. E. 1945. Wildlife values of the lespedezas. J. Wildl. Manage. 9(1):1-9.

Day, A. 1966. Wildlife habitat management as a means of increasing recreation on public lands. U.S. Bur. Land Manage. Rep. 73 p. (mimeo).

Dixon, J. S. 1934. A study of the life history and food habits of mule deer in California. Calif. Fish & Game 20:1-146.

Driscoll, R. S. 1967. Managing public rangelands. U.S. Dep. Agr. Inform. Bull. 315.

Drury, W. H., Jr. 1966. Birds at airports. *In* A. L. Nelson and A. Stefferud (ed.), Birds in our lives. U.S. Bureau of Sport Fisheries and Wildlife. 561 p.

Edminster, F. C. 1941. Wildlife management through soil conservation on farms in the northeast. U.S. Dep. Agr. Farmers' Bull. 1868. 53 p.

Edminster, F. C., and R. M. May. 1951. Shrub plantings for soil conservation and wildlife cover. U.S. Dep. Agr. Circ. 887. 68 p.

Einarsen, A. S. 1948. The pronghorn antelope and its management. Wildlife Management Institute, Washington, D.C. 238 p.

Erickson, A. W. 1965. The brown-grizzly bear in Alaska. Alaska Dep. Fish & Game, F.A. Proj. W-6-3-5, Work Plan F.

Errington, P. L. 1945. Some contributions of a fifteen-year local study of the northern bobwhite to a knowledge of population phenomena. Ecology Monogr. 15(1):1-34.

Ferber, A. E. 1958. Windbreaks in conservation farming. U.S. Soil Conserv. Serv. Misc. Publ. 759. 22 p.

Ferrel, C. M., and H. R. Leach. 1950. Food habits of the pronghorn antelope of California. Calif. Fish & Game 36(1):21-26.

Fox, A. C. 1942. Windbreaks and their value to wildlife. Soil Conserv. 7(10):259-260.

Gambel, E. L. 1967. Greenspan provisions of the cropland adjustment program. 54th Annu. Mtg. Ass. So. Agr. Workers. 5 p.

Gates, J. M., and G. E. Ostrom. 1966. Feed grain program related to pheasant production in Wisconsin. J. Wildl. Manage. 30(3):612-617.

George, J. L. 1966. Farmers and birds, p. 396-403. *In* A. L. Nelson and A. Stefferud (ed.), Birds in our lives. U.S. Bureau of Sport Fisheries and Wildlife. 561 p.

Good, E. E., and C. A. Dambach. 1943. Effect of some land use practices on breeding birds in Ohio. J. Wildl. Manage. 7:291-297.

Graham, E. H. 1941a. Wildlife management as a part of soil conservation. U.S. Soil Conserv. Serv. Misc. Publ. 23. 50 p.

Graham, E. H. 1941b. Legumes for erosion control and wildlife. U.S. Dep. Agr. Misc. Publ. 412. 153 p.

Graham, E. H. 1942. Grasses for soil and wildlife conservation. Soil Conserv. 7(10):244-247, 250.

Graham, E. H. 1944. Natural principles of land use. Oxford University Press, New York. 274 p.

Graham, E. H. 1947. The land and wildlife. Oxford University Press, New York. 232 p.

Griffith, G. K. 1962. Guidelines for antelope management. Interstate Antelope Conf. Trans. p. 102-114.

Hanson, H. C. 1965. The giant Canada goose. Southern Illinois University Press, Carbondale. 226 p.

Hawbecker, A. C., and R. M. Bond. 1942. Wildlife increased by erosion control practices. Soil Conserv. 7(10):255-256.

Hedge, A. M., and A. A. Klingebiel. 1957. The use of soil maps, p. 400-411. *In* Soils. The yearbook of agriculture 1955. U.S. Department of Agriculture. U.S. Government Printing Office, Washington, D.C.

Hervey, D. F. 1961. Improving sagebrush ranges: progress report of the Great Divide Experimental Range. Colo. Agr. Exp. Sta. Gen. Ser. 761. 10 p.

Hill, R. R. 1956. Forage, food habits, and range management of the mule deer. *In* W. P. Taylor (ed.), The deer of North America. Wildlife Management Institute, Washington, D.C. 668 p.

Hoover, M. D. 1962. Water action and water movement in the forest, p. 31-80. *In* Forest influences. FAO Forest. and Forest Prod. Stud. No. 15. Food and Agriculture Organization, Rome.

Hoover, R. L., C. E. Till, and S. Ogilvie. 1959. The antelope of Colorado. Colo. Game Fish Dep. Tech. Bull. No. 4.

Hubbard, R. L. 1962. The place of browse seeding in game range management. 27th N. Amer. Wildl. Natur. Resour. Conf. Trans. p. 394-401.

Huss, D. L. 1964. A glossary of terms used in range management. American Society for Range Management, Denver, Colo.

Hyatt, S. W. 1966. Sagebrush control: costs, results, and benefits to the rancher. J. Range Manage. 19(1):42-43.

Hyder, D. F., and F. A. Sneva. 1958. Herbage response to sagebrush spraying. J. Range Manage. 9(1):34-38.

Jackson, A. S. 1962. A pattern to population oscillations of the bobwhite quail in the lower plains grazing ranges of northwest Texas. S.E. Ass. Game Fish Comm., 16th Annu. Conf. Proc., p. 120-126.

Johns, W. 1965. Where the livestock, but not the antelope, can play. Conserv. News 30(20):7-10.

Johnson, E. A. 1952. Effect of farm woodland grazing on watershed values in the southern Appalachian Mountains. J. Forest. 50:109-113.

Julander, O. 1951. Utah's big game, livestock, and range relationship research project. J. Range Manage. 4:330-334.

Julander, O. 1955. Deer and cattle relations in Utah. Forest. Sci. 1:130-139.

Julander, O. 1958. Techniques in studying competition between big game and livestock. J. Range Manage. 11:18-21.

Julander, O. 1962. Range management in relation to mule deer habitat and herd productivity in Utah. J. Range Manage. 15:278-281.

Julander, O., and D. E. Jeffrey. 1964. Deer, elk and cattle range relations on summer range in Utah. 29th Wildl. & Natur. Resour. Conf. Trans. p. 404-413.

Julander, O., and W. L. Robinette. 1950. Deer and cattle range relationships on Oak Creek range in Utah. J. Forest. 48:410-415.

Julander, O., W. L. Robinette, and D. A. Jones. 1961. Relation of summer range condition to mule deer herd productivity. J. Wildl. Manage. 25:54-60.

Kell, W. V. 1938. Strip cropping, p. 634-645. *In* Soil & men. The yearbook of agriculture 1938. U.S. Department of Agriculture. U.S. Government Printing Office, Washington, D.C.

Kirsch, L. 1964. The value of soil bank lands to breeding prairie grouse. U.S. Bureau of Sport Fisheries and Wildlife. 5 p.

Komarek, R. 1966. A discussion of wildlife management, fire, and the wildlife landscape, p. 177-194. *In* 5th Tall Timbers Fire Ecol. Conf. Tall Timbers Research Station, Tallahassee, Fla.

Küchler, A. W. 1964. The potential natural vegetation of the conterminous United States. American Geographical Society, New York.

Lack, D. 1954. The natural regulation of animal numbers. Oxford University Press, Cambridge, England. 134 p.

Lay, D. S. 1956. Effects of prescribed burning on forage and mast production in southern pine forests. J. Forest. 54:582-584.

Lay, D. S. 1957. Browse quality and the effects of prescribed burning in southern pine forests. J. Forest. 55:342-347.

Leach, H. R., and A. L. Hensley. 1954. The sage grouse in California with special reference to food habits. Calif. Fish & Game 40(4):385-394.

Leedy, D. L. 1940. Natural pheasant production in relation to agricultural land-use. Ph.D. Thesis. Ohio State University, Columbus. (Diss. Abstr. 33:115-124.)

Leedy, D. L. 1949. Ohio pheasant nesting surveys based on farmer interviews. J. Wildl. Manage. 13(3):274-286.

Leedy, D. L., and E. H. Dustman. 1947. The pheasant decline and land-use trends, 1941-1946. 12th N. Amer. Wildl. Conf. Trans. p. 479-490.

Lehmann, V. W. 1953. Bobwhite population fluctuations and vitamin A. 18th N. Amer. Wildl. Conf. Trans. p. 199-246.

Leithead, H. L. 1950. Field methods used to demonstrate range conservation. J. Range Manage. 3:95-99.

Leopold, A. 1933. Game management. C. Scribner's Sons, New York, 481 p.

Line, L. 1964. The bird worth a forest fire. Audubon Mag. 66:370-375.

Longhurst, W. M., A. S. Leopold, and R. F. Dasmann, 1952. A survey of California deer herds. Calif. Dep. Fish Game Bull. No. 6.

Lull, H. W. 1959. Soil compaction on forest and range lands. Forest Serv. Misc. Publ. No. 768.

Marshall, W. H. 1953. A survey of farm-game habitat restoration programs in fifteen states. 18th N. Amer. Wildl. Conf. Trans. p. 390-411.

McAtee, W. L. 1941. Plants useful in upland wildlife management. U.S. Fish & Wildl. Serv., U.S. Dep. Interior Conserv. Bull. 7. 50 p.

Miller, J. P., and B. B. Powell. 1942. Game and wild-fur production and utilization on agricultural land. U.S. Dep. Agr. Circ. 636. 58 p.

Mohler, L. L., J. H. Wampole, and E. Fichter. 1951. Mule deer in Nebraska National Forest. J. Wildl. Manage. 15:129-160.

Morris, M. S., and J. E. Schwartz. 1957. Mule deer and elk food habits on the National Bison Range. J. Wildl. Manage. 21(2):189-193.

Murie, O. J. 1951. The elk of North America. The Stackpole Co., Harrisburg, Pa. 376 p.

Nelson, B. A. 1953. Pheasant habitat improvement in South Dakota. 32d Annu. Western Ass. State Game Fish Comm. Conf. Proc. p. 123-126.

Nunns, F. K. 1958. The classification of rural land, p. 362-370. *In* Land. The yearbook of agriculture 1958. U.S. Department of Agriculture. U.S. Government Printing Office, Washington, D.C.

Orell, B. L. 1964. Private responsibilities for resources. 29th N. Amer. Wildl. & Natur. Resour. Conf. Trans. p. 10-16.

Parker, K. W. 1954. Application of ecology in determination of range condition and trend. J. Range Manage. 7:14-21.

Parker, K. W., and S. C. Martin. 1952. The mesquite problem on southern Arizona ranges. U.S. Dep. Agr. Circ. 908.

Patterson, R. L. 1952. The sage grouse in Wyoming. Sage Brooks, Denver. 341 p.

Pechanec, J. F., A. P. Plummer, J. H. Robertson, and A. C. Hull, Jr. 1944. Eradication of big sagebrush. U.S. Forest Serv. Intermountain Forest Range Exp. Sta. Res. Paper No. 10.

Pechanec, J. F., G. Stewart, A. P. Plummer, J. H. Robertson, and A. C. Hull. 1954. Controlling sagebrush on rangelands. U.S. Dep. Agr. Farmers' Bull. 2072. 36 p.

Pickford, G. D., and E. H. Reid. 1943. Competition of elk and domestic livestock for summer range forage. J. Wildl. Manage. 7(3):328-332.

Plummer, A. P., D. R. Christensen, and S. B. Monson. 1965. Job completion report of game forage revegetation project. Utah State Fish & Game Dep. Inf. Bull. No. 65-10.

Read, R. A. 1957. Effects of livestock concentration on surface soil porosity within shelterbelts. J. Forest. 55:529-530.

Renner, F. G., and B. W. Allred. 1962. Classifying rangeland for conservation planning. U.S. Dep. Agr., Soil Conserv. Serv., Agr. Handb. No. 235.

Rhoades, E. D., et al. 1964. Water intake on sandy range as affected by 20 years of differential cattle stocking rates. J. Range Manage. 17:185-190.

Ridd, M. F. 1965. Area-oriented multiple use analysis. U.S. Forest Serv. Intermountain Forest Exp. Sta. Res. Paper No. 21, 14 p.

Riley, C. V. 1952. An evaluation of reclaimed coal strip-mined lands as wildlife habitat. Ph.D. Thesis. Ohio State University, Columbus. (Diss. Abstr. 18:740-743, 1958.)

Robinette, W. L., O. Julander, J. S. Gashwiler, and J. G. Smith. 1952. Winter mortality of mule deer in Utah in relation to range condition. J. Wildl. Manage. 16:289-299.

Rogers, G. E. 1964. Sage grouse investigations in Colorado. Colo. Game, Fish Parks Dep. Tech. Publ. No. 16.

Rosene, W., Jr. 1950. Quail studies on a river floodplain. J. Soil Water Conserv. 5(3):111-114.

Rosene, W., Jr. 1952. Care and maintenance of bicolor lespedeza. Soil Conserv. 17(7):151-153.

Rosene, W., Jr. 1956. An appraisal of bicolor lespedeza in quail management. J. Wildl. Manage. 20(2):104-110.

Sampson, A. W., and B. S. Jesperson. 1963. California range and brushlands browse plants. Calif. Agr. Exp. Sta. Ext. Serv. Manual 33. 162 p.

Sandfort, W. W. 1952. Ring-necked pheasant production in north-central Colorado. M.S. Thesis. Colorado A&M College, Fort Collins. (Unpublished.)

Sayers, W. B. 1966. To tell the truth, 25 years of American Forest Products Industries, Inc. J. Forest. 64(10):657-663.

Scott, R. F. 1965. Problems of multiflora rose spread and control. 30th N. Amer. Wildl. Natur. Resour. Conf. Trans. p. 360-378.

Skeete, G. M. 1966. Can ranchers adjust to fluctuating forage production? J. Range Manage. 19:258-262.

Smith, A. D. 1950. Sagebrush as a winter feed for deer. J. Wildl. Manage. 14(3):285-289.

Smith, A. D. 1959. Adequacy of some important browse species in overwintering of mule deer. J. Range Manage. 12(1):8-13.

Smith, D. R. 1961. Competition between cattle and game on elk winter range. Univ. Wyo. Agr. Exp. Sta. Bull. 377.

Smith, J. G., and O. Julander. 1953. Deer and sheep competition in Utah. J. Wildl. Manage. 17:101-112.

Society of American Foresters. 1964. Forest terminology. 3d ed. Society of American Foresters, Washington, D.C. 35 p.

Stearns, F. W. 1967. Wildlife habitat in urban and suburban environments. 32d N. Amer. Wildl. & Natur. Resour. Conf. Trans. p. 61-69.

Steen, M. O. 1950. Road to restoration. 15th N. Amer. Wildl. Conf. Trans. p. 356-362.

Stevens, D. R. 1966. Range relations of elk and livestock, Crow Creek Drainage, Montana. J. Wildl. Manage. 30(2):349-363.

Stoddard, H. L. 1931. The bobwhite quail; its habits, preservation, and increase. C. Scribner's Sons, New York. 559 p.

Stoddart, L. A., and A. D. Smith. 1955. Range management, 2d ed., McGraw-Hill Book Co., New York.

Swanson, C. V., and C. F. Yocum. 1958. Upland game-bird populations in relation to cover and agriculture in southeastern Washington. 23d N. Amer. Wildl. Conf. Trans. p. 277-290.

Taylor, W. P. 1934. Significance of extreme or intermittent conditions in distribution of species and management of natural resources, with a restatement of Liebig's Law of Minimum. Ecology 15:374-379.

Taylor, W. P., and H. K. Buechner. 1943. Relationship of game and livestock to range vegetation in Kerr County, Texas. The Cattleman (March).

True, G. H., Jr., and B. Glading. 1946. Catchment and other devices for supplying water for wildlife in California. 26th Annu. Western Ass. State Game & Fish Comm. Conf. Proc. p. 156-160.

Twiss, R. H. 1969. Conflicts in forest landscape management. J. Forest. 67:19-23.

U.S. Bureau of the Census. 1960, 1965. Historical statistics of the United States. U.S. Government Printing Office, Washington, D.C.

U.S. Department of Agriculture. 1962. Major uses of land and water. Agr. Econ. Rep. No. 13, p. 17.

U.S. Department of Agriculture. 1965. Soil and water conservation needs. U.S. Dep. Agr. Misc. Publ. 971.

U.S. Department of Agriculture. 1967. Agricultural Conservation Program, summary fiscal year 1966. Agr. Stabilization and Conserv. Service. 133 p.

U.S. Department of the Interior. 1960. Project twenty-twelve: A long-term program for our public lands. U.S. Government Printing Office, Washington, D.C.

U.S. Forest Service. 1965. Timber trends in the United States. U.S. Dep. Agr. Forest. Res. Rep. No. 17.

Van Dersal, W. R., and E. H. Graham. 1946. The land renewed. Oxford University Press, New York. 110 p.

Wandell, W. N. 1948. Agricultural and wildlife values of habitat improvement plantings on the Illinois Black Prairie. 13th N. Amer. Wildl. Conf. Trans. p. 256-270.

Wilbert, D. E. 1963. Some effects of big sagebrush control on elk distribution. J. Range Manage. 16(2):74-78.

Workman, D. R., K. R. Tefertiller, and C. L. Leinweber. 1965. Profitability of aerial spraying to control mesquite. Tex. Agr. Exp. Sta. MP-784. 12 p.

Yoakum, J. 1962. Interstate antelope range—its research and management needs. Interstate Antelope Conf. Trans. p. 52-58.

CHAPTER 5

Special Problems of Waters and Watersheds

As noted in preceding chapters, hydrologic developments have been important since primitive times in radically altering the face of the land. Both dewatering and flooding have been used to convert the natural drainage pattern of the continent into what we find today in many regions—the efficient utilization of land for adapted crops and the use of water for power, irrigation, and other purposes. These changes are still in progress, and pertinent questions arise as to how far and at what cost they should be pursued.

On a wide variety of aquatic sites, as well as on watersheds directly affecting streams and slack waters, what man does has important environmental impact. As one such impact, wildlife habitats may be either degraded or improved. Effects of this kind were touched upon in the survey of major changes on land and water (Chapter 3). In this chapter, several of the more far-reaching problems are explored in more detail, with the view that they offer particular challenge to resource planning in the public interest. The analysis may also help to provide guidance on the local front where, in the last analysis, the test of policy is made.

WETLANDS OF THE NORTHERN PRAIRIES

The importance of the northern prairie pothole country as a breeding ground of North American waterfowl has been mentioned in various sections of this report. This region provides a classic example of the conflict between land-use practices and a wildlife resource of national and international importance.

The land in this region is characterized by small marshes that in some localities are thickly scattered over the former tall-grass and mixed prairies. It is some 300,000 square miles in extent, stretching in a broad arc from Iowa north and west to Winnipeg and Edmonton. Since Iowa marshes have largely been drained (Sieh, 1948), the present distribution of potholes south of the border is principally in the Dakotas and western Minnesota. Combined, the prairies of Canada and the northern United States comprise about 10 percent of the waterfowl breeding grounds of North America, and it is estimated that they produce more than half of the annual crop of dabbling and diving ducks on the continent (Smith *et al.*, 1964). The density of potholes on the land varies from as many as 100 per square mile to "Blocks of prairies as large as 20 thousand square miles in the Dakotas [that] average fewer than 10 potholes per square mile."

In some years nearly every depression in glaciated northcentral United States and the Prairie Provinces holds water in the spring. The wet areas may be small temporary ponds and puddles, or they may be lakes covering hundreds of acres. It is during these years of high precipitation that our continental "duck factory" is most productive. It is also during these years that water damage to farm crops is most severe.

Birds frequently court and develop their pair bonds on the temporary waters. Dabbling ducks nest in fields and grassy borders and rear their broods in the marshes. Diving ducks incubate their clutches on mats of dead plant material in the emergent vegetation of shallow waters. For all ducks, the deep sloughs that hold water through the summer are critical habitat for maturing the young.

The northern location of the breeding ground undoubtedly has certain advantages, as pointed out by Day (1966):

... the pothole area North has traditionally demonstrated advantages in the production of marsh dwelling duck species. These shallow natural depressions freeze each winter to depths that eliminate natural predators such as pike, bass and turtles. Also, freezing prevents infestation by carp, which roil the waters and discourage the production of aquatic plants.

The coming of the ducks in spring was described by Smith *et al.* (1964):

The first mallards, pintails, and canvasbacks begin to arrive on prairie potholes in late March or early April, depending upon the severity of the weather. On the western prairies, spring usually arrives earlier than in eastern sections. . . . Mallards and pintails may appear in Alberta and northern Montana in mid-March, while great concentrations of the same species may be held up in the Dakotas for another month by freezing temperatures.

American widgeons, gadwalls, shovelers, green-winged teal, lesser scaup, and redheads usually follow in a few weeks. . . . Blue-winged teal, normally the last to migrate, may appear anytime from late April to mid-May.

Recent ecological studies have shown that periods of drought, when most of the potholes go dry, are important in the long-term dynamics of waterfowl productivity. At these times, humus deposits that have been preserved under water are again exposed to the air. Through oxidation they break down and become soluble nutrients that contribute to fertility and the production of all plant and animal life when the rains come again. Oxidation and subsidence, as well as occasional peat fires, are processes that slow the eutrophication, filling, and natural drying out of the prairie lakes and marshes (Jahn and Hunt, 1964).

In decades past, the contribution of potholes to groundwaters was largely discounted, it being the view of some hydrologists that the tight soils of the region largely precluded this movement. In times of drought, however, many landowners discovered that their only source of stockwater was a shallow well dug into the dry bottom of a pothole. More recently, studies of the Geological Survey have brought about a new evaluation of the "insoak" from potholes (quoted by Mann, 1966):

The rates calculated seldom exceed 0.01 foot per day and usually are much less. Even if the rate were only 0.0025 foot per day, in a season of 200 days and an average area of 1 million acres in North Dakota, this would mean 500,000 acre-feet seeping into the ground. The maximum seepage rates that might be significant for the pothole region are now being investigated.

On this basis it appears that prairie marshes do have at least a limited hydrologic function in replenishing aquifers beneath these glacial deposits.

Pothole Losses, Past and Present

The first general wetland inventory in the pothole region south of the Canadian border was taken in 1964. Biologists of the Bureau of Sport Fisheries and Wildlife surveyed a 25 percent sample in every section of each township. On this basis they estimated that 2.7 million acres of permanent wetlands remain. In primitive times the acreage was perhaps twice as great.

There has been a progressive loss of waterfowl habitat in the northern prairie region from a combination of causes, including agricultural drainage, land leveling and filling, soil washing and siltation, wind erosion, road building and urban occupancy, and pollution. Of these, the first is undoubtedly the most important.

From an agricultural standpoint, drainage in the wheat-growing lands of the former grass country can be good business for a landowner. It permits him to harvest a crop from sites that formerly caused trouble. When seedbeds are prepared each spring, low areas of a field may be too wet to be worked; the farmer must detour and seed them at a later date or forgo planting crops in these spots. Often he wastes time when equipment bogs down. When a wetland does get planted, it is not uncommon for a heavy rain to drown the crop.

Economist H. W. Herbison (1967) of North Dakota State University discussed the shallow and temporary types of field depressions in a report on wetlands use and management:

Losses due to incomplete drainage for Type 1 and 2 wetlands . . . in about 30 counties east of the Missouri would figure out to an average annual toll of North Dakota's economy of at least $15 million in terms of income from delayed seeding . . . the cost of incomplete drainage in terms of marketability and lost grain associated with harvesting following periods of heavy rainfall would likely average out in this same area at about $5 million annually.

Herbison indicated that, by conservative estimates, farmers of one district of the Devils Lake Watershed should benefit by about $3 to $4 for every $1 expended on updating facilities for removing excess sheet water and floodwater from valuable croplands. This, of course, does not apply to the deep marshes on which ducks chiefly depend, but it illustrates the importance of adequate drainage to the agricultural enterprise.

As early as 1938, Kenney and McAtee stated that the drainage of productive waterfowl marshes to create more wheat land in the northern Great Plains was a major reason for the decline of the continental waterfowl population. They commented that

Drought has now shown us that drainage of that region was carried on to a degree harmful even to the direct interests of man and that it would have been well to have left a great deal of this territory in its original undrained condition.

Evidently the progress of land reclamation, mainly through private drainage operations, was well along at that time. In spite of such admonitions, in the period after World War II, with government encouragement to increase production, farmers of the northern prairies greatly intensified their land-use practices. A long-term record specific to wetland drainage does not exist. However, the U.S. Department of Agriculture (1963) reported drainage benefiting 6,237,000 acres in Minnesota, North Dakota, and South Dakota from 1936 to 1963. Biologists of the Bureau of Sport Fisheries and Wildlife investigated the significance of these figures as an indication of actual wetland losses and concluded that approximately 25 percent of the reported drainage represented a significant reduction of waterfowl habitat. On this basis, the loss of productive wetlands is about one and one-half million acres, or about 57,000 acres per year. Loss of waterfowl production is estimated at 1,840,000 (chiefly ducks) per year. Annual duck losses as a result of all habitat destruction since the late 1800's are thought to be of the order of 6 million.

There is major disagreement between the Bureau of Sport Fisheries and Wildlife and the Soil Conservation Service relative to both statistics and their interpretation. On the basis of data compiled by the Soil Conservation Service, 205,984 potholes, totaling 246,918 acres, were drained in the tri-state area from 1946 to 1965. The waterfowl production lost to drainage is estimated at an average of 327,613 ducks per year. Although this 20-year period is not the same as the 27-year survey interpreted by the Bureau of Sport Fisheries and Wildlife, a difference in the figure on annual waterfowl losses by a factor of nearly 6 to 1 indicates a fundamentally different approach to the problem.

More reliable indications of the extent of recent drainage are studies made by the Bureau of Sport Fisheries and Wildlife since 1950, when more intensive work in this field was initiated. Cooperation of the Soil Conservation Service and the Agricultural Conservation Program Service has made more drainage records available, and field appraisals in terms of wetland categories have aided interpretation. The prairie wetlands are now described as ranging from class I (the most transitory type of field depression that holds water for a few days or weeks in spring) to class V (deep marshes that retain some water even in time of drought) (Schrader, 1955).

A study of drainage records for 1949 and 1950 indicated that an average of nearly three potholes to the square mile were drained in west-central Minnesota. There remained 14.2 water areas to the square mile at that time (Burwell and Sugden, 1964).

Some 46 thousand potholes, whose total surface area was 188 thousand acres, were destroyed in Minnesota and North and South Dakota in 1949 and 1950. That was done with subsidy payments; many others were drained without payments and did not appear in the record.

As part of the intensified program, a survey of subsidized agricultural drainage in relation to waterfowl habitat losses in the tri-state region was carried out from 1954 to 1958 (Bureau of Sport Fisheries and Wildlife, 1961). This work was restricted to the 93 counties of greatest importance to waterfowl at that time. Thus counties largely drained before 1954 were not included. For the 5-year period a minimum of 50,410 waterfowl habitat areas, totaling 60,440 acres, were drained with federal assistance. The average was 12,088 acres per year. From 1959 to 1966 more data on subsidized drainage in the tri-state region indicated that approximately 31,032 acres of habitat were destroyed, with the rate of loss considerably reduced after 1962, when Public Law 87-732 was passed, followed by the Reuss Amendment to the Agricultural Appropriations Act in 1963.

The foregoing figures indicate that waterfowl habitat losses involving government-sponsored programs are reasonably well known; the extent of private drainage was not well documented, however, until 1964 when the Bureau of Sport Fisheries and Wildlife made its total inventory of existing production habitat (wetland classes III, IV, and V). In this 25-percent sampling, the most recent aerial photographs were used, followed by field checks to verify the typing. Data were corrected for losses that occurred after the photographs were taken. This survey is the base from which the reduction of waterfowl habitat has been calculated in an annual inventory since 1964.

These yearly studies indicate that recent wetland losses are primarily the result of privately constructed farm drainage systems (Haddock and DeBates, 1969). The outlets used are those established through the small watersheds program (see p. 163 for discussion of Public Law 566), flood control projects of the Corps of Engineers, and local highway and other ditching systems. The sampling of the tri-state area, utilizing 4.6 percent of the 1964 inventory, from 1965 through 1968 indicated that approximately 125,000 acres of the best waterfowl habitat (i.e., classes III, IV, and V) had been drained in the 4-year period. The most intensive operations were in Minnesota, with North Dakota and South Dakota following in that order.

In Canada, land reclamation through drainage has lagged behind similar operations in the United States, although the availability of heavy machinery has given impetus to the movement in recent years (Burwell and Sugden, 1964). There has been some provincial participation in drainage projects, most notably in Alberta. There, a survey by Ducks Unlimited indicated that by 1960 registered ditches and drainage projects had affected 115,000 acres, and licensed "flood irrigation projects" had drained 27,000 acres of wetlands and 55,580 acres of large lakes and marshes. Prior to 1960, water rights legislation in the Prairie Provinces did not recognize nonconsumptive uses of water, such as wildlife and recreation, as a legitimate claim.

The general significance of trends in land use north and south of the border appears to be the same. Almost irrespective of the degree of accuracy attributed to drainage statistics, there is no real question that this and other types of habitat destruction and degradation in the prairie nesting ground have been extensive. The continental waterfowl population reached its low point in historic times during the drought years of the 1930's, when habitats of this region were largely out of production. Correspondingly, it may be concluded that the disappearance of a major portion of the prairie waterfowl habitat has had an important influence in the long-term downward trend of the duck population.

Regulation and Mitigation of Drainage

By the late 1940's, field staffs of the Soil Conservation Service and the Fish and Wildlife Service were attempting to reconcile their differences. Predictably they did not make great progress, even though administrators and biologists of both agencies realized that public money was being used on the one hand to destroy waterfowl habitat and on the other to restore it (in the national wildlife refuge system and also in state federal-aid programs). The fact that Congress, under the urging of national agricultural organizations, continued to provide drainage subsidies meant that agencies of the Department of Agriculture would continue to carry out their missions.

Within the limits of its position, however, the Department of Agriculture recognized the problem. Attention was called to it in the regulations for 1954, and in the following year cost sharing was not allowed on drainage for the primary purpose of bringing new land into production. This principle was further invoked in guidelines applying to open ditches in 1958. Drainage for improving existing croplands (lands with a crop history in at least 2 of the 5 years preceding an application for assistance) and for improving land-use efficiency was recognized as legitimate.

These regulations necessarily left the drainage of land up to local option and definitions. They slowed the destruction of waterfowl habitat where work unit conservationists took a strong stand. They were not generally effective, however, in part because landowners could plow up potholes in years of drought, thus establishing a crop history and making the area eligible for drainage assistance. The Bureau of Sport Fisheries and Wildlife (1961) concluded that

> It is clearly evident from an evaluation of the foregoing data and considerations, that as long as Federal cost-shares and/or technical assistance for drainage are available in the primary waterfowl-producing zone of the United States, waterfowl habitat will continue to be destroyed both directly and indirectly as a result of such assistance until the waterfowl habitat is gone.

The inconsistency of this situation was increasingly realized in the Congress as the representations of many wildlife conservation groups were heard during the fifties. In 1958 Public Law 85-585 made possible the purchase or leasing of waterfowl breeding habitat, and in 1962 Public Law 87-732 required that all requests for drainage of land in the prairie pothole region be referred to the Bureau of Sport Fisheries and Wildlife for a prior determination of their wildlife value. The Bureau, or a state, was afforded an opportunity to buy areas of importance, and if the landowner refused to sell, he was not eligible for drainage assistance during the ensuing 5 years.

Significant action in 1963 was passage of the Reuss Amendment to the Agricultural Appropriations Act of that year—a measure that has been a part of subsequent annual appropriations acts. On a nationwide basis, the use of Agricultural Conservation funds is prohibited for the drainage of wetland classes III, IV, and V. This law limits drainage subsidies in an important way, but it does not disqualify individuals or groups from obtaining other kinds of assistance in drainage projects. Government help is thus still contributing to the loss of valuable wetland areas.

The foregoing aspects of the waterfowl-wetlands problem must be considered in the light of a recent study by Goldstein (1967). This broad economic appraisal indicated that the cost of drainage of permanent wetlands is sufficiently high that it would be uneconomical for a landowner if he paid the entire cost and if the market were free and competitive for agricultural products. Thus, without price supports and government subsidies, the destruction of high-quality waterfowl habitat would be a socially inefficient process. Goldstein suggested that legislation prohibiting drainage of permanent wetlands would be appropriate if it included a suitable appeals system under which the public value of a marsh might be determined with a view to equitable adjustments.

Public Acquisition and Easements

On the northern prairies, state conservation agencies and organizations have long been concerned over the disappearance of wetlands. This is particularly evident in Minnesota, where Vesall (1963) estimated that these habitat types were being lost at a rate of 5 percent per year. He reported that under a program begun in 1951—Save Minnesota's Wetlands—the state had optioned or purchased 122,835 acres of prime habitat at a cost of nearly $4 million in sportsmen's funds. The state increased the small game license fee by $1 for this purpose. Within 10 years it was expected that the goal of 250,000 acres would be achieved—areas that would be preserved and developed for wildlife. At that time the state had created or improved about 60,000 acres of marshlands on state wildlife areas. In the Dakotas, federal aid acquisition and development programs have featured wetlands, and in South Dakota $9 of every out-of-state license fee is allocated to this purpose.

A citizen's organization dedicated to preserving waterfowl habitat was formed in Milwaukee in 1961. "Wetlands for Wildlife" purchases key areas, which are then given to a state or the federal government. Although not a part of the prairie pothole country, the State of Wisconsin has been outstanding for its historic surveys and program of preservation and restoration for waters and marshlands. Dahlberg (1960) said that in 20 years 141,532 acres of wetlands had been acquired at a cost of more than 2 million dollars. Significantly, he called this the sportsman's "best investment," and observed that such areas are growing steadily in value. Acquiring these habitat areas was essential to preserving them from drainage even though full development of their productive potential for wildlife must await the future availability of funds. Among the spectacularly successful waterfowl areas that the state has developed (in some cases jointly with federal projects) are the Horicon, Neceda, Meadow Valley, and Crex Meadows wildlife areas.

The federal program to preserve valuable wetland habitat from drainage through the acquisition of land or rights was initiated in 1958 with passage of an amendment to the Duck Stamp Act of 1934. This effort requires cooperative arrangements with the Minnesota Department of Conservation; the North Dakota Department of Game and Fish; the South Dakota Department of Game, Fish and Parks; and the Nebraska Game, Forestation, and Parks Commission. Since funds were inadequate, an accelerated program was provided for in 1961 with passage of the Emergency Wetlands Loan Act (Public Law 87-383, 75 Stat. 813). This act authorized an appropriation up to $105 million over a 7-year period on a countrywide basis for waterfowl conservation purposes. The act was extended for an additional 8 years in 1967.

A part of the wetlands conservation effort is concentrated in the north-central states (about a third of the above funds are so earmarked) and is known as the Waterfowl Production Habitat Preservation Program on Private Lands. This program provides for purchasing easements, in perpetuity, extending to the owner's right to drain, burn, or fill small water or marsh areas, so that they may be preserved permanently to benefit waterfowl and other wildlife. Some key areas are purchased outright. By the end of April 1968, more than 590,000 acres of privately owned waterfowl habitat were so protected.

The initial objections of county officials and landowners created difficulties for this program, and delayed approval by state governors. One basis for objections was removed in 1964 when the Refuge Revenue Sharing Law allocated three fourths of one percent of the purchase price of a federally acquired tract to counties for the use of schools and roads. It has long been established that 25 percent of the income from products sold (such as crops or timber) on the national wildlife refuges goes to counties for the above purposes.

Under drainage referral arrangements through March 1967, more than 91 percent of landowners requesting assistance refused offers of the Bureau of Sport Fisheries and Wildlife that would have preserved their wetland areas through easement or purchase. Other limitations are that easements do not protect a marsh from siltation, and there is no guarantee that there will be adjacent nesting cover as required by most dabbling ducks. In Herbison's study (1967), an informal survey of farmers indicated that about 7 out of 10 showed interest in maintaining class III, IV, and V wetlands for the accommodation of ducks in return for governmental assistance with economic drainage of excess flood and sheet waters from valuable croplands currently classified as class I and II wetlands. He indicated that such willingness was hedged with a desire to have competent soils technicians establish the class III and IV classifications for the areas under consideration. An obvious difficulty is that these are habitat classes, not soil classes.

As of March 1969, in the critical tri-state area covered by the 1964 wetlands inventory, state game agencies had acquired some 83,000 acres of waterfowl habitat. Another 86,000 acres had been purchased under the federal Small Wetlands Program, and the bureau had obtained easements on about half a million acres of class III, IV, and V potholes.

Another significant effort toward government responsibility for key waterfowl lands is being made in Canada. Jahn (1968) stated that

Canada launched a 10-year program, beginning in 1967 to control, through landowner agreement, about two thirds of the 6,000,000 prairie sloughs and potholes that are of major importance in the production of three-fourths of North America's important game ducks.

At a research and management workshop held at the Northern Prairie Wildlife Research Center at Jamestown, North Dakota, in 1967, biologist Graham Cooch said that the Canadian effort includes acquisition of selected wetlands and a system of easements to preserve waterfowl habitat in the pothole country. These multimillion-dollar programs are expected to secure 4.4 million acres of prime duck habitat and provide for research, public use, and depredation control. A complete inventory of lands, including wetlands, will be available in 1970 (Flyway Council Memo by Raymond E. Johnson, June 26, 1967).

A promising aspect of wetland acquisitions, state and federal, is that many areas in public ownership can be improved as breeding habitat for waterfowl. The Northern Prairie Wildlife Research Center is carrying out studies that have this objective. Soil Conservation Service biologists (Hamor *et al.*, 1968) have made useful suggestions to landowners for improving natural and man-made wet areas for waterfowl. Fencing, damming, "level ditching," opening up dense vegetation, and creating "loafing areas" are appropriate measures where the owner has an interest in wildlife. Progress in creating such interest among farmers would be speeded by establishing an adequate federal-state extension program on wildlife problems.

The Changing View

Although positive programs, both public and private, have developed in the United States and Canada for preserving and managing portions of the waterfowl breeding areas, the efforts to date probably are not on a scale that can maintain this wildlife resource on a generally useful level. As Jahn (1968) pointed out, something more effective is needed, and he cited the "water bank" idea being studied by an interagency committee in North Dakota. This would be a system of waters and wetlands reserved and administered through the county offices of the

Agricultural Stabilization and Conservation Service. Financial incentives would be provided by payments from a special appropriation. Since no agricultural program at present encourages farmers to retain water areas on their land, the water bank could be a valuable means of supplementing other efforts.

Such a program would help maintain these hydrologic units of the landscape and thereby help to hold runoff waters and nutrients within the watershed, maintain ground water recharge, and enhance wildlife values.

The preliminary plan for a national water bank has been approved in recent meetings by the National Wildlife Federation, the National Association of Soil Conservation Districts, and the Mississippi Flyway Council. Implementation of the idea could reverse the present trend toward drainage and destructive management of wetland areas.

It has been suggested frequently that major areas of the northern prairies might be utilized appropriately in a grass-livestock economy. W. M. Myers, of the University of Minnesota, has stated (Kimball, 1954) that:

Grassland farming will save and restore soil, reduce production costs, and in most cases, result in higher food yields per acre. . . . This is true in the level deep soils of southern Minnesota and the need for more grassland farming greatly increases as we get into the rolling shallow-soiled country. The advantages of grass over corn increases by leaps and bounds as we move north.

In a report on waterfowl habitat losses, the Bureau of Sport Fisheries and Wildlife (1961) discussed the advantages of such a system:

It is known that a farm economy based on livestock production, particularly beef production founded on grassland farming, is generally compatible with the retention of wetland areas. The wetland areas provide water and forage for the livestock. A good distribution of natural wetland areas assists in proper distribution of grazing intensity so that parts of the range are not overgrazed due to the distance from water. During dry periods, livestock find better grazing in the areas normally occupied by wetlands when precipitation is adequate. The wetland vegetation remains green longer than the vegetation of surrounding uplands, and judging by the natural gathering of grazing cattle in such vegetation during local drought, the more succulent wetland plants are preferred to the cured upland growth.

Drying out of potholes through siltation and wind erosion would be greatly decreased under grassland farming as compared with the present regime of wheat farming. The outlook for pothole preservation can be materially improved by encouragement of the Great Plains Conservation Program of the Soil Conservation Service, under which a large area of the central grasslands, including portions of the northern prairies, would be converted to a more durable economy in grass and livestock. A broad outlook on this question was described by the National Advisory Commission on Food and Fiber (1967). The Commission suggested that programs designed to convert excess croplands to grass, forestry, and recreation should be expanded and noted that:

New technology in agriculture is increasing both yields per acre and output per man-hour at a much faster rate than the increase in demand for farm products. As a result, the U.S. has more cropland than it needs, and more workers on farms than can earn incomes comparable to nonfarm workers. . . . This excess manpower and the excess crop acres are the heart of the U.S. agricultural adjustment problem.

The report questioned public payments for drainage and irrigation to reclaim land and increase crops at a time when efforts are being made to adjust production downward.

NEW WATERS IN THE BREEDING RANGE

As discussed in Chapter 3, the development of small artificial waters on private lands is a national movement of growing popularity. Cost sharing and technical assistance are provided for in the agricultural conservation programs, and the improvement of conditions for wildlife is now a recognized objective along with stock water and other agricultural benefits.

The construction of stock watering ponds or "tanks" is of particular importance on northern grazing lands from the plains of Montana north and eastward. This region is breeding range for ducks wherever local conditions are suitable. The ponds are typically impounded behind an earthen dam, and they vary in size from a fraction of an acre up to many acres. Another type of water development, the "dugout," is an excavation into the water table (i.e., in a naturally wet area) or at a site where surface runoff can be utilized. Bue *et al.* (1964) said that most dugouts are in the small grain and livestock areas of the eastern Dakotas, Minnesota, and the Prairie Provinces. Relative to the numbers of artificial water areas, they stated that:

The number of stock ponds and dugouts is hard to determine. The Department of Agriculture has an annual accounting of the number of structures in which its agencies participate, but those made by individual operators without assistance are not recorded. According to the records and our estimates, approximately 220 thousand stock ponds, and 40 thousand dugouts have been constructed in North Dakota, South Dakota, western Minnesota, and Montana.

Favorably situated artificial waters produce ducks, and an important factor is the degree of grazing of adjacent land. Bue *et al.* (1952) reported on the first major study of this kind. They found that over-grazing destroyed the minimum of grass cover needed by nesting dabbling ducks such as blue-winged teal, mallards, and pintails. Thus, the most important management measure was to limit grazing pressure to a recommended level of about 15 cattle-days per acre-year. Under some conditions, fencing a part of the shoreline of a pond was advisable, although long-continued protection from grazing promoted the over-growth of tall emergents such as bulrush and cattail. In short, regulated grazing was beneficial in creating variable densities of nesting cover, edges, and sodded shorelines.

Relative to these matters in Canada, Munro (1967) stated that:

Stock-raising is generally more compatible with waterfowl production than is grain-growing. Construction of stock-watering dams, which usually have shallow edges at least part way around, is quite beneficial in expanding waterfowl habitat. The typical steep-sided dugout is less useful. Some attention is being given to modifying the design of dugouts to provide at least one gently sloping edge. Haying on temporary sloughs is not detrimental to waterfowl unless the hay is cut too early and the cover that nesting ducks need, or the nests themselves, are destroyed; but reclamation of semi-permanent potholes and sloughs to provide more land for fodder production is a loss to waterfowl. Light grazing of slough edges is probably beneficial by controlling the density of cattails. Heavy grazing is detrimental.

As indicated by Smith (1953), who studied the use of stock ponds in eastern Montana, these areas are not so productive of diving ducks (canvasback, redhead, ruddy, scaup) as are the natural potholes. Ponds do not commonly have as much emergent vegetation as is required by diving ducks, and they do not fulfill another need—that of associated water areas. Large marshes within a quarter-mile of large lakes are most favorable to the divers (Low, 1945), and isolated stock ponds are used only as seasonal resting and feeding spots.

These relationships need to be included in any comparison of productivity between artificial and natural water and wetland areas as related to waterfowl breeding. There has been some tendency to regard the construction of stockponds and dugouts as compensation for the drainage and destruction of natural waterfowl habitat. It appears more realistic to consider each program on its merits as an agricultural enterprise that affects wildlife. Within valid economic and social limitations each should be handled for the best management of all values, including wildlife. This is the perspective from which we are considering other uses of land and water.

SMALL WATERSHEDS AND PUBLIC LAW 83-566

The Watershed Protection and Flood Prevention Act, the so-called small watersheds act, was passed by Congress in 1954 and has since been amended several times. It embodies the sound logic that the management of land and water resources is best accomplished through a plan for the watershed as a natural ecological unit. As amended, the law authorizes the Department of Agriculture to cooperate through planning and cost sharing with state and local agencies in projects to reduce flooding and to preserve and improve the renewable resources of headwater drainages, including soil, water, wildlife, forests, and associated recreational features (see Kimball, 1964).

The small watershed program may be considered, in part, an answer to longstanding criticism of the traditional "big dam" approach to flood control, which tended to disregard watershed conditions. As Sears (1956) stated the case,

On general principles we would expect denuded and exploited headwater regions to intensify the destructive character and frequency of floods. While this is assumed as a basic element in national forest policy, far greater funds are expended upon efforts to control flood *after* water has reached the river channels than are devoted to securing proper land use on the tributary upland to retain the water where it falls. This is an interesting aspect of a technological culture whose emphasis is on engineering rather than on biological controls.

Grizzell (1960) mentioned that, in contrast with the *downstream* approach to watershed management involving dams and levees, "Upstream projects deal with water conservation and treatment of all watershed lands." He described the featured practices as: land treatment with all applicable soil and water conservation measures on agricultural areas, establishing vegetation on other silt-producing sites such as road cuts and ditchbanks, building farm ponds and floodwater retarding structures, and improving stream channels.

Through 1959, in approximately the first 5 years of the small watersheds program, some of the nationwide accomplishments of principal significance to wildlife were (Grizzell, 1960):

1,114 floodwater retaining structures
79,198 farm ponds
287,773 acres wildlife habitat improvement
334,114 acres critical areas vegetated

Allan and McKeever (1962) discussed the extremely broad range of benefits to both rural areas and municipalities that amendments to Public Law 566 had made possible. Relative to wildlife they said:

Federal technical and financial aid are both available for the enhancement of fish and wildlife resources in connection with small watershed programs. Enhancement measures are those that create, increase or improve fish and wildlife habitat. The measures, to qualify for cost-sharing, must be related to water-management; must significantly benefit fish or wildlife; must significantly benefit the public; and must be accessible to the public.

These authors cited six projects in eastern Pennsylvania that were particularly well adapted to increasing wildlife benefits and that would tie in with work of the Pennsylvania Game Commission and the Fish and Wildlife Service. A similar involvement of the Pennsylvania Fish Commission in small watersheds work was described by Day (1964). In 11 projects there were 13 reservoirs, aggregating "more than 4,500 surface acres for fishing and waterfowl."

Problems of Direction and Emphasis

The strategy of Public Law 566 was well calculated to provide opportunity for the balanced development of upstream lands and waters, and this concept has been embraced enthusiastically by administrators and biologists in the Soil Conservation Service (see Williams, 1957; Allan and McKeever, 1962; Hamor, 1965). However, major problems have arisen because plans for individual projects are made locally, as set forth in the enabling legislation. Among relative values to be stressed, and among various practices that might be employed, the choices made by landowners, county boards of supervisors, county agents, and soil and water conservation districts are likely to reflect traditional viewpoints. Thus, drainage, channel dredging, and impoundments have been the common choices in small watershed projects. Recognizing that wildlife habitat frequently is destroyed when headwater marshes are converted to cropfields, or when a brushy meandering stream gives way to a ditch, efforts frequently are made to mitigate such damage by a substitute development of new habitat elsewhere in the project.

In the decade following passage of Public Law 566, general dissatisfaction with the program became evident among state and federal workers concerned with the management of wildlife. Perhaps representative of these misgivings was a report by the Tennessee Game and Fish Director (Durand, 1963), himself a former employee of the Soil Conservation Service. He indicated that in southeastern states some 50 million acres were covered by Public Law 566 applications, and he expressed concern over the plans:

... 2,865 miles of channel work are already actually scheduled or under construction. ... A total of 258,000 acres of idle lands are in process of conversion to cropland, pasture or woodland, the latter mostly pine. The total plus side of new woodlands of this 258,000 acres is 26,000 acres. This might at first seem an asset from a Game and Fish administrator's view but unfortunately a good deal of this comes from idle land providing at the present good habitat for which purpose pine trees are no substitute. Then in the process, many prime and irreplaceable bottom-land hardwood areas providing good wildlife habitat are being converted to cropland and pasture fields. As an example of this, one of the watersheds in Tennessee plans to reforest 4,410 acres but the net gain in woodlands is only 568 acres.

Relative to the important wooded floodplain habitat, Cain (1966) also expressed a concern shared by many wildlife professionals in the region:

... bottomland hardwood habitat in the Southeast is gradually disappearing before channelization projects sponsored by the Department of Agriculture under the Small Watershed Program and the programs of the Agricultural Stabilization and Conservation Service. Each project by itself seems to take away only a little piece of habitat, but together they add up to alarming damages to fish and wildlife of many types. These losses are almost impossible to mitigate because habitat like that exists only in the valley bottoms.

Although creating new fishing waters by impounding streams for flood control has been welcomed in most areas, it has not been favored where structures block trout streams.

Both state and federal biologists have expressed dissatisfaction over the extent to which watershed projects have contributed to the drainage problem on northern prairies, discussed earlier in this chapter. In connection with such an appraisal, Southwick (1966) discussed the shortcomings of the mitigation principle and, in particular, the question of financing:

If a flood control channel (100 percent paid by PL 566, except land) drains a marsh it can (theoretically) be replaced with 100 percent PL 566 funds, EXCEPT that a local sponsor must buy the land; this in many cases can mean most of the cost! Here, also the problem is that most sponsoring organizations under state law do not have authority to levy assessments or take land for mitigation. Result? Habitat lost *is not replaced* unless the state game and fish agency can find the funds to assume the local costs. This proves to be a hardship on the state agency and usually means that some other project has to be cancelled.

The author was critical of "Laws and policies which make it comparatively easy to obtain a favorable cost-benefit ratio in drainage but not in other land treatment practices. . . ." In the northern prairie region there appeared to be a tendency for Public Law 566 projects to cover watersheds ". . . where drainage may not have been economically feasible or desired without watershed plan funding."

Needed Coordination

Jahn (1966) summarized various aspects of the discontent over Public Law 566 operations from the standpoint of the Wildlife Management Institute. His general comment was that:

Highlights of the historical record emphasize the need for modifying the small watershed program to consider fish and wildlife more adequately. Transactions of the National Watershed Congress (1956, 1957, 1958, 1963, 1964, 1965) and the North American Wildlife and Natural Resources Conference (1963, 1966) contain reports emphasizing major wildlife habitat losses in small watersheds. For a number of years resolutions of the International Association of Fish, Game, and Conservation Commissioners have urged greater consideration of fish and wildlife in small watershed projects.

Jahn pointed out that

Public funds were and are being used in small watershed projects to destroy, as well as benefit, public values associated with private lands. Losses exceed gains. This conversion of wildland to cropland was and still is inconsistent with accelerated private and local, state, and federal governmental efforts to maintain and restore wetlands and other types of wildlife habitat.

It was in response to these conflicting developments that a joint review committee was formed by the Soil Conservation Service and the Bureau of Sport Fisheries and Wildlife. After field studies in South Dakota and North Carolina in 1965, the group made a number of recommendations for improving the cooperative direction of watershed projects.

The committee suggested more frequent communication between personnel of the Soil Conservation Service and the state fish and game agency—the state agency taking part in planning from the inception of a project. This would include an exploration of all possible means of fish and wildlife enhancement, in which Soil Conservation Service biologists would participate, and the making of professional judgments before plans were presented to the sponsors. Cooperative inspections should be made during the construction phase.

There is an increasing tendency for agencies to work together in resolving problems, particularly in the states that are important to waterfowl nesting. North Dakota, Minnesota, and Wisconsin brought about major improvements in planning by appointing joint-agency task forces to carry out biological and hydrological surveys and make reports on specific watersheds. Reports include the designation of key wetlands to be preserved or "mitigated," of bottomland timber to be similarly handled, of sections of streams that should not be impounded, of erosion and siltation problems on streams, of sites that can be made to hold excess or runoff water, and of possibilities for wildlife developments through structures.

Jahn (1966) further suggested the drafting of "model development plans for watersheds, based on combined ecological-engineering principles for stated soil, water, vegetation, and land use conditions." Contributions to such a guidance program could be made by all public agencies, including universities.

State and local agencies have faced important financial obstacles to their participation in small watershed projects. Poole (1968) cited the need for broader authority in the use of federal funds, especially for enhancing water quality and for the acquisition of land and easements. He emphasized the severe limitations on funds available to the states themselves and the wide margin by which they were failing to keep up with the national watershed program. Federal appropriations for this purpose were equal to about 43 percent of the total money

... available to all state fish and game departments for a program involving about one-thousandth as much land. If you subscribe to dollar-power as a measure of intensity of application, you have to agree that the state agencies are woefully ill-equipped for a confrontation of this kind.

The small watersheds program typifies the difficulty of preserving the democratic element of local choice and planning for community resources, while at the same time invoking the broader perspective of public interest through technical and administrative guidance. By the very nature of existing mechanisms of local government, it is to be expected that the skills of soil scientists, crop specialists, and drainage engineers are more readily available and more readily accepted than those of biologists. To reach a meeting of minds is likely to require the kind of special undertaking that crosses long-established lines of agency interest and jurisdiction. By this means it appears that the frequent overemphasis on land reclamation aspects in Public Law 566 projects will gradually give way to something that will better serve a wide range of community and national needs.

WATERSHED OVERVIEW

Nearly every use of the earth's surface is concerned with the flow of waters from land masses into the oceans. In natural ecosystems plant cover slows the rate at which elevated lands are eroded, and in so doing contributes to the persistence and welfare of many living things.

Accelerated erosion of the watershed is a liability of far-reaching consequences in the management of renewable resources, and also in the recovery of such fund resources as minerals. Disturbance of the land is often unavoidable, but provisions for the early recovery of soil stability should now be recognized as an obligation of entrepreneurs in all land-use operations. It is to be expected that a recognition of a common social interest will lead eventually to the development of new ethical imperatives in the husbandry of land and water. However, Americans are still emerging from the pioneer period of open-ended exploitation, and there are but minimal beginnings of the mores that a stabilizing ecosocial system should bring. Thus, the earlier phase of progress in such matters as watershed protection must entail effective public controls. The development of standards, workable practices, and regulatory mechanisms is progressing in certain fields of major concern. Relatively little has been accomplished in others.

Siltation—Product of Disturbance

On uplands the subsoil exposed by water and wind erosion is largely barren as wildlife habitat. In addition, the topsoil and silt from many sources are highly significant in hastening eutrophication and in degrading the quality of downstream water habitats. Phosphorus, nitrogen, and other nutrients build up fertility, and pesticide pollutants are absorbed by particulate matter and carried by running water.

Man's agricultural pursuits, his timber cutting, livestock grazing, waste disposal, and construction activities have had an incidental impact on wildlife much greater than his deliberate wildlife management efforts. Unfortunately, the effects are commonly unfavorable. Probably the vast majority of damaging practices are associated with the degradation of the watershed. Among these practices are plowing and cultivating steep slopes, tearing up mountainsides for logging and mining, overgrazing rangelands—including high alpine meadows and tundras—by sheep, making extensive highway cuts with inadequately treated banks, and laying bare large areas during urban construction.

Resulting sediments are carried into streams, lakes, reservoirs, and estuaries, bringing about major changes in aquatic life. As a direct effect, silt may cover fish-spawning beds and bottoms long productive of shellfish. For example, in the Patuxent River, Maryland, deposits of sediment have accumulated during the past century to depths of 40 feet over former oyster beds. High turbidity commonly damages the gills of fish, reduces the photosynthetic activity of aquatic plants, and raises the temperature of water.

In assessing the magnitude of the total siltation problem in the United States, Freeman and Bennett (1969) calculated that some 4 billion tons of soil material is transported by water and deposited each year. "The impact of fluvial sediment on the national economy and on the quality of our environment is of tremendous significance. Sediment damage . . . has been estimated at more than 500 million dollars annually." Total costs undoubtedly would be difficult to appraise. It is evident that turbidity is a major factor in degrading water as used for recreational purposes, even aside from adverse effects on wildlife resources.

Progress in the conservation of topsoil on agricultural lands has been steady, it being the primary mission of the Soil Conservation Service since the mid-thirties. Despite this, it continues to be true that (Freeman and Bennett, 1969):

Because of the tremendous area, agricultural land supplies the greatest amount of sediment to the total load carried by streams. Numerous measurements on plots on which conservation measures have not been used have shown losses from land in continuous row crops ranging from 10,000 to 70,000 tons per square mile per year, depending on soil characteristics, crops, tillage practices, and topographic and climatic factors.

In this connection, there probably is ample justification for a much greater effort in the field of remedial soil conservation. Of equal significance, crop ecology as a discipline might well be more clearly concerned with the integrity of the watershed as a primary objective in all cultural innovations. Practices involving seedings in deep mulch, minimum tillage, and the return of humus to the soil present unending challenges to the agronomist and agricultural engineer. Important advances of these kinds have been made and undoubtedly will continue.

The soil-stabilizing vegetation that forms wildlife coverts on riparian lands sometimes receives little consideration in land uses. Surveys indicate that there are at least 300,000 miles of streambanks undergoing severe erosion. In the intermountain West, from 66 to 90 percent of the sediment load of many streams has this origin. Commonly the streamside vegetation important to fish and other wildlife has been destroyed by heavy grazing.

Streambank cover is beneficial to fish as shade and as a source of insect foods. It is habitat for fur animals, squirrels, wood ducks, and many kinds of songbirds. A survey of streambank wildlife habitat in Kentucky (Russell, 1966) showed that of 226 miles of stream margins surveyed, including 18 streams or sections thereof, 93.5 miles (41.4 percent) had been altered. The practice most frequently adverse to wildlife was agricultural clearing; others included refuse dumping, gravel operations, and bulldozing in connection with flood-control operations.

In the Southwest, the introduced salt cedar occurs on floodplains of the Rio Grande, and the Colorado and Gila rivers. It serves as important nesting habitat for the white-winged dove and mourning dove. Arizona Game and Fish Department studies indicated that the salt cedar thickets along the Gila River channel between Gillespie Dam and the confluence with the Salt River provided about 98 percent of the habitat for a nesting population of more than 360,000 doves in this area.

Salt cedar appears to take the place of dryland thickets of mesquite that were destroyed by woodcutting and land clearing and thus has been important in maintaining the dove population. If the salt cedar, a phreatophyte that occasions a large loss of water through evapotranspiration, were destroyed on a large scale, the number of doves would inevitably be reduced.

Likewise, if the cottonwoods, sycamores, alders, and maples of mountain canyons in southern Arizona and New Mexico were to be cut without consideration of the habitat requirements of certain rare and endangered birds, these species might well be decimated in the United States. Among the species utilizing such areas are the coppery-tailed trogon (*Trogon elegans*), grey hawk (*Buteo nitidus*), black hawk (*Buteogallus anthracinus*), whiskered owl (*Otus trichopsis*), rose-throated becard (*Pachyramphus aglaiae*), thick-billed kingbird (*Tyrannus crassirostris*), varied bunting (*Passerina versicolor*), blue-throated hummingbird (*Lampornis clemenciae*), and the violet-crowned hummingbird (*Amazilia violiceps*).

These cases perhaps exemplify the local involvements of wildlife that come to light when operations are planned and carried out by agencies having a single purpose. Water management in the West has been notable in this regard.

Since pioneer times, siltation has been a major factor in changing the ecology of streams and influencing their productivity for many kinds of vertebrate life. Whereas initially the streams of forested areas were characteristically deep, shaded, and spring-fed, today many are shallow and intermittent—a general reflection of the instability of watersheds.

The storage capacity of artificial reservoirs in the country is being reduced by sedimentation at the rate of 1 million acre-feet per year (Freeman and Bennett, 1969). This has obvious implications for the future, as stated by Leopold (1956):

Most projects will yield benefits equal to costs during their economic life, but there will come a time when great lengths of major river valleys will consist of reservoirs more or less filled with sediment. When that time comes, the problems of water control and of water use will be of a distinctly different character from those which concern us today. . . .

Problems that will be created on built-up floodplains when this situation becomes widespread have received minimal consideration. Information on the useful life of proposed reservoirs has been notably lacking among the economic criteria available to the public.

Mining the Watershed

Directly or indirectly, surface mining has adversely affected wildlife habitat involving 12,898 miles of stream, 281 natural lakes, 168 reservoirs, and 1,687,288 acres of land (U.S. Department of the Interior, 1967). In Kentucky the average sediment yield from coal-stripping spoil banks was 27,000 tons per square mile, as compared with 25 tons on adjacent forested watersheds (Freeman and Bennett, 1969). From active and abandoned mining operations of all types it is estimated that some 4 million tons of acid equivalents are being discharged annually into the nation's streams (Udall *et al.*, 1968).

An approach to the rehabilitation of areas damaged by surface mining has been suggested by special committees formed at the request of the 89th Congress through Public Law 89-4. Their report, issued by the Department of the Interior (1967), indicates that much can be done to prevent damage and to reclaim mined lands. It proposes a co-ordinated program involving government at all levels, plus the industries concerned, and calls for specific legislation, regulations, and action programs relating to: (1) prevention of future damage; (2) repair of past damage; (3) research and investigations; and (4) administration. This report, as submitted to Congress, could be an effective guide to all branches of the government in regulating an activity that involves the return of more than 5,000 square miles of disturbed areas to usefulness as wetlands, forests, ranges, croplands, and special wildlife habitats and greatly affects the public welfare.

Listings in bibliographies on strip-mine reclamation by Limstrom (1953), Knabe (1958, in German), Bowden (1961), and Funk (1962) indicate that the majority of the research has been concerned with basic problems of reclaiming and revegetating or reforesting mined areas. Yeager (1940), Riley (1958), and Klimstra (1959) studied the potential of strip-mined coal lands of Illinois, Indiana, and Ohio as wildlife habitat. Their studies indicate that the surface-mined areas on which trees, shrubs, and herbaceous vegetation had been re-established either naturally or artificially provided desirable habitat for at least ten species of game mammals and three species of game birds, plus numerous species of other birds and mammals. Wetlands within the strip-mined area supported several kinds of fish, waterfowl, shorebirds, reptiles, and amphibians. Such studies show the need for additional research to determine, for the various parts of the United States, interrelationships between wildlife, surface mining, and rehabilitation of mined areas.

The states have varied in their approach to reclamation of strip-mined areas, some having laws requiring a high degree of reclamation and others permitting a minimum of grading and revegetating under broad regulations. In recent years Kentucky and Pennsylvania have enacted reclamation laws that require contour leveling where this is possible, and bench leveling on steeper lands. Where the land cannot be reclaimed, stripping is not permitted.

Particularly in the Appalachian region, the extensive mining of steep mountain slopes has severely damaged recreation lands and waters. On the other hand, in the more level lands of the Midwest certain benefits are recognizable and may be enhanced through reclamation operations.

In this respect, surface mining is leaving ponds and lakes of high recreational value, and leveling the land surface would destroy these if carried to the extreme. The irregular surface of mined areas, including the breaking up of rock strata, forms an effective catchment for the recharging of groundwaters. Mined lands also impound runoff and may have some flood-control value. Mined lands, with their associated waters, have in some areas become choice suburban home sites and bring a high price as real estate.

The Kentucky state law that requires reclamation grading back to the original contour probably means that most of the land will become pasture or otherwise lose its primary value for wildlife. However, most surface-mined lands are likely to yield their major benefits in forestry and recreation, and specific planning for these purposes is appropriate. Thus, to promote better access by hunters and other recreationists, Pennsylvania guidelines require that slopes not exceed 25 percent (Davis, 1965).

In Indiana, the Patoka State Fish and Game Area has been established on surface-mined lands and will encompass some 7,000 acres when lease arrangements with a coal company are completed. It includes seven coal-pit lakes up to 14 acres in size that offer public fishing, and quail shooting is reported to be good. As part of this project, which was begun in 1963, the state plans a management program for other small game and for deer.

Other states are giving emphasis to wildlife habitat development in reclaiming stripped lands, and many more such areas are likely to be developed intensively for hunting and fishing. Natural processes of rock fragmentation and plant succession work rapidly to aid the recovery of mined lands where attention is given to the burial of acid-producing materials and to a reasonable shaping of contours. Where mining results in long-term degradation, as on steep mountainsides, the working of coal or other deposits should be postponed until acceptable methods can be developed.

WILDLIFE IN WATER RESOURCES DEVELOPMENT

Legislative recognition that wildlife values should be considered in water development operations began with passage of the Fish and Wildlife Coordination Act of 1934 (Public Law 48-401). An amendment of 1946 provided that reports and recommendations of the Secretary of the Interior relative to wildlife losses and measures to be taken would be made a part of the construction reports for federal water projects. A further amendment in 1958 gave authority to the construction agencies to improve and develop wildlife resources, with the stated purpose of providing ". . . that fish and wildlife conservation shall receive equal consideration . . . with other features of water-resource development programs." A final step in this direction was taken in 1965 with passage of the Anadromous Fish Act (Public Law 89-304), which stated that:

Water resource projects which are determined by the Secretary to be needed solely for the conservation, protection, and enhancement of such fish, may be planned and constructed by the Bureau of Reclamation in its currently authorized geographical area of responsibility, or by the Corps of Engineers, or by the Department of Agriculture, or by the States.

In noting this important progress, Assistant Secretary of the Interior Cain (1966) remarked that the Fish and Wildlife Service had now become one of that select group of federal agencies that could institute water project plans. "Progress has been made, but problems are still with us. Federal actions still are being taken in the water resources field that are inimical to fish and wildlife resources, and we can do little about them."

Particular areas of difficulty, said the Assistant Secretary, were the lack of control over thermal pollution by steam electric plants, and the insistence by some of the construction agencies that dollar values be placed on wildlife losses. In the latter connection he quoted the Senate Committee report on the 1958 amendment to the Coordination Act:

It is the understanding of your committee, however, that these measures would not have to be justified under the usual benefit-cost type analysis. They would not produce 'benefits.' These measures would be for reducing or compensating for losses.

As a final major problem area, "We are almost always frustrated in trying to maintain fish and wildlife values in connection with water resource development of coastal and estuarine areas of the Nation as a result of dredging and filling operations." Since the waters of concern are navigable, a permit for such operations must come from the Corps of Engineers. But this agency has no jurisdiction over values other than navigation. Thus the destruction continues:

All along the Atlantic and Gulf Coasts and in some parts of the Pacific Coast, dredges by the score are busy tearing up the estuarine environment. Much of their purpose is to build new residential areas for Venetian-type developments, that is, with navigable canals leading to each residence. This situation is particularly acute in Florida, where all around the peninsula estuarine fish and wildlife values are suffering huge losses from dredging and filling. The situation is almost as bad in Long Island and along the New Jersey coast.

Since prehistoric times, the rich biological resources of coastal wet-lands and tidal waters have been important to mankind. Odum (1961) has shown that estuaries in Georgia produced 10 tons of dry matter during their year-round growing season—more than the best European wheat and corn lands. The zone of shallows where fresh and salt waters mix serves as a "nutrient trap" where a wide variety of living things benefit from the changing depths and currents.

Coastal waters and their associated saltmarshes, mudflats, and tidal creeks and pools are used seasonally by great numbers of migratory waterfowl and resident birds of many kinds. They are the habitat of certain aquatic and semiaquatic mammals, the alligator, and a vast ar-ray of economically important marine life.

It is estimated that there are some 27 million acres of these seaside environments bordering the United States and its territories. Here is where such seafoods as oysters, clams, abalone, shrimp, crabs, and lob-sters are produced, and estuaries are the nursery waters for juvenile stages of fish that support the commercial fisheries of offshore conti-nental shelves (see Milton, 1968; U.S. Bureau of Sport Fisheries and Wildlife, 1967; Walford, 1967; Lynch, 1967).

Cooper (1968) stated that about 5,000 commercial fishermen and 400,000 sportsmen of North Carolina take an annual harvest of marine products that is the equivalent of a $100 million industry. This yield is primarily dependent on more than 2 million acres of "sounds and marshes" bordering the state.

The importance of estuaries as fish and wildlife habitat places a high premium on the preservation of essentially natural conditions. How-ever, these are also the areas of greatest promise for the artificial cul-ture of marine mollusks and crustaceans (Webber, 1968). It is clearly in the national interest to promote an understanding of their ecology and leave their use options open for the future.

It has been suggested that the Secretary of the Interior be given authority to protect estuarine biological resources; this appears to be a logical arrangement. In 1967, however, Cain reported gratifying moves that were made possible through increased communication and cooperation between the Department of the Interior and the Corps of Engineers:

On a basis of protection to fish and wildlife habitat, a dredging per-mit was denied in Boca Ciega Bay, Florida. There has been increasing evidence that the Corps of Engineers and the State of Florida are rec-ognizing the right of Everglades National Park (a major estuarine habi-tat) to a share of water diverted by the central and south Florida flood-control and water-development project. A memorandum of understanding between the Secretary of the Army and the Secretary of the Interior ". . . provides a firm basis for the two Departments to cooperate in controlling pollution and conserving fish and wildlife, recreation and esthetic values that may be involved in dredging and similar operations under Corps permits."

Under this agreement district engineers of the Corps will notify state, federal, and other interested parties when a permit application is received and hold public hearings when appropriate (Cain, 1967).

Despite persistent liabilities, important benefits have accrued from the Coordination Act and its amendments. Various states and the Division of River Basin Studies of the Bureau of Sport Fisheries and Wildlife have worked consistently to retain conservation pools in reservoirs, provide for minimum water releases for fish, and avoid excessive water releases. Increasing attention has been given to wildlife values and to mitigation measures when construction activities are expected to result in fish and wildlife damage. In 1965, some 196,000 acres were purchased by the Corps of Engineers and the Bureau of Reclamation for additions to the National Wildlife Refuge System. These lands were not only for the reduction of losses but also for enhancement of the wildlife resource. In North Dakota, 70 units of waterfowl habitat are being supplied in dry periods with water from the Garrison Diversion Unit on the Missouri River.

Progress is being made in integrating the hitherto widely divergent programs of federal agencies. The intent of Congress to preserve and improve wildlife resources for public use is evident and should have a salutary effect as an example to states where wildlife management still is not recognized as a beneficial competing use of water.

Much of the loss of wildlife habitats incident to water management has come about through the widespread urge to replace natural dynamics with mechanized controls. The extensive development of floodplains for intensive uses, discussed in Chapter 3, exemplifies this trend. When these effects are added to the accumulative results of drainage, the total destruction of natural aquatic scenes and environments reaches catastrophic proportions. The question of what is worth saving for future purposes becomes an issue pressing for clear-cut decisions.

Further restructuring of natural drainageways in North America involves a high proportion of large-scale, expensive, and marginal projects that must be studied in terms of long-term effects and objectives. The valid considerations include a philosophical outlook on the future of mankind in this part of the world. The support of maximum numbers of human beings under highly artificial conditions is a choice opposed to the alternative of limiting population at a level where the living standard can include the esthetic and recreational values found in spacious hinterlands. The viewpoint is growing that the summary writing off of scenic, space, and recreational values, as has been common in resource developments, is not acceptable public policy. The emergence of revised quality criteria for the human environment is suggested in a statement by the President's Council on Recreation and Natural Beauty (1968) [ed. note: the original is in italics]:

The Council proposes that Federal flood control and other water resource development programs and projects seek to retain or restore natural channels, vegetation, and fish and wildlife habitats on rivers, streams, and creeks and apply the same policy to federally assisted public and private projects. . . .

In view of the rapidly developing signs of overdemand and overuse in the industrialized part of the world (see Jackson *et al.*, 1968; Mayer, 1969), accompanied by an overburden of pollution for which no adequate provision is now in sight, the need for more conservative resource policies is evident. It is prudent to assume that not enough is known of ultimate human needs to permit further extensive and irreversible changes in the natural aspects of land and water.

REFERENCES

Allan, P. F., and I. McKeever. 1962. Multiple purpose developments in small watersheds. 27th N. Amer. Wildl. & Natur. Resour. Conf. Trans. p. 122-132.

Bowden, K. L. 1961. A bibliography of strip-mine reclamation: 1953-1960. Univ. Mich. Dep. Forest. & Conserv. 13 p. (processed.)

Bue, I. G., L. B. Blankenship, and W. H. Marshall. 1952. The relationship of grazing practices to waterfowl breeding populations and production on stock ponds in western South Dakota. 17th N. Amer. Wildl. Conf. Trans. p. 396-414.

Bue, I. G., H. G. Uhlig, and J. D. Smith. 1964. Stock ponds and dugouts, p. 391-398. *In* J. P. Linduska and A. L. Nelson (ed.), Waterfowl tomorrow. Bureau of Sport Fisheries and Wildlife, Washington, D.C.

Bureau of Sport Fisheries and Wildlife. 1961. Waterfowl production habitat losses related to agricultural drainage. Br. of River Basin Stud. Rep. 39+A-23.

Burwell, R. W., and L. G. Sugden. 1964. Potholes—going, going . . . , p. 368-380. *In* J. P. Linduska and A. L. Nelson (ed.), Waterfowl tomorrow. U.S. Bureau of Sport Fisheries and Wildlife, Washington, D.C.

Cain, S. A. 1966. Coordination of fish and wildlife values with water resources development goals. 2nd Ann. Amer. Water Resour. Ass. Conf. 11 p. (processed.)

Cain, S. A. 1967. Estuaries: our most endangered natural habitats, p. 41-48. *In* J. D. Newson (ed.), marsh and estuary management symposium, Louisiana State University, Baton Rouge.

Cooper, A. W. 1967. Salt marshes and estuaries: cradle of North Carolina fisheries. N.C. Architect 15(6,7).

Dahlberg, B. L. 1960. Wetlands: The sportsman's best investment. Wis. Conserv. Bull. 25(8):3-5.

Davis, G., *et al.* (editorial committee). 1965. A guide to revegetating bituminous strip-mine spoils in Pennsylvania. Research Committee on Coal Mine Spoil Revegetation in Pennsylvania. 46 p.

Day, A. M. 1964. Developing fish and wildlife resources through Public Law 566 projects. 29th N. Amer. Wildl. & Natur. Resour. Conf. Trans. p. 112-118.

Day, A. M. 1966. Wildlife habitat management as a means of increasing recreation on public lands. Bureau of Land Management. Unpublished Report. 73 p.

Durand, F. V. 1963. Small watershed projects and wildlife. 28th N. Amer. Wildl. & Natur. Resour. Conf. p. 308-313.

Freeman, O. I., and I. L. Bennett, Jr. 1969. Control of agriculture-related pollution. U.S. Department of Agriculture and Office of Science and Technology, Washington, D.C. 102 p.

Funk, D. T. 1962. A revised bibliography of strip-mine reclamation. Cent. States Forest Exp. Sta., Misc. Release 35. 19 p.

Goldstein, J. H. 1967. An economic analysis of the wetlands problem in Minnesota. University of Minnesota, unpublished thesis. 115 p.

Grizzell, R. A. 1960. Fish and wildlife management on watershed projects. 25th N. Amer. Wildl. Conf. Trans. p. 186-192.

Haddock, J. L., and L. W. DeBates. 1969. Report on drainage trends in the prairie pothole region of Minnesota, North Dakota and South Dakota. Bureau of Sport Fisheries and Wildlife. 8 p. (unpublished.)

Hamor, W. H. 1965. An analysis of fish and wildlife developments in watershed projects in the midwest. Ass. Midwest Fish & Game Comm. Proc. 32:29-34.

Hamor, W. H., H. G. Uhlig, and L. V. Compton. 1968. Ponds and marshes for wild ducks on farms and ranches in the northern plains. U.S. Dep. Agr. Farmers' Bull. 2234. 16 p.

Herbison, H. W. 1967. A progress report on aspects of North Dakota wetlands use and management. N.D. State Univ., Agr. Econ. Rep. 58. 35 p.

Jackson, H. M., *et al.* 1968. Congressional white paper on a national policy for the environment. 90th Cong., 2nd Sess., Senate Committee on Interior and Insular Affairs, House Committee on Science and Astronautics. U.S. Government Printing Office, Washington, D.C. 19 p.

Jahn, L. R. 1966. A wildlife organization's view of P.L. 566. Soil Conservation Service, Midwest Biological Workshop, Madison, Wis. 24 p.

Jahn, L. R. 1968. "Water Bank" proposed to maintain wetlands. Ducks Unlimited 31(3):14.

Jahn, L. R., and R. A. Hunt. 1964. Duck and coot ecology and management in Wisconsin. Wis. Conserv. Dep. Tech. Bull. 22. 212 p.

Kenney, F. R., and W. L. McAtee. 1938. The problem: drained areas and wildlife habitat, p. 77-83. *In* Soils and Men. The Yearbook of Agriculture 1938. U.S. Department of Agriculture. U.S. Government Printing Office, Washington, D.C.

Kimball, J. W. 1954. Ducks, potholes, and good farming. Flicker. 26(4):131-135.

Kimball, J. W. 1964. Recreation, fish and wildlife in watershed development. 11th Nat. Watershed Cong., Comm. Rep. p. 42-54.

Klimstra, W. D. 1959. The potential of wildlife management on strip-mined areas. Ill. Wildl. 14(2):5-10.

Knabe, W. 1958. Beiträge zur Bibliographie über Wiederurbarmachung von Bergbauflächen. Wiss. Z. Humboldt-Univ., Berlin. 7:291-304.

Leopold, L. B. 1956. Land use and sediment load, p. 639-643. *In* W. L. Thomas (ed.), Man's role in changing the face of the earth. University of Chicago Press, Chicago.

Limstrom, G. A. 1953. A bibliography of strip-mine reclamation. Cent. States Forest Exp. Sta., Misc. Release 8. 25 p.

Low, J. B. 1945. Ecology and management of the redhead (*Nyroca americana*) in Iowa. Mon. Ecol. 15:35-69.

Lynch, J. J. 1967. Values of the south Atlantic and Gulf Coast marshes and estuaries to waterfowl, p. 51-63. *In* J. D. Newson (ed.), Marsh and estuary management symposium, Louisiana State University, Baton Rouge.

Mann, G. E. 1966. Wetlands–liquid assets. Conserv. Volunteer 29(166):30-38.

Mayer, J. 1969. Toward a non-Malthusian population policy. Columbia Forum (summer), 5-13.

Milton, J. P. 1968. Coastal conservation. Conservation Foundation. 22 p. (mimeo.)

Munro, D. A. 1967. The prairies and the ducks. Canadian Geogr. J. (July)

National Advisory Commission on Food and Fiber. 1967. Food and fiber for the future. U.S. Government Printing Office, Washington, D.C. 361 p.

Odum, E. P. 1961. The role of tidal marshes in estuarine production. N.Y. State Conserv. 15(6):12-15.

Poole, D. A. 1968. Weaknesses in the Public Law 566 watershed program. 15th Nat. Watershed Cong., Proc.

President's Council on Recreation and Natural Beauty. 1968. From sea to shining sea. A report on the American environment. U.S. Government Printing Office, Washington, D.C. 304 p.

Riley, C. V. 1958. An evaluation of reclaimed coal strip-mined lands as wildlife habitat. Diss. Abstr. 18:740-743.

Russell, D. M. 1966. A survey of streambank wildlife habitat. Southeastern Ass. Game & Fish Comm., 20th Ann. Meeting, Proc.

Schrader, T. A. 1955. Waterfowl and the potholes of the north central states, p. 596-604. *In* Water. Yearbook of Agriculture 1955. U.S. Department of Agriculture. U.S. Government Printing Office, Washington, D.C.

Sears, P. B. 1956. The processes of environmental change by man, p. 471-484. *In* W. L. Thomas (ed.), Man's role in changing the face of the earth. University of Chicago Press, Chicago.

Sieh, J. G. 1948. The waterfowl story in Iowa. 14th Midwest Wildl. Conf. (mimeo.)

Smith, A. G., J. H. Stoudt, and J. B. Gollop. 1964. Prairie potholes and marshes, p. 39-50. *In* J. P. Linduska and A. L. Nelson (ed.), Waterfowl tomorrow. U.S. Department of the Interior, Bureau of Sport Fisheries and Wildlife.

Smith, R. H. 1953. A study of waterfowl production on artificial reservoirs in eastern Montana. J. Wildl. Manage. 17(3):276-291.

Southwick, H. C. 1966. Small watershed projects, friend or foe of wildlife? Naturalist 17(1):24-28.

Udall, S. L., *et al*. 1968. The nation's water resources. Report of the Water Resources Council, Washington, D.C.

U.S. Bureau of Sport Fisheries and Wildlife. 1967. Estuarine programs interim report. U.S. Department of the Interior, Fish and Wildlife Service, Washington, D.C. 29 p.

U.S. Department of Agriculture. 1963. Summary by states of the Agricultural Conservation Program. Washington, D.C.

U.S. Department of the Interior. 1967. Surface mining and our environment. Special Report. Washington, D.C. 124 p.

Vesall, D. B. 1963. Your wetlands . . . blue chip investment. Conserv. Volunteer 26(152):4-7.

Walford, L. A. 1967. Values of the south Atlantic and Gulf Coast marshes and estuaries to sport fishery resources, p. 79-82. *In* J. D. Newson (ed.), Marsh and estuary management symposium, Louisiana State University, Baton Rouge.

Webber, H. H. 1968. Mariculture. BioScience 18(10):940-945.

Williams, D. A. 1957. Benefits from watershed projects. U.S. Dep. Agr., Soil Conserv. Serv., Watersheds Memo. SCS-66 (Rev. 4). 50 p.

Yeager, L. E. 1940. Wildlife management on coal-stripped land. Fifth N. Amer. Wildl. Conf. Trans. p. 348-353.

CHAPTER 6

Pesticides and Wildlife

Modern pesticides* have accounted for impressive gains in food production both here and abroad; they have been responsible for saving many human lives through control of disease vectors; they have become components of twentieth-century technology. It is appropriate, however, to examine the evidence of harmful environmental effects and to weigh the benefit-risk equation in the use of pesticides, with special reference to their effect on wildlife. It may well be that the gains sought through pesticide use can be had only at some sacrifice in wildlife values, but the risks involved should be understood as fully as possible to provide a basis for establishing policies in the best public interest.

THE NEED FOR PESTICIDES

Strong pressures—biological, economic, sociological, and esthetic—favor the use of pesticides. It is extremely important that these influences be understood if there is to emerge a system of regulating pesticides that strikes a balance between adequate safeguards and undue restriction.

*As used here, the term "pesticides" includes chemicals employed to kill living organisms that are considered pests. The major groups of pesticides considered here are insecticides, fungicides, and herbicides. The term "pesticide" may also include chemicals used against pests to repel, attract, or interrupt a vital function such as reproduction (sterilants). Other chemicals sometimes considered as pesticides are plant growth regulators, desiccants, and defoliants.

The Biological Struggle

Man recognizes the need to protect his sources of food and fiber from the ravages of pests. Similarly, he is concerned with pests that spread disease and affect his health and comfort. To combat living organisms he considers harmful, while protecting those he considers beneficial, is a challenge of great complexity. So-called pest species are to be found in most of the major groups of living organisms—viruses, bacteria, fungi, nematodes, insects, birds, mammals, and plants.

All living organisms occur in communities, or ecosystems, interacting and arriving at some kind of balance that is constantly in a state of flux. To maintain conditions favorable to man requires that he impose many controls. Pesticides are valuable tools in making some of these adjustments.

The problem is intensified because modern commerce has introduced many pests to new areas where they are not under the restraints imposed by the biological checks and balances present in their native habitat. Approximately 50 percent of the pests in the United States are introduced.

In addition, domesticated varieties of plants and animals are often selected because of desirable qualities other than their natural resistance to pests. For instance, the McIntosh apple, introduced about 1870, remains a favorite despite its high susceptibility to apple scab, a fungus disease requiring intensive use of fungicides.

The system of monoculture whereby large numbers of a single species are cultivated in close proximity renders the population vulnerable to attack and subject to violent cyclic fluctuations.

It is evident that modern agriculture, rather than having built-in biological regulators to hold it in equilibrium, is extremely artificial and is dependent upon intensive pest-control programs. Chemical pesticides have been very effective as tools in the struggle.

The Need for More Food

Two thirds of the world's inhabitants are underfed, and we are in the midst of a population explosion that has a potential for doubling the world population by the year 2000. Every optimistic projection for overcoming worldwide food shortages is based on the assumption that the technology responsible for the impressive increase in agricultural production since about midcentury can be extended to other countries and that it can be further improved (President's Science Advisory Committee, 1967). The developed countries of the world have increased the use of pesticides chiefly to increase food production, while developing countries have employed them largely to control vectors of human diseases. Although pesticides are but one of the numerous elements of modern agricultural technology, the various elements interact in such a way that the withdrawal of any one of them sets off a chain of limiting effects. Despite the promise of alternative methods of pest control, they are not likely to account for major reductions in the use of chemical pesticides in the immediate future.

Public Health

The value of DDT in disease control through the reduction of insect vectors was dramatically demonstrated during World War II. Since the war extensive programs in public health have been sponsored by the World Health Organization (WHO) and other agencies. Because of the desire to put "first things first," high priorities have been placed on saving human lives in developing countries and perhaps secondary priority was given to environmental considerations which, at the moment at least, did not involve human lives. The sense of responsibility and concern of WHO leadership in the use of DDT is well stated in the following passage:

The general attitude and feeling of WHO towards the use of DDT is at present agonizingly ambivalent. On the one hand it is proud of its amazing record, of having been the main agent in eradicating malaria in countries whose populations total 550 million people, of having saved about 5 million lives and prevented 100 million illnesses in the first 8 years of its use, of having recently reduced the annual malaria death-rate in India from 750,000 down to 1,500, and of having served at least 2 billion people in the world without causing the loss of a single life by poisoning from DDT alone.

On the other hand WHO is still pressing its search for new compounds with the view of finding some to validate as DDT substitutes. It has investigated the possibilities of biological control since 1959 and has not given up although the outlook appears so unpromising. It is pushing the development of genetical control, not only for *Culex fatigans* in which cytoplasmic incompatibility offers real practical possibilities, but also for *Anopheles gambiae*, the principal malaria vector of Africa. In fact, the bulk of the research promoted by WHO in the past 10 years has been devoted to the search for substitute materials and methods. And it intends forthwith to repair the omission of not having investigated quantitatively the fate of the DDT that has been applied to the houses over the years.

In short, WHO has been working towards a progressive transfer away from DDT in public health operations. But the problem is to effect this transfer without jeopardizing the large amount of human life and health which is at stake, and without making control so expensive, complicated and uncertain that the developing countries will lose heart in their operations against diseases transmitted by disease vectors. Certainly an attempt to force the pace by advocating the immediate discontinuation of the use of DDT would be a disaster to world health.*

Economic Stress

In a free enterprise system the entrepreneur can adopt any legal means to protect his investment and insure a favorable competitive position. Indeed, his success is measured in terms of his ability to do this. In response to this well-known economic principle, modern agriculture seeks to adopt all measures that can enhance its efficiency. This means converting to large production units, using hybrid seed, and adopting mechanization to reduce labor and insure timely cultivation and harvesting. Pesticides have proven their worth as elements in modern technology, and sound economics dictates that they be used, for example, in weed control, or insect control as a substitute for more costly hand operations.

Similarly, the economic pressure favors using the least expensive pesticide. Although the trend is away from persistent pesticides, they are often chosen as less costly than unstable ones requiring more applications, but having less potential for environmental pollution.

All trends in modern agriculture suggest that these economic pressures will increase. If so, the regulations governing the use of such components of the technology web as pesticides need to be re-examined and clear guidelines established.

The present regulatory system places the responsible agricultural producer in the difficult position of choosing between practices that are economically sound and legally acceptable, but that may well be harmful to environmental quality—a matter he understands only vaguely and for which he recognizes no direct responsibility—and more expensive, less environmentally troublesome measures.

Standards of Quality

The American public has come to expect high standards of quality and, in response to this expectation, regulatory agencies have estab-

*World Health Organization, Vector Biology and Control. 1969. The present place of DDT in world operations for public health. Statement presented at the symposium "The Biological Impact of Pesticides in the Environment," at Oregon State University, Corvallis, August 19, 1969.

lished exacting standards that producers must meet to qualify for marketing grades and to avoid condemnation. Thus, more is involved than the grower's desire to produce attractive fruits and vegetables. The housewife would be reluctant to buy wormy apples, nor would wormy apples qualify for existing marketing grades. Again, though the housewife is unlikely to detect fragments of aphids on broccoli, the Food and Drug Administration of the Department of Health, Education, and Welfare has established tolerance limits for insect fragments. To meet these the grower resorts to control programs of which chemical control is the most effective. The Food and Drug Administration is also charged with responsibility for establishing residue tolerances for pesticides (discussed later in this chapter). Purity standards that insure freedom of food products from insect fragments, excreta of rats, and other extraneous filth is in the best public interest; these standards must be realistically established; however, undue emphasis on the use of pesticides is to be avoided. In terms of human health and environmental quality, a few more insect fragments may be the lesser of two evils.

When the foregoing factors are considered, it is evident that pesticides are an indispensable component of our technology for producing food and fiber and protecting man's health and comfort. All responsible studies agree with this conclusion. The choice is not whether pesticides will be used, but which ones and under what circumstances.

ASSESSMENT OF THE PESTICIDE PROBLEM

Chemical pest control in the modern sense began around the middle of the last century. Sulfur was used against powdery mildew of grapes in 1821; Paris green was successfully used to control an outbreak of Colorado potato beetle in 1867; and the fungicidal properties of Bordeaux mixture, which is still used, were discovered in 1883.

Reservations about effectiveness and concern for hazard to non-target organisms were expressed early in the development of chemical pest control. An editorial in the first number of the *Practical Entomologist*, October 30, 1865 (Entomological Society of Philadelphia, 1865), raised doubts as to the value of chemical pesticides in insect control and suggested the importance of biological studies. In 1894 it was proven that arsenicals killed bees when sprayed on fruit trees in bloom, and in 1903 a tolerance for arsenicals on foods was established by the British.

The era of the synthetic organic pesticides began with the development of DDT as an insecticide in 1939. The effectiveness of DDT was highlighted through its use during and after World War II to control vectors of human diseases.

After World War II, the chemical industry, government, and universities joined forces in adapting DDT and related compounds to peacetime uses. The discovery of many new synthetic compounds followed. This was augmented by equally rapid developments in formulation and methods of application. Thus, in a matter of a decade or so, synthetic organic pesticides became commonplace in agriculture, in industry, and in the home. Indeed, by 1962 some 500 compounds, in more than 54,000 formulations, were registered for use as pesticides in the United States.

It was at this point that Rachel Carson's *Silent Spring* appeared (Carson, 1962). The combination of timing, her literary skill, the popular cause she espoused, and the misgivings that had already arisen touched off a great debate. This debate extended throughout government, the scientific community, the chemical industry, and agriculture and conservation organizations, and provided a public forum whereby the advantages and disadvantages, the gains and the losses, the facts and the fantasies could be aired.

This controversy led to numerous investigations. Of these, five are especially pertinent to the impact of pesticide use on wildlife:

1. The President's Science Advisory Committee's (PSAC) Panel on the Use of Pesticides began a study of the problem in the summer of 1962. This group's report is of particular interest because it represents the first official pronouncement after the outbreak of the pesticide controversy (President's Science Advisory Committee, 1963). The theme of the report, simply stated, is that the use of pesticides must be continued to insure adequate supplies of food and fiber, but that their use may endanger beneficial plants and animals as well as man himself. The report recommended:
   a. assessment of the level of pesticides in man and his environment;
   b. development of measures to allow greater safety in pesticide use;
   c. research on safer and more specific methods of pest control;
   d. amendments to strengthen public laws governing the use of pesticides; and
   e. public education of pesticide benefits and hazards.
2. At about the same time, the Subcommittee on Reorganization and International Organization of the Committee on Government

Operations began its study entitled "Inter-Agency Coordination in Environmental Hazards (Pesticides)" under the chairmanship of Senator Abraham Ribicoff. Hearings continued for 15 months and massive testimony was compiled on many aspects of the problem. The hearings served not only as a fact-finding forum, but also as a public sounding board for the diverse interests represented by the many witnesses. The final report of the subcommittee (United States Senate, 1966) was released in August, 1966.

Particularly significant is the broad ecological context within which the committee viewed the pesticide issue. The following is indicative of its view:

The public debate over pesticides is but one facet of a wider debate which reflects a greater sensitivity to the fundamental questions raised by the continuing and accelerating pace of man's modification of his total environment. Pesticides are but one factor and we are increasingly aware that our environment is being altered even more dramatically by air and water pollution, atomic fallout and the population explosion.

As we come to appreciate more keenly the significance of this fast accelerating, irreversible alteration of our environment, we recognize the need for stock-taking and the necessity of endeavoring to take into account all the multitude of complex relationships between man and his natural and artificial surroundings.

3. In a comprehensive report titled "Restoring the Quality of Our Environment," the PSAC Environmental Pollution Panel (President's Science Advisory Committee, 1965) considered pollution in its broadest context and made more than a hundred specific recommendations. The philosophy of the panel was based on the assumption that pollution is a by-product of a technological society and that pollution problems will grow with increases in population and improved living standards unless drastic counter-measures to reduce it are taken.

The panel offered some sweeping recommendations that placed problems of pollution in a new perspective. The report stated that freedom from pollution should be recognized as a human right, that responsibility for pollution control rests with the polluter, and that the polluter should bear the cost of pollution abatement and pass it on to the consumer as part of the cost of operation. Finally, the need for considering all pollution as a single problem was stressed; the responsibility for leadership in pollution abatement should be assumed by the federal government.

The study by the PSAC Environmental Pollution Panel was attuned to the needs of the times and the report provides a broad blueprint for constructive action. The philosophy, recommendations, and much of the material in the appendixes of that report are relevant to the question of land use and wildlife.

Although the approach was different, the recommendations growing out of the Ribicoff hearings (United States Senate, 1966) agree essentially with those of the Environmental Pollution Panel report. This is not surprising since the counsel of many of the same individuals or agencies was sought by the two groups in the course of their investigations.

4. In early 1966, a symposium on "Scientific Aspects of Pest Control," sponsored by the National Academy of Sciences-National Research Council (1966) was held in Washington, D.C. The objective was to bring together the current scientific knowledge of the various aspects of pest control, and communicate it not only to the scientific community, but to lay leaders, the press, and government policymakers as well.

The symposium provided an opportunity for review of the progress made on the recommendations of the PSAC Panel almost 3 years earlier. It was a unique experiment in seeking to bridge the communication gap between persons developing specialized knowledge and persons responsible for translating that knowledge into broad policy and future environmental quality goals.

5. The most recent report was by the Committee on Persistent Pesticides, which was established by the National Academy of Sciences-National Research Council (1969b) at the request of the U.S. Department of Agriculture. This report is of special interest because it addresses the problem of persistent pesticides as they relate to wildlife. The report reiterates many earlier findings regarding the benefit-risk features of persistent pesticide use. In addition, it stresses that while present methods of pesticide regulation adequately protect man's food supply, "they do not appear to insure the prevention of environmental contamination."

These five reports provide useful assessments of the relationship of pesticides and, to a lesser degree, other pollutants to wildlife. Many other studies have contributed to our knowledge of the problem. Two committees established by agencies of the federal government in the late 1960's undertook to study the relationship of pesticides to human health and environmental pollution—the Commission on Pesticides and Their Relationship to Environmental Health, an 11-member committee appointed by Secretary Finch of the Department of Health, Education, and Welfare, and the Environmental Quality Council established by executive order of President Nixon. In all of these studies the problem of pesticide pollution as it affects wildlife was recognized. The plea for more research is common to all of them. Lacking, however, are statements fixing responsibility for well-being of the ecosystem and specific proposals to reduce inputs of persistent pesticides to avoid the adverse consequences that are foretold in these reports if their use continues unabated.

REGULATING THE USE OF PESTICIDES

The three major concerns in the use of pesticides are: (1) direct poisoning of humans and wildlife through accidents or exposure during manufacture, transport, storage, or use; (2) toxic residues that may pose a hazard to the consumer; and (3) environmental pollution arising from introduction of pesticides in the ecosystem.

The need has long been recognized for legislation to regulate the use of pesticides and minimize the undesirable effects. The original Federal Insecticide Act of 1910 controlled the sale of pesticides in the United States to protect consumers from substandard or fraudulent products. The concern for human health was first demonstrated with the Federal Caustic Poison Act of 1927, which regulated the labeling of any dangerous, caustic, or corrosive substance put up in containers suitable for household use. The present regulatory responsibilities of the U.S. Department of Agriculture and the Department of Health, Education, and Welfare have been described in detail (National Academy of Sciences-National Research Council, 1966:385-398).

It was not until after World War II, when the variety of pesticides had greatly increased and commercial use became widespread, that concern for protection of human health led to the replacement of the Insecticide Act of 1910 with the Federal Insecticide, Fungicide and Rodenticide Act of 1947 (FIFRA), administered by the Pesticides Regulation Division of the Department of Agriculture. This law is the basic federal act governing pesticides in interstate commerce. A 1959 amendment to the FIFRA added nematocides, plant regulators, defoliants, and desiccants. Further amendments in 1964 (a) eliminated the controversial section of the 1947 act that allowed sale of an unregistered product when a protest had been filed, (b) required a federal registration number on each label and conspicuous precautionary labeling of poisonous and potentially hazardous pesticides and (c) required manufacturers to remove unwarranted safety claims from the labels. The 1964 act requires:

1. Registration of economic poisons prior to their sale or introduction into interstate or receipt from foreign commerce;
2. Prominently displayed warnings on the labels of all pesticides with an LD_{50} of less than 5,000 mg/kg;*
3. The coloring or discoloring of certain economic poisons to prevent their being mistaken for flour, sugar, salt, baking powder, or other similar articles used in preparing foodstuffs;
4. Prominently displayed statements on the label of the economic poison to advise the user of potential hazards to man, wildlife, vegetation, and other nontarget organisms; and
5. Instructions for use to provide adequate protection and to assure effectiveness of the formulations against stated target organisms.

Besides the above requirements, a three-way agreement was concluded in 1964 between the Departments of Agriculture, of the Interior, and of Health, Education, and Welfare on the review of pesticide registration applications relative to considerations of human health and hazards to wildlife. The Department of the Interior reviews for implications as to hazard to wildlife all data on compounds submitted to the Department of Agriculture for registration or re-registration. When a hazard to wildlife is believed to exist, the Department of the Interior advises the Department of Agriculture of appropriate action to restrict use, to require additional warnings, or to eliminate certain use patterns.

In addition to the 1947 FIFRA and its amendments and regulations, the Federal Food, Drug and Cosmetic Act of 1938 and its "Miller Amendment" of 1954 (Public Law 83-518) further control the use of pesticides. This act and its amendments are administered by the Secretary of Health, Education, and Welfare through the Food and Drug Administration. They provide that tolerance levels be established for pesticide residues in raw agricultural commodities upon which pesticides are used. Any raw agricultural commodity may be condemned as adulterated if it contains a residue of any pesticide that has not been formally exempted or that is present in excess of the tolerances. This law is also concerned with the adulteration of foods with insects, insect fragments, hair, excreta of rodents, and any other extraneous filth that may offend the sensitivities of consumers or endanger their health.

*LD_{50}—Lethal dose for 50 percent of the test populations (a computed, not observed, figure) reported in milligrams toxicant per kilogram body weight of test species (mg/kg).

These two federal statutes (FIFRA and Miller) in their present form supplement each other and are interrelated by law and practical operation. Both require stringent evaluation of the safety and effectiveness of the toxicants. Both are primarily concerned with the protection of the health of the user, the consumer, and the public in general. Because both statutes apply to interstate sale of the chemical or commodities treated with pesticides, there is no provision for federal control over the final use of a USDA-registered pesticide. Control of actual use of pesticides rests with the states. Present pesticide use laws vary considerably between states. However, many of the states now have pesticide control boards or panels that include representation from fish and wildlife groups as well as from agricultural and industrial interests and that are working in the public's behalf to reduce pollution by pesticides and to minimize their harmful effects on fish and wildlife.

By 1969, 48 states regulated the marketing of pesticides within their own borders through labeling or tolerance laws, or both, patterned after the federal acts. In addition, 37 states regulate the use and commercial application of pesticides, which includes the licensing of commercial applicators. Unfortunately, many states use pesticide laws as a means of providing additional revenue and exercise little regulatory authority. The need for state legislation and enforcement, in addition to the federal, is based on two facts: (1) Federal legislation applies only in interstate commerce, and there are many instances where sale either of the pesticide or of the agricultural commodity is transacted completely within a single state; and (2) neither of the two federal laws (FIFRA and Miller) provides for control of the actual use of a given chemical.

State legislation frequently deals specifically with the use of toxicants for control of birds, mammals, or fish. In 1967, for example, 12 states prohibited completely the use of poisons for eliminating such birds as starlings, feral pigeons, or house sparrows, which frequently become a nuisance. The use of rotenone or other toxicants to control or eliminate unwanted fish is usually regulated by the state fish and game laws. The use of these materials ordinarily requires a permit from the state.

As indicated above, numerous legislative regulations exist at both state and federal levels designed to control residues and promote safe use of pesticides. These impose direct legal controls on the manufacturer and shipper to insure proper labeling and acceptable standards of quality. The chief control over the user is the regulations on residue tolerances that must be met if the commodity is to be safe from condemnation. For the commercial farmer this is a strong incentive for compliance, but there are obviously many uses that do not fall within these regulations.

How effective have state and federal regulations been in protecting the public? The evidence suggests that existing regulations are effective in avoiding excessive residues in food, if established tolerances are in fact realistic. The so-called Market Basket Surveys lend support to this view (Duggan *et al.*, 1967; Martin and Duggan, 1967), and the recent report of the Committee on Persistent Pesticides (National Research Council, 1969b) reaffirms this presumption.

In the matter of direct human poisoning the record indicates that the number of poisonings by pesticides is reasonably low compared with poisonings by common drugs, household chemicals, and similar substances. The National Clearing House of Poison Control Centers, reporting on 83,704 poisoning cases among all ages, stated that in 1967, 51.5 percent of accidental ingestions involved medicines; cleaning and polishing agents ranked second with 14.3 percent; cosmetics third with 6.1 percent; and pesticides fourth with 6.0 percent (U.S. Department of Health, Education, and Welfare, Public Health Service, 1968).

In the third area of concern, environmental pollution, the regulatory framework provides inadequate safeguards. There are a number of reasons for this. Early concern over pesticide use centered chiefly on matters of human health, and experience in regulatory control for environmental quality is therefore limited. Responsibility could be rather easily established with respect to the manufacturer, shipper, and user in the case of food products. For the user not concerned with residue tolerances there is little or no control. While label directions can specify the timing, concentration, and number of applications, compliance is essentially voluntary. Into this gap in the regulations fall numerous uses such as municipal and public health programs and treatment of turf, soil, and ornamentals.

Another void in the regulations is the virtual exemption of the homeowner, who is free to purchase numerous pesticides in countless formulations and to use them as he likes. The cabinet at a summer cottage attests to industry's innovativeness and the buyer's eagerness for a vast array of pesticides for pushbutton use.

The welfare of wildlife is presumably represented in the pesticide regulations issued by the Department of the Interior; however, that agency's judgments must be made without full knowledge of the errors and abuses that may result from the human factor. And fully adequate information on the quantity of pesticides involved in various uses and the movement of a pesticide in the ecosystem is not available. Of increasing concern is the chance of accidents in transporting pesticides that could lead to poisoning of humans or massive pollution of an area. These possibilities are increased when pesticides are employed in area treatments in conjunction with military operations.

The striking feature of our dilemma is that the persistent pesticides, which are so widely distributed and are in some cases adversely affecting wildlife, were acquired chiefly through practices that conformed to existing regulations. This fact alone speaks to the inadequacy of existing regulations. As this situation has become clear, public interest has focused on more stringent legislation designed to halt the accumulation of pesticides known to be serious environmental contaminants.

A number of bills have been introduced or suggested to ban DDT and other persistent chlorinated hydrocarbons. Restrictive regulations are in effect in several states and action at the municipal level is increasing.

There are, of course, arguments for and against a total ban on persistent pesticides. General prohibition denies the public the benefits of uses that do not seriously contribute to environmental contamination. Such action substitutes legislative fiat for the exercise of judgment, and reduces the diversity of pesticides available to meet varied needs. Because pesticides are mobile, local prohibition may create a sense of false security unless it is applied so generally as to have an effect on area pollution.

A point in favor of legislative bans is that while many voluntary measures could have been adopted to reduce pollution, progress by this route has been disappointing. A number of factors—economics, market standards, and provincial environmental concepts—operate against concerted action on a voluntary basis. A system of licensing or issuing of permits has been employed with reasonable success in the case of commercial pest-control operators, but issuing permits involves costly overhead and is of questionable effectiveness for control of the diverse uses of pesticides.

The ultimate solution to the problem of pesticides and, indeed, of environmental quality in all its aspects will require both regulatory and educational programs. At best, regulations can be effective only as they reflect the understanding of the public at large. The greatest factor in insuring a viable environment will be an informed public.

PRODUCTION AND USE OF PESTICIDES

The total worldwide production of pesticides is not accurately known, a fact that complicates assessments of the inputs of pesticides in the ecosystem. General trends in pesticide production and use are, however, available. The reports on production and use published annually by the U.S. Department of Agriculture are particularly useful. Based on information from this source (Agricultural Stabilization and Conservation Service, USDA, 1968) it is estimated that in 1967 the United States produced from 50 to 75 percent of the total worldwide supply of pesticides. It is expected that this proportion will decrease as other countries improve their capacity to produce these chemicals. In both domestic and foreign use, total quantities showed an overall increase of 37 percent during the 5-year period 1963-1967. In the United States, use of herbicides continued to increase more rapidly than did the use of either fungicides or insecticides. This trend did not apply overseas, where insecticides and fungicides are expected to dominate, reflecting the close relationship of herbicides to advances in mechanization of agriculture.

Total production of chlorinated hydrocarbons in the United States for domestic use and export increased by about one third in the ten-year period ending June 30, 1966, but the 225 million pounds produced in 1967 represents a decline over the levels of the preceding five years. The reduction is greater for DDT than for the related compounds of the "aldrin-toxaphene group." Production of DDT reached a peak of 185 million pounds in 1962-63 and declined by 40 percent by 1966-67. Thus, in terms of total production of persistent insecticides, there was no dramatic change between 1957 and 1967.

Insecticide exports of 1967 comprised 59 percent of the total value of pesticide exports; DDT accounted for 8 percent of the total and related chlorinated hydrocarbons added another 14 percent.

There are certain striking features in domestic and foreign patterns of pesticide use. Data compiled for 1964 indicate that 42 percent of the total production of pesticides was used in agriculture in the United States, the remainder going for export and domestic nonagricultural purposes. Farmers applied two thirds of the total quantity of all insecticides used on farms that year to three crops—cotton, corn, and apples. The cotton market accounted for more than half of this total—70 percent of the DDT, 86 percent of the endrin, and 69 percent of the toxaphene. It is recognized, of course, that there are other agricultural pollutants (Secretary of Agriculture and the Director of the Office of Science and Technology, 1969).

While similar comparisons cannot be made for foreign insecticide use, it is known that over half of the DDT exported is used for control of the mosquito vector of malaria. In both foreign and domestic use patterns, a few insects account for a high proportion of insecticide application; alternative methods of control of these pests could result in marked reductions in insecticide consumption.

Another major domestic use of insecticides is for control programs conducted by the Plant Pest Control Division, U.S. Department of Agriculture, in cooperation with the various states. Municipal programs of pest control and the operations of resort owners, homeowners, etc., must also be considered as sources of pesticide pollution.

The significance of these points in terms of environmental pollution are:

1. Systems of reporting on pesticide production and use are not adequate for accurate determinations of total production and specific uses, and for identification of site of employment.

2. There has been no dramatic decrease in the production of persistent chlorinated hydrocarbon insecticides.

3. Total production of synthetic organic pesticides has increased consistently since their introduction, and this pattern is expected to continue.

OUTLOOK FOR IMPROVED PEST-CONTROL PRACTICES

The accumulation of pesticides in the environment could be reduced by: (1) adopting improved methods of pesticide use, (2) adopting alternative methods of control, and (3) using pesticides that are less troublesome as pollutants. The series of six volumes on principles of plant and animal pest control published by the National Academy of Sciences (National Research Council, 1968a, 1968b, 1968c, 1968d, 1969a, 1970) provides useful background information on these alternatives. Other pertinent summaries are available (National Academy of Sciences-National Research Council, 1966, p. 39-218; and President's Science Advisory Committee, 1965, p. 230-291).

It is obvious that much progress can be made in methods and application, in formulations, and in timing of treatments. Likewise, biodegradable pesticides can often be substituted for persistent ones. There is also great promise for control methods that do not require chemicals. In practice, however, these possibilities have thus far had but limited impact on the problem of pesticide pollution, and the outlook for marked change within the existing economic and regulatory framework is limited.

Chemical control has continued as the first line of defense against pest outbreaks because it can be employed as needed and the results are immediate. These advantages weigh heavily whenever other possibilities are considered as alternatives. There has been no great tendency to shift to biodegradable pesticides except where there are advantages other than those pertaining to environmental quality. The development of resistance to certain pesticides has, in some cases, been responsible for some instances of changing to less persistent pesticides. Persistence is, in many cases, a prerequisite to effectiveness, and industry has for many years sought broad-spectrum, persistent pesticides because of their more general use and sales appeal. This is a natural response on the part of industry, considering the several million dollar investment required to develop and market a new pesticide. As indicated earlier, economics is a major factor in the selection of a pesticide and no appreciable change can be expected as long as "raw" economics is the major factor in decision-making by the individual who is not in a position to place a price tag on environmental quality.

In addition, the side-effects of shifting to pesticides believed to involve less hazard to the environment cannot be predicted with accuracy. It is, therefore, essential that vigilance be maintained as changes are made in materials and practices.

While the lists of alternative methods of pest control are impressive and promising, research on their refinement is a time-consuming effort that cannot be programmed with certainty, and their effective employment requires precise supporting information if sound judgments are to be made.

PESTICIDES AS POLLUTANTS

While not all factors in the benefit-risk equation of pesticide use will be known to our satisfaction, a few facts are highly pertinent. We should have rather complete knowledge of the quantities of pesticides produced, where they are applied, and for what purpose. In addition, we need to know the chemical characteristics of these compounds as regards toxicity, stability, and solubility. Information is also needed on mobility in the ecosystem and on levels in living organisms and components of the biosphere.

Toxicity

In seeking chemicals useful as pesticides, the search is for those that interfere with an essential link in the biochemical chain of events. It is therefore not surprising that chemicals selected to kill pests also affect other species. This follows because, in the evolution of organisms, successful biochemical processes have been passed on to higher forms with the result that there is far less diversity in physiological machinery than in morphology among the countless species of living things. This is well illustrated by the similarity in biochemical pathways in yeast and man whereby glucose is converted to pyruvic acid in eight chemical steps; the same steps occur in a primitive unicellular plant and in a highly developed mammal.

Despite these similarities there is the apparent contradiction that differences in susceptibility to a given chemical occur even among closely related species, and data from one species cannot be extrapolated with certainty to another. The basis for such differential susceptibility may lie in differences in entry, transport, metabolism, excretion, or action at an active site.

Of the various classes of pesticides currently in general use, insecticides pose a greater hazard to wildlife than do fungicides and herbicides, since the physiological processes of insects have more in common with those of wildlife than do those of plants and fungi. In addition, the chlorinated hydrocarbons, the first family of insecticides, are more stable than are most fungicides and herbicides.

Our concern at this point is chiefly over DDT and its relatives, which are already widely distributed in the ecosystem. This group is toxic to a broad spectrum of living organisms through their action as nerve poisons, although the precise manner in which they exert toxicity is not known.

While focusing chiefly on insecticides of the chlorinated hydrocarbon class, because they represent our major concern at this time, we should recognize that substitute pesticides will likely involve some adverse side-effects. The chief replacements for chlorinated hydrocarbons are presently organophosphorus and carbamate compounds and, although these are less stable, they are, in general, also toxic to a broad spectrum of organisms.

Chemical Stability

The range in chemical stability of pesticides includes those that are bio-degradable within a few hours following application and those having a half-life of days or years. The chlorinated hydrocarbons fall in the class of very stable compounds. Unfortunately, existing knowledge of degradation in soil, water, plants, and animals has many voids. Some persistent pesticides are decomposed photochemically, whereas others are subject to biological degradation. The sequence of degradation and the identity and biological activity of the products formed must be known in order to make meaningful assessments of toxicity and duration of residency.

The ideal would be to develop compounds that are relatively stable in soil and water and selectively biodegradable in plants and animals. Such compounds are not beyond the realm of chemical possibility.

Solubility

The solubility properties of a pesticide greatly influence its potential activity as a pollutant. Those that are water soluble are subject to dilution within living organisms and within the ecosystem as well as to chemical reaction with water. The chlorinated hydrocarbons are insoluble in water and soluble in lipids. Since lipids occur in all living organisms, they act as built-in solvents for chlorinated hydrocarbons, thus imparting to this class of pesticides an affinity for living organisms.

Mobility

Pesticides such as DDT have become widely distributed throughout the biosphere. They have been found beyond points of application in run-off water (Weaver et al., 1965), in air and rainwater (Abbott et al., 1965), and in animals from diverse parts of the world. In addition to pesticides applied as dusts and sprays in the air, additional amounts enter the air on soil particles and by co-distillation in the evaporation of water. Their high affinity for colloidal surfaces makes them susceptible to transport on soil particles during soil erosion.

Once circulating in the biosphere they can travel great distances and be deposited by physical forces that tend to concentrate them in strata in the biosphere. Such mobility accounts for the general distribution of DDT in organisms that have not been directly exposed to the pesticide. This mobility phenomenon as it has been disclosed through continued use was not generally anticipated and has, therefore, not been taken into full account in establishing policy on the use of persistent pesticides.

Biological Magnification

Another factor that bears an important relationship to the effect of pesticides on wildlife is biological magnification. This is the process whereby pesticides accumulated in one organism are passed on through the food chain to other organisms, thus leading to higher concentrations at each level in the food chain. Each organism eats many organisms from the lower step in the food chain. A large fish, for instance, feeds on many smaller fish, which in turn feed on still smaller fish, the smallest feeding on plankton, which may acquire the initial concentration of a pesticide introduced into the environment.

A classic example of biological magnification is one that occurred at Clear Lake, California, after the lake was treated with DDD to control gnats in 1957 (Hunt and Bischoff, 1960). The level of DDD in the lake was calculated to be 0.02 ppm. Residue levels of DDD in samples taken 13 months later were 10 ppm in plankton, 903 ppm in fat of plankton-eating fish, 2,690 ppm in fat of carnivorous fish, and 2,134 ppm in fat of fish-eating birds. This represents a 100,000-fold increase in fish-eating birds over levels in lake water after treatment.

Ecosystems are characterized by countless intricate food chains and the end result of interference in food chain relationships cannot be predicted. The end result of practices that might interfere with some basic organism in the food chain such as algae in marine food chains is, therefore, viewed with concern.

Another form of biological magnification involves transfer of a pesticide directly from the environment rather than indirectly through the food chain. Fish, for instance, may acquire DDT from water in contact with the gills (Holden, 1962).

MONITORING PESTICIDES IN THE ENVIRONMENT

The need to monitor residues in the environment was stressed by the President's Science Advisory Committee (1963). The committee specifically recommended that current pesticide levels and their trends in man and his environment be determined and that a continuing network be established to monitor residue levels in air, water, soil, man, and wildlife. In response to this recommendation the interagency Federal Committee on Pest Control provided guidelines for establishing the National Pesticide Monitoring Program (NPMP). The findings of NPMP, as well as the monitoring findings of other agencies, are reported in the *Pesticides Monitoring Journal* which began publication in June 1967 under sponsorship of the Federal Committee on Pest Control. This monitoring program is described in the first issue of the journal (Federal Committee on Pest Control, 1967).

Phases of the NPMP designed to measure pesticides in humans follow the levels in selected communities. Pesticides in foods are considered in terms of average levels in a standard diet as well as in selected components of basic diets. These findings provide baselines for determining changes and also for calculating average values.

Soil monitoring is based on sampling of agricultural, range, and forest soils. Monitoring of water is based on sampling of rivers at selected sites. Oysters and clams, freshwater fish, waterfowl, and starlings have been selected as representative substrates for monitoring residues in wildlife. The importance of comprehensive air monitoring is obvious, particularly in view of the growing recognition of air as a transport medium in the movement of pesticides.

It is perhaps too early to judge the adequacy of the monitoring program, but it would appear in view of their mobility that persistent pesticides should be monitored on a global scale, with emphasis on the pattern of pesticide "fallout" in the biosphere.

PESTICIDES IN WILDLIFE AND THEIR SIGNIFICANCE

A voluminous literature establishes the fact that persistent insecticides are widely distributed in the biosphere and occur in a wide variety of animals throughout the world. A review of some pertinent evidence on this topic has been provided by Stickel (1968).

The mere presence of a pesticide in a living organism does not mean, *per se*, that it has a harmful effect. In fact, the tolerances established for DDT in the human diet are based on the assumption that, at these levels, DDT will accumulate in the fat, but at levels that are not harmful to human health.

Unfortunately, diagnosing a cause of mortality as it relates to residue content in the animal is fraught with difficulty. Much research has been directed to this question in insect toxicity studies and many anomalies remain. Such studies are complicated by the fact that the mode of action of chlorinated hydrocarbons is not precisely known. Even in the case of organophosphate insecticides, whose mode of action is known to be generally through the inhibition of cholinesterase of the nervous system, the relationships between dosage levels, inhibition rates, and toxicity are not readily established experimentally; these relationships would be even more difficult to establish in animals taken in their natural habitats. Despite these considerations, the literature includes many reports of residue content of tissues or whole bodies of animals on the assumption that such evidence is diagnostic of pesticide poisoning. Some meaningful correlations have apparently been established for the relationship between DDT residue levels in the brain and DDT poisoning that do apply to a wide range of species (Bernard, 1963; Dale *et al.*, 1962; Stickel *et al.*, 1966). Obviously, it will not be possible to regulate pesticides effectively unless the significance of pesticide levels in living organisms is better understood.

Levels of pesticide residues in animals are influenced by many variables, such as contamination of the food supply and the abilities of different species to absorb, metabolize, and excrete the toxicant. In birds, for instance, raptorial and fish-eating species in general have higher residue levels than do plant-feeding and omnivorous species because of magnification through the food chain.

The effects of pesticides on living organisms may be acute or chronic. Acute effects generally become evident soon after treatment, and are readily apparent by symptoms of abnormal behavior or death. Chronic effects, on the other hand, are in many cases not readily detected and may manifest themselves by death or in subtle ways over an extended time span. Chronic poisoning is of major concern as it might relate to mortality or physiological disturbance resulting in reproductive impairment or behavioral change. Mortality of wildlife due to pesticide poisoning has been reported for a number of species and under varied circumstances (e.g., Robbins *et al.*, 1951; DeWitt, 1956; Rudd and Genelly, 1956; Wallace, 1959, 1962; Hunt, 1960; Hickey, 1961; Roelofs and Shick, 1962; Rosene, 1965; Ames, 1966; Keith, 1966).

More recently, concern has centered on less obvious effects of pesticide residues, such as reproductive failure. Estrogenic activity of DDT in mammals and birds has been demonstrated by Bitman *et al.* (1968). In both fish and birds, cases of reproductive failure have been established. Burdick *et al.* (1964) showed that the reduced hatch of eggs of lake trout in Lake George, New York, was due to DDT. Similar cases have been reported elsewhere. Apparently, in the maturation of eggs, the female draws on fat reserves containing DDT, which is transferred to lipids in the egg and acts on the embryo as it metabolizes this source of food in the yolk sac.

The evidence on impaired reproduction in birds by chlorinated hydrocarbon residues has been reviewed by Wurster (1968a). DDT apparently stimulates the liver to produce enzymes that act on steroids; these in turn control metabolism of calcium and its deposition in eggshells. Decrease in eggshell weight, resulting in breakage and reproductive failure, has been cited in the United States and Great Britain (Ratcliffe, 1967; Hickey and Anderson, 1968). Laboratory studies have confirmed that DDT may cause reproductive decline through reduction in eggshell thickness, resulting in mechanical breakage, and through behavioral changes, resulting in abandonment of eggs. Retardation in sexual maturity has also been reported (Jefferies, 1967).

Behavioral responses that could have important survival implications have been reported for New Brunswick salmon from DDT-sprayed rivers. Very low doses resulted in increased sensitivity to low temperatures, causing a shift in temperature selection (Ogilvie and Anderson, 1965). Behavioral changes have also been cited in gulls on Lake Michigan where high DDT levels were associated with aggressive behavior and high egg breakage (Ludwig and Tomoff, 1966). In a study of cowbirds that were fed DDT, mortality was reported following the stress of disturbance (Stickel, 1965).

While birds and fish are of general interest and are subject to observation and study with relative ease, some other important components of the biota are less conspicuous, and possible ill effects may escape detection. For instance, marine algae, which are important components of marine food chains and which play a major role in total photosynthetic activity, show reduced photosynthesis at low concentrations of DDT under laboratory conditions (Wurster, 1968b). It has also been shown that microorganisms accumulate DDT and dieldrin from soils and culture media (Chacko and Lockwood, 1967). Changes in such essential components of the ecosystem could have profound biological implications. Thus, the evidence on wildlife is important not only as it relates to wildlife directly, but to wildlife as living monitors of the environment that they share with man.

It is clear from the evidence cited that:

1. Pesticide residues occur very generally in wildlife—in some cases at high levels.
2. Pesticide residues may in some species cause death, or physiological disturbances that result in reduced reproductive potential and behavioral changes.

3. The numbers of some species of wildlife are declining and the evidence strongly implicates pesticides as a causative factor.

The conclusion seems inescapable that pesticides, as currently employed, constitute a threat to wildlife, and that future practices for their use should be formulated with this in mind.

IMPLICATIONS FOR EDUCATION AND RESEARCH

The evidence cited above establishes a number of points as the framework for consideration in the future employment of pesticides.

1. During two decades of use, some adverse side-effects of persistent pesticides on wildlife have become evident.
2. In terms of biological adjustments in the global ecosystem, two decades has been insufficient to assess the ultimate effect of these pesticides.
3. No decrease is anticipated in worldwide production and use of pesticides.
4. Persistent pesticides continue to play an important role in providing for man's food, fiber, health, and comfort.
5. The replacement of persistent pesticides and adoption of alternative methods of control are desirable but have proceeded slowly for lack of economic and other incentives and because so much time is needed for research on other methods.
6. While pesticide regulations in the United States are believed to provide adequate safeguards for human health, they are inadequate for controlling pesticide levels in the environment.
7. Knowledge of the movement of pesticides in the environment, their degradation, and fate is inadequate.
8. Contamination of the biosphere with pesticides is a worldwide problem, but no international body is charged with responsibility for environmental quality.

These conclusions have strong implications for programs in education and research. While these are somber conclusions, there is encouragement in the national awakening to abuses of the environment and the need for constructive programs to restore its quality. Central to this point are the questions, "What level of environmental quality does society want?" and "What level is it prepared to pay for?"

It seems reasonable to proceed from the premise that knowledge of the relationship of man to his environment is an essential component of an educational program at both the secondary and college levels. It is entirely practical to make such training an integral part of the high school curriculum and to provide it for college students in the humanities as well as those in the sciences.

Beyond this general need is the special need to provide training for a cadre of scientists and technicians who can conduct research on the myriad problems associated with environmental pollution. Challenging opportunities are available for young people interested in careers in improving environmental quality (President's Science Advisory Committee, 1965: 39-56).

It is particularly important that narrow specialization be avoided in training scientists. In retrospect, the failure to consider pest control in terms of ecological principles accounts for some failures in the tactics employed in pest control. It is equally clear that interdisciplinary effort will be required to solve problems of environmental quality and that receptiveness to such team effort is greatly influenced by the breadth of training provided.

In addition to more adequate formal education in high schools and colleges, there is the need for education of the general public on environmental quality in all its aspects. The pesticide problem is typical of the kind of issue that will continue to arise in a technological society. In the end, society must decide, but our system of informing the public is rather ineffective in providing a useful fund of knowledge on which the concerned individual can draw. Furthermore, the existing options are not made clear and the result is a polarization of opinion "for" or "against," with little regard for the consequences of either course. In the present debate on regulating the use of persistent pesticides, no estimates have been provided on the cost of food produced without benefit of these materials.

In considering the problem of public understanding of the impact of science and technology, an intriguing proposal has been offered by Morison (1969):

As for less formal methods for presenting science to adults, we should devise some analogy that would do for the general public what agricultural extension courses have done for the farmer and his wife. The average successful farmer, although he is far from being a pure scientist, has an appreciation for the way science works. Certainly he understands it well enough to use it in his own business and to support agricultural colleges and the great state universities that grew out of them.

The important point is that in terms of an informed public, we can do far better than we have done and an immediate objective should be that of developing an informed and responsible public to which alternatives may be directed.

We are only beginning to understand the delicate interrelationships among living creatures in biological communities. Similarly, there are great voids in our knowledge of cellular functions on which the survival of the individual organism depends. When these matters are considered, it should be recognized that most pesticides were developed empirically rather than by designing a molecule that would induce toxicity in a predictable manner. Thus, the mode of action of the most intensely studied insecticide, DDT, is still unknown—a striking example of the kind of bottlenecks that exist.

It is obvious that a tremendous research effort is needed at the basic and applied levels, that research is costly, that achievement of research goals cannot be predicted with accuracy, and that competition for able young minds is always keen.

It is reassuring, however, to note the progress that can be made in science and technology, once clear national goals are established. The success of Apollo 11 in placing men on the moon is a dramatic case in point. The current public interest in pesticide pollution offers promise for significant advances in our knowledge through research.

REFERENCES

Abbott, D. C., R. B. Harrison, J. O'G. Tatton, and J. Thomson. 1965. Organochlorine pesticides in the atmospheric environment. Nature 208:1317-1318.

Agricultural Stabilization and Conservation Service. 1968. The pesticide review. U.S. Department of Agriculture, Washington, D.C. 54 p.

Ames, P. L. 1966. DDT residues in the eggs of the osprey in the north-eastern United States and their relation to nesting success. J. Appl. Ecol. 3(Suppl.): 87-97.

Bernard, R. F. 1963. Studies on the effects of DDT on birds. Publ. Mus. Mich. St. Univ. 2(3):155-192.

Bitman, J., H. C. Cecil, S. J. Harris, and G. F. Fries. 1968. Estrogenic activity of o,p'-DDT in the mammalian uterus and avian oviduct. Science 162(3851):371-372.

Burdick, G. E., E. J. Harris, H. J. Dean, T. M. Walker, J. Skea, and D. Colby. 1964. The accumulation of DDT in lake trout and the effect on reproduction. Trans. Amer. Fish. Soc. 93(2):127-136.

Carson, R. 1962. Silent spring. Houghton Mifflin Co., Boston. 368 p.

Chacko, C. I., and J. L. Lockwood. 1967. Accumulation of DDT and dieldrin by microorganisms. Can. J. Microbiol. 13:1123-1126.

Dale, W. E., T. B. Gaines, and W. J. Hayes, Jr. 1962. Storage and excretion of DDT in starved rats. Toxicol. Appl. Pharmacol. 4(1):89-106.

DeWitt, J. B. 1956. Chronic toxicity to quail and pheasants of some chlorinated insecticides. Agr. Food Chem. 4(10):863-866.

Duggan, R. E., H. C. Barry, and L. Y. Johnson. 1967. Pesticide residues in total diet samples II. Pestic. Monit. J. 1(2):2-12.

Entomological Society of Philadelphia. 1865. Practical entomologist, Vol. 1-2. Philadelphia.

Federal Committee on Pest Control. 1967. Pestic. Monit. J. 1(1).

Hickey, J. J. 1961. Some effects of insecticides on terrestrial birdlife in the middle west. Wilson Bull. 73(4):398-424.

Hickey, J. J., and D. W. Anderson. 1968. Chlorinated hydrocarbons and eggshell changes in raptorial and fish-eating birds. Science 162:271-273.

Holden, A. V. 1962. A study of the absorption of C^{14} labeled DDT from water by fish. Ann. Appl. Biol. 50:467.

Hunt, B. L. 1960. Songbird breeding populations in DDT-sprayed dutch elm disease communities. J. Wildl. Manage. 24(2):139-146.

Hunt, E. G., and A. I. Bischoff. 1960. Inimical effects on wildlife of periodic DDD applications to Clear Lake. Calif. Fish Game 46(1):91.

Jefferies, D. J. 1967. The delay in ovulation produced by p,p'-DDT and its possible significance in the field. Ibis 109:266-272.

Keith, J. A. 1966. Reproduction in a population of herring gulls (*Larus argentatus*) contaminated by DDT. J. Appl. Ecol. 3(Suppl.):57-70.

Ludwig, J. P., and C. S. Tomoff. 1966. Reproductive success and insecticide residues in Lake Michigan herring gulls. Jack-Pine Warbler 44(2):77-84.

Martin, R. J., and R. E. Duggan. 1967. Pesticide residues in total diet samples III. Pestic. Monit. J. 1(4):11-20.

Morison, R. S. 1969. Science and social attitudes. Science 165:150-156.

National Academy of Sciences-National Research Council. 1966. Scientific aspects of pest control. Publ. 1402. Washington, D.C. 470 p.

National Research Council. 1968a. Plant-disease development and control. Principles of plant and animal pest control, Vol. 1. Publ. 1596. National Academy of Sciences, Washington, D.C. 205 p.

National Research Council. 1968b. Weed control. Principles of plant and animal pest control, Vol. 2. Publ. 1597. National Academy of Sciences, Washington, D.C. 471 p.

National Research Council. 1968c. Control of plant-parasitic nematodes. Principles of plant and animal pest control, Vol. 4. Publ. 1696. National Academy of Sciences, Washington, D.C. 172 p.

National Research Council. 1968d. Effects of pesticides on fruit and vegetable physiology. Principles of plant and animal pest control, Vol. 6. Publ. 1698. National Academy of Sciences, Washington, D.C. 90 p.

National Research Council. 1969a. Insect-pest management and control. Principles of plant and animal pest control, Vol. 3. Publ. 1695. National Academy of Sciences, Washington, D.C. 508 p.

National Research Council. 1969b. Report of Committee on Persistent Pesticides to Administrator, Agricultural Research Service, U.S. Department of Agriculture, Washington, D.C. 34 p.

National Research Council. 1970. Vertebrate pests: problems and control. Principles of plant and animal pest control, Vol. 5. Publ. 1697, National Academy of Sciences, Washington, D.C. 164 p.

Ogilvie, D. M., and J. M. Anderson. 1965. Effect of DDT on temperature selection by young Atlantic salmon, *Salmo salar*. J. Fish. Res. Board Can. 22:503-512.

President's Science Advisory Committee. 1963. The use of pesticides. U.S. Government Printing Office, Washington, D.C. 25 p.

President's Science Advisory Committee. 1965. Restoring the quality of our environment. Report of Environmental Pollution Panel. U.S. Government Printing Office, Washington, D.C. 317 p.

President's Science Advisory Committee. 1967. The world food problem. Panel on World Food Supply. U.S. Government Printing Office, Washington, D.C. p. 138-139.

Ratcliffe, D. A. 1967. Decrease in eggshell weight in certain birds of prey. Nature 215:208-210.

Robbins, C. S., P. F. Springer, and C. G. Webster. 1951. Effects of five-year DDT application on breeding bird population. J. Wildl. Manage. 15(2):213-216.

Roelofs, E. W., and C. Shick. 1962. Spray programs and wildlife. Mich. State Univ. Coop. Ext. Serv. E-375:1-8.

Rosene, W. 1965. Effects of field applications of heptachlor on bobwhite quail and other wild animals. J. Wildl. Manage. 29(3):554-580.

Rudd, R. L., and R. E. Genelly. 1956. Pesticides: their use and toxicity in relation to wildlife. Calif. Fish Game Bull. 7. 209 p.

Secretary of Agriculture and the Director of the Office of Science and Technology. 1969. A report to the President—control of agriculture-related pollution. U.S. Government Printing Office, Washington, D.C.

Stickel, L. F. 1968. Organochlorine pesticides in the environment. Special Scientific Report—Wildlife No. 119. Bureau of Sport Fisheries and Wildlife. U.S. Government Printing Office, Washington, D.C. 32 p.

Stickel, L. F., W. H. Stickel, and R. Christensen. 1966. Residues of DDT in brains and bodies of birds that died on dosage and in survivors. Science 151(3717): 1549-1551.

Stickel, W. H. 1965. Delayed mortality of DDT-dosed cowbirds in relation to disturbance. Effects of pesticides on fish and wildlife. U.S. Fish and Wildlife Service, Circ. 226.

U.S. Department of Health, Education, and Welfare, Public Health Service. 1968. National clearinghouse for poison control centers bulletin. Washington, D.C.

U.S. Senate. 1966. Pesticides and public policy. Report of the Committee on Government Operations. Made by its Subcommittee on Reorganization and International Organization. Senate Report No. 1370. U.S. Government Printing Office, Washington, D.C. 86 p.

Wallace, G. J. 1959. Insecticides and birds. Audubon Mag. 61(7):10-12, 35.

Wallace, G. J. 1962. The seventh spring die-off of robins at East Lansing, Michigan. Jack-Pine Warbler 40(1):26-32.

Weaver, L., C. G. Gunnerson, A. W. Breidenbach, and J. J. Lichtenberg. 1965. Chlorinated hydrocarbon pesticides in major U.S. river basins. Publ. Health Rep. 80:481-493.

Wurster, C. F., Jr. 1968a. Chlorinated hydrocarbon insecticides and avian reproduction: How are they related? *In* First Rochester Conference on Toxicity, Chemical Fallout, Current Research on Persistent Pesticides. University of Rochester, Rochester, New York.

Wurster, C. F., Jr. 1968b. DDT reduces photosynthesis by marine plankton. Science 159(3822):1474-1475.

CHAPTER 7 **Wildlife Damage and Control**

Just as agriculture and land use have changed tremendously in the United States during the past 100 years, so have attitudes toward wildlife. This has been as true of the scientist as of the general public and the agriculturist. The early premise was simple, i.e., animals were either harmful or beneficial, in varying degrees. The government program, begun in the 1880's by the Division of Economic Ornithology and Mammalogy to determine which birds and mammals were harmful and which were beneficial, concentrated for years upon the food habits of birds and mammals in order to establish their economic relationship to man.

These attitudes naturally were reflected in the legislation of that day. State bird protection laws left unprotected or even provided bounty payments for destroying birds considered harmful, such as the hawks and owls that were known to feed upon smaller birds.

Many factors have contributed to the changing attitude toward wildlife, so that no longer can a species be designated simply as friend or foe. Increasing emphasis on ecology and recognition of many of its principles by the public as well as at the congressional level have been important. At the same time there has been an increasingly widespread interest in conservation and a recognition of the value of preserving our natural environment. The Wilderness Act and the Rare and Endangered Species Act reflect the concern of Congress, and President Nixon has established an official council of environmental advisers to the Executive Office.

As public and official attitudes have changed the pressures upon resources have increased and become more complex. These factors combine and result in a number of situations where wildlife and agriculture are in some degree of conflict.

PREDATION AND THE LIVESTOCK INDUSTRY

Predation upon livestock by large carnivores is one of the earliest, most sustained, and most widely recognized types of wildlife damage. As early as the 1600's colonists shot, trapped, and offered bounties for the destruction of wolves and cougar to protect their livestock, so these large predators were eliminated rather early over most of the East. Even in the western states the timber wolf has been exterminated, and the red wolf of the South is considered an endangered species. In several states the cougar and the black bear have now come to be recognized as valued game species, rather than pests. The coyote is the species against which most predator control is now directed. In some situations its depredations upon sheep are unquestioned, but unbiased assessments of the extent of damage are difficult to obtain because many sheepmen tend to attribute most or all of their losses to coyotes. Accurate evaluation of coyote damage is complicated by the animal's carrion-eating habits. It is often difficult to determine whether a fed-upon lamb was dead or moribund from some other causes when the coyote found it. The magnitude of the coyote control program is indicated in the Leopold report (1964), which shows that in the federal and cooperative predator control program nearly 90,000 coyotes were taken in one recent year, out of a total of 190,763 predators of all kinds.

Another species widely accused of predation upon lambs is the golden eagle, especially in Texas and New Mexico. After World War II literally thousands of these raptors were killed, largely by private gunners in aircraft. Federal protection was accorded the golden eagle in 1962, but the law provides that governors of states where ranchers could show evidence of eagle predation upon livestock, preimarily young sheep and goats, can obtain permission from the Secretary of the Interior for the ranchers to shoot and trap the birds (but not to hunt them from airplanes or to employ poisons).

The economic effects of golden eagles are being studies by biologists from several agencies. Most recently the National Audubon Society, the National Wool Growers Association, and the Department of the Interior have sponsored a study by Texas Technological College, on the basis of which the subject of golden eagle regulation is being evaluated by the Department. However, more information is still needed on the economics of the golden eagle, and studies should continue.

WILDLIFE CONFLICTS WITH CROPS

Birds may often cause severe damage to fruit or agricultural crops, and for several reasons the incidence of damage seems to be increasing. The nature of modern agriculture, with its emphasis upon monoculture and highly specialized crops, and the high cost of bringing the crop to the harvesting stage, when bird damage usually occurs, are among the factors involved.

Accurate estimates of the value of fruit or grain destroyed by birds are extremely difficult to obtain. Numerous field surveys have been made; among the most convincing are those involving ducks and small grain in the Canadian Prairie Provinces and California, blackbirds and rice in Arkansas, and blackbirds and corn in Ohio and several other states.

Losses of grain in Canada have become so serious that major efforts have been made to alleviate them. Devices of various kinds to frighten the birds, and spreading grain near the marshes to lure the birds from the unharvested grainfields, are two methods that have been used. Both are cumbersome and expensive, and they are not always effective.

Another program, inspired by the success of crop insurance against losses from hailstorms and similar "acts of God," was initiated by Saskatchewan in 1953 and by Alberta in 1961. Paynter (1966) summarized the experience of the first 13 years of the Crop Depredations Insurance program in Saskatchewan, showing that 4,395 farmers had been insured for liabilities totaling $9,557,828. They paid insurance premiums of 2 percent (over $180,000), and claims that totaled more than $745,000 were paid. Claim payments beyond those covered by the 2-percent premiums are covered by a $1 surcharge on each hunting license sold in the province.

The insurance plan alone, however, cannot be considered completely successful in Canada. Many farmers feel they should not be required to pay any premium to defend their interests against legally protected birds, and such a high proportion of those insured are being paid claims for damage that the fund appears likely to be inadequate.

Although waterfowl depredations upon grain in the Dakotas, Minnesota, and Nebraska have been estimated at hundreds of thousands of dollars in some years, the Canadian insurance plan, though considered, has not actually been tried in the United States.

Jahn (1969), in an excellent review of crop depredations by migratory birds, has pointed out that in some counties of the United States the all-risk crop insurance available through the Federal Crop Insurance Corporation of the U.S. Department of Agriculture includes losses to bird depredations among the items eligible for payment. The arrangement is different from that in Canada, since the policy guarantees a specified number of bushels per acre and quality of crop harvested. The number of farmers taking out the all-risk crop insurance has increased since 1937, when it was first made available, so that in 1968 nearly a third of a million farmers insured almost 20 million acres of crops. However, the losses due to wildlife depredations are so minor compared to those from drought, excessive rainfall, hail, insects, and similar causes, that they are included only among the "other causes" that comprise 5 percent of the total.

Farmes (1969) reports that an interagency team, after evaluating waterfowl crop depredations in Minnesota, concluded that with appropriate changes the federal crop insurance program might be more effective in handling losses caused by waterfowl, and that the Federal Crop Insurance Corporation has the staff and experience to deal with a wildlife insurance program.

In California, damage to rice and other small grains by waterfowl has been reduced through a combination of several management procedures. Plantings of waterfowl foods on areas purchased especially for this purpose attract ducks from nearby commercial crops. Improvements in rice-farming practices have also been aided by creating more continuous stands and reducing openings, which are expecially attractive to ducks. Finally, state and federal officials have developed with farmers a "self-help" crop protection program that includes bird harassment and the use of fright devices.

Depredations by several kinds of blackbirds upon rice, especially in Arkansas (Neff and Meanley, 1957), and upon corn in several states in the eastern half of the country are still exceedingly serious and, despite a long-term research program, the problems remain unsolved. Only a few examples of the many other situations in which birds or mammals cause damage to fruit or agricultural crops can be included here.

Lesser sandhill cranes, strictly protected since the Migratory Bird Treaty Act of 1918, have been reported in several western states to cause damage to sorghum, alfalfa, winter wheat, and peanuts. Experimental hunting seasons, in strictly limited areas in New Mexico and

Texas, were initiated in 1961, and complaints of damage have decreased. This suggests that the institution of hunting seasons has provided successful control.

In Maine, blueberries are a multimillion-dollar crop on 80,000 acres, and depredations on the ripening fruit by gulls are estimated by specialists at the University of Maine at 2 percent of the crop annually. The total damage appears small, but individual growers may lose the greater part of their crop in a single day.

In California several specialized crops are damaged by legally protected birds of many kinds. Horned larks destroy lettuce; linnets (local name in California for house finch) eat the buds of apricot and almond trees; band-tailed pigeons damage several orchard and truck crops; and coots feed upon hay and truck garden produce.

The problems of bird conflicts with crops are so numerous, complex, and varied that no one solution can be expected. Some effective control measures have been developed, but many more are needed, adaptable to the peculiarities of the problem faced. Nonlethal methods are particularly appropriate, for many of the birds that cause trouble in one situation are valued in others. Where lethal methods are deemed necessary, it is important that they be specific, or selective, so that they will not needlessly destroy nontarget species or have a long-lasting effect upon the environment as do so many of the pesticides now commonly employed.

WILDLIFE PROBLEMS INVOLVING THE FOREST AND RANGE

Damage to the forest by wildlife is widely scattered and usually attracts little attention. Perhaps the commonest effect is upon tree reproduction, because a large number of birds and mammals feed upon tree seeds (Smith and Aldous, 1947). Both artificially seeded and natural forest reproduction have been severely damaged by a variety of small mammals, particularly mice, chipmunks, and squirrels. Areas cleared through logging or fire are particularly vulnerable to wildlife damage during the stage of reseeding and growth of seedlings and saplings, because many species of wildlife are attracted into the openings (Kverno, 1964).

Two other types of damage widespread in the forest are clipping and browsing of timber species by big game, rabbits and hares, and others; and the bark and root damage caused by rodents, such as pocket gophers, mice, and porcupines.

Deer, elk, and other ungulates have frequently become so numerous that their feeding has caused severe damage to forests, especially to seedlings and saplings. In most areas, however, population control is now being achieved through regulated hunting and this type of damage is far less widespread than in the past.

Studies of the effect of rabbit and rodent activity on range forage have shown that rabbits eat mostly leaf and stem material as do meadow voles (*Microtus*), pocket gophers (*Thomomys, Geomys*), and some species of ground squirrels (*Citellus*); most other rodents eat such foods as seeds and insects and may have a beneficial effect on rangelands.

In north-central Colorado studies have shown that the plant genera *Vicia, Lathyrus,* and *Agoseris* are important foods for meadow voles; these plants also are consumed by cattle. Pocket gophers eat some of the same plants as do cattle, and show a high preference for certain grasses (e.g., *Stipa comata*) at the very season when cattle show similar preference. In a variety of areas pocket gophers, ground squirrels, and jack rabbits all compete to some degree with cattle for food.

It is clear that small mammals consume range forage plants, but to what extent? In some annual grassland areas in the Central Valley of California, jack rabbits commonly reach a population level of one rabbit for every two acres. At this level rabbits would eat approximately 115 pounds of air-dry herbage per acre per year. In the same areas pocket gophers occur regularly at population densities of approximately 10 per acre; at this level they would eat about 220 pounds of air-dry herbage per acre per year. The aggregate consumption of these small mammals—about 330 pounds per acre per year—is about a third of the total allowable annual forage utilization.

In the subalpine parklands of the Rocky Mountains the two small mammals of greatest importance as consumers of vegetation are the northern pocket gopher (*Thomomys talpoides*) and the montane vole (*Microtus montanus*). In studies made in the summer of 1965 in Colorado, these rodents occurred at population levels of about 20 and 8 animals per acre, respectively. In such numbers, they would consume about 460 pounds of air-dry herbage per acre per year, or approximately one quarter of the yearly herbage production.

Not all of the vegetation eaten by these rodents is suitable for livestock forage and it is likely that their most important effect is not from consumption of herbage, but from their burrowing, mound building, and food storage activities. Jameson (1958) has estimated that the California vole destroys as much vegetation through these activities as in its food consumption. Fitch and Bentley (1949), in their work on

the rodents of a California annual grassland, showed that they ate but
10 percent of the vegetation they destroyed. In a 1966 study of subalpine rangeland in north-central Colorado, about 22 percent of the
ground was found to be covered with soil brought to the surface during winter or spring by pocket gophers, and only a few plants were able
to establish themselves on the fresh workings.

The total ecological impact of rodents on rangelands is clearly the
result of a variety of factors. Both native and domestic animals affect
vegetation; it is of primary importance to determine precisely what
these effects are and how they are brought about. A final and more
difficult step is to develop management practices that maintain a vegetational complex such that there will be minimum rodent and rabbit
damage and maximum forage for livestock and game animals.

NONAGRICULTURAL WILDLIFE PROBLEMS

Wild birds and mammals act as carriers or reservoirs for certain diseases
of man and domestic animals. A few of these, such as rabies, are of
great economic importance, but the majority are local or temporary
and do not usually result in control demands of any magnitude.

In certain urban and industrial situations, however, birds have become serious pests and have created unusually difficult control problems. Best known are starling and pigeon roosts on buildings or the
roosting in city shade trees of tremendous aggregations of starlings and
other birds. A variety of control methods are partially successful, but
most are awkward, expensive, and ineffective.

Perhaps the most spectacular conflict between birds and man involves
the bird-airplane problem, which was brought dramatically to public
attention in 1960 when a jet plane crashed at Logan International Airport, Boston, killing a number of persons. In this instance a flock of
starlings was sucked into the jet engines.

In Canada one commercial airline (Air Canada) has maintained
records of strikes with birds and costs of repairing the damage. Strike
rates are highest during the spring and fall bird migrations, and the
greatest annual damage was $350,000, sustained in 1961. Since then
the damage and costs have declined as a result of habitat modification
and other measures to disperse birds from the vicinity of the airports.

In the United States, records appear to be less accurate, but at 28 of
the nation's busiest commercial airports from 1962 through 1966, approximately 1,000 bird strikes were recorded. In 1965 the U.S. Air

Force recorded 839 strikes, necessitating 75 engine replacements at a cost of four to five million dollars (Seubert and Solman, 1968; U.S. Air Force, 1966).

More accurate data must be obtained as a basis for remedial action, but the one simple fact that has come through most clearly is that habitat conditions particularly attractive to birds cannot be tolerated in the immediate vicinity of jet airports.

POSITIVE VALUES OF PREDATORS AND RODENTS

Predators and rodents have positive values as well as the negative ones discussed above. This, in fact, was the first tenet of the Leopold report (Discussed later in this chapter) and it underscores the expressed policy of the Department of the Interior that control measures when instituted must be specific and selective and must avoid destroying the innocent individuals with the guilty.

The American public, as it has become more affluent with more leisure time for recreation, has developed a stronger and more sophisticated interest in nature and the out-of-doors. This interest is expressed in many ways. While the number of hunters and fishermen continues to grow, the number of people interested in the "nonconsumptive" uses of wildlife has shown a far greater increase. National parks and other nature reserves are used far more than ever; and books, binoculars, and cameras sell as never before to the growing number of bird-watchers and other amateur naturalists.

Not many decades ago, few would have challenged the statement that "the only good coyote is a dead coyote," but today many thrill to hear or see a coyote. It is a common sight in some of the national parks to see traffic jams where motorists have stopped to enjoy the sight of a coyote hunting. The timber wolf population in Algonquin Provincial Park, only 200 miles from Canada's largest city, is regarded by many as the park's proudest possession, and hundreds have gathered in an evening along the road through the park to hear the wolves respond to recorded howling.

While the value is sometimes intangible and difficult to translate into monetary terms, it is clear that the American public has come to place a high premium on wildlife in general, and particularly upon predatory species that only recently were almost universally condemned as pests and that, in certain situations, must still be controlled to prevent damage. In this context the growing interest in the predators for sport has special significance, especially if their use in sport can aid in necessary control.

POTENTIAL OF LARGE PREDATORS FOR SPORT HUNTING

The value of large predators for sport has received little attention in the United States, though the contrary is true in northern Europe. Where the Europeans hunted such carnivores for sport, the American tradition was to trap, poison, and bounty them. This attitude was understandable on the frontier, where wildlife was more important for food than for recreation; therefore, deer, turkey, or ducks were far more welcome quarry than a fox. Neither economic nor social conditions in the United States favored a leisure class that could afford the luxury of fox hunting.

In recent years, however, the sporting potential of these predators has become more widely recognized. In its 1965 National Survey of Hunting and Fishing the U.S. Bureau of Sport Fisheries and Wildlife included for the first time a survey of participation in the sport of "varmint hunting," and came up with a surprising estimate of 2,573,000 participants—more even than had hunted migratory game birds that year. The term "varmint" is loosely used; in the sporting literature it includes many species of commonly unprotected wildlife such as crows, magpies, marmots, and jack rabbits as well as predators, but coyotes and foxes are favored on the long list of "varmints."

The inconsistencies even in adjacent states indicate clearly how our traditions relating to these predators are changing. The mountain lion, for example, is a game animal in Colorado and hunting it requires a special license. In Arizona and South Dakota a bounty is paid on it, and in seven western states it is unprotected. In 1967, Oregon declared the cougar a game animal and provided a year-round closed season pending study to determine if its population was sufficient to merit a hunting season. The previous year eight counties in Oregon had offered a bounty on the cougar.

Although the coyote is a prime target of state and federal predator control programs, it is increasingly a favorite of sportsmen, who have a variety of hunting methods from which to select. "Calling" coyotes is remarkably successful, permitting even close-up photography at times. The use of trained hounds, particularly greyhounds, is not uncommon in the western plains states.

The growing popularity of coyote hunting for sport is indicated in western states by the existence of such groups as the Arizona Varmint Callers Association, which reports seven clubs with a paid membership of 550. California, Colorado, Nevada, and New Mexico report similar clubs and a growing interest in this sport.

In New York State in 1964 and 1965 an attempt was made to coordinate predator hunting with control when the statewide raccoon hunters' organization, as part of its effort to keep the raccoon a legally protected game animal, offered the services of its members in the control of any raccoons causing damage to corn or garden crops. Properly organized, this type of cooperation could accomplish needed control where animals are doing damage, and at the same time provide recreation.

As the recreational value of hunting certain predators becomes more widely recognized, this sport might well replace some of the expensive control efforts. It should be emphasized, however, that the hunting of what are not ordinarily considered to be game animals should be done only when such animals are sufficiently abundant to sustain an annual kill without hazard to their populations or ecological values. Examples of such abundant and successful species, in much of their range, are the woodchuck, crow, coyote, and raccoon. In states where it is still to be found, the status of the cougar should be guarded to make certain that is not overhunted.

FEDERAL PREDATOR AND RODENT CONTROL

Control of predators and rodents by the federal government, in response to state and local requests, is a well-established activity that had its beginnings in the Bureau of Biological Survey, U.S. Department of Agriculture. The Bureau began conducting experiments in control methods for predators in 1909, and for range rodents in 1914. In 1915 Congress appropriated funds to control predatory animals that were killing livestock and transmitting rabies. Since then the activity has grown until in 1964-65 the cost of these programs was nearly $7 million, of which about a third was federal funds. This federal activity was invariably in response to requests by states, lesser divisions of government, and in some cases private organizations; these private organizations provided substantial contributions to the work.

In some areas efforts have been made to provide educational programs on the control of rodents and predators, particularly through established extension agencies. In eastern states the Fish and Wildlife

Service developed extension services for landowners and others who needed rodent control, and some of the states employed extension specialists who had as one of their duties the development of educational programs relating to rodent control. In the fruit-growing areas of several eastern states, particularly New York and Virginia, mice and rabbits are a considerable threat to fruit trees; here the states have been active in both research and extension to prevent losses to the orchards.

The concept of having either the state or federal government provide the landowner with information on methods he himself can use to protect his crops, instead of furnishing actual control services, is similar to policies and practices related to disease and insect control. In Kansas and Missouri, state extension specialists in predator control have been operating since before 1950.

There are compelling reasons for continuing the federal control program in some areas. In western states federal land is intermingled with private holdings, and ranchers graze their stock under permit on public lands. Thus animal damage control traditionally has been regarded as a federal responsibility. The lands on which control is practiced are extensive, and the methods used often are potentially dangerous to other animals and man. Given these conditions it is argued that control by professionals is more likely to meet acceptable standards of safety and effectiveness than that by the owners of livestock or other property. The fact that animal control left to nonfederal agencies has often employed the outmoded and inefficient bounty system is a case in point.

The administration of control programs and the setting of control policies face inherent difficulties. Until recently the Fish and Wildlife Service carried on predator and rodent abatement operations where field workers and supervisors judged them to be needed. Criteria for deciding when and where operations were desirable or necessary were not clearly established, and decisions too often reflected the personal ideas and biases of individuals. Under these conditions, and with two thirds of the funds coming from stockmen's associations and local levies, a steadily expanding and not highly discriminating program against predators and range rodents was carried on. The Service was under long-standing demand from both scientists and laymen to increase the objectivity of its methods for determining control needs and to adjust field activities accordingly.

Predator control problems and policies have been reviewed by a number of writers. A few recent representative publications include those of Allen (1963), Balser (1964), Berryman (1966), Hall (1966), U.S. Congress (1966), and Gottschalk (1967).

As a result of the concern at highest levels of government that public programs involving wildlife damage and control be in tune with modern thinking, an important study was conducted dealing specifically with these problems.

The Leopold Report

The so-called Leopold report (Leopold, 1964) on predator and rodent control in the United States was written at the request of then Secretary of the Interior Stewart L. Udall. The board of five that produced this report after a period of intensive study has an impressive record of experience in the biological sciences and in public service in wildlife management, and their conclusions and recommendations have been widely accepted.

Two basic assumptions adopted by the board were that:

1. All native animals are resources of inherent interest and value to the people of the United States. Basic governmental policy therefore should be one of husbandry of all forms of wildlife.

2. At the same time, local population control is an essential part of a management policy, where a species is causing significant damage to other resources or crops, or where it endangers human health or safety. Control should be limited strictly to the troublesome species, preferably to the troublesome individuals, and in any event to the localities where substantial damage or danger exists.

After its appraisal the board concluded:

It is the unanimous opinion of this Board that control as actually practiced today is considerably in excess of the amount that can be justified in terms of total public interest. As a consequence many animals which have never offended private property owners or public resources values are being killed unnecessarily. The issue is how to sharpen the tools of control so that they hew only where cuts are fully justified.

The board included in its report six recommendations:

1. Appointment of a continuing advisory board of predator and rodent control which should be widely representative of the livestock and agricultural interests, conservation organizations, and technical organizations. The Leopold board recognized the controversial nature of animal control programs and the need for a "forum for the wide spectrum of opinions" regarding control.

2. Reassessment of its own goals by the Branch of Predator and Rodent Control of the Fish and Wildlife Service, and a break with the tradition that it ". . . is primarily responsible to livestock and agricultural interests. . . ."

3. Some specific suggestions for the control program:

a. Continuation in the West of the system of trained professional hunters as being most effective.

b. Continuation of the cooperative arrangement under which at least half of the costs are borne by nonfederal sources.

c. Requirement of more proof and documentation of the need for any local control program, including statistics on the "true extent of the damage."

d. Encouragement of extension educational programs wherever feasible (generally the eastern half of the country).

e. Replacement of bounty systems with extension programs.

f. Use, in the eastern United States, of "flying squads of federal control agents" where rabies outbreaks or similar temporary situations occur.

4. An amplified research program, particularly to develop more specific controls, so that innocent animals are not so often the victims, and also to develop repellents and other protective devices that do not involve killing.

5. Selection of a new name for the Branch of Predator and Rodent Control—one that suggests a broader management function.

6. Adoption of stricter legal control over the use of poisons, particularly over 1080, which the report states has resulted in much secondary poisoning. Mentioned specifically were the need to guard against the "ecological abuses" of secondary poisoning of nontarget species, and the need to prohibit export to foreign countries where the danger of misuse is high.

Official Acceptance of the Leopold Report

The Leopold report, released to the public on March 9, 1964, at the North American Wildlife and Natural Resources Conference, was accepted officially by Secretary Udall on June 22, 1965, after 15 months of study, as a "general guidepost for Department policy," but ". . . not as a policy mandate." However, several tangible results of the report's recommendations have been evident:

On July 1, 1965, the Branch of Predator and Rodent Control became the Division of Wildlife Services, and new leadership and direction were provided. As the name suggests, the Division has far broader responsibilities than did its predecessor. In addition to control activities the Division has responsibility for surveillance and monitoring of pesticides in the environment, and for "wildlife resource enhancement work," with emphasis upon migratory species; initial efforts are to be concentrated upon Indian, military, and Interior lands (Berryman, 1966).

In May 1967 the Bureau of Sport Fisheries and Wildlife issued a statement of policy for animal damage control (Gottschalk, 1967). In announcing it, Director Gottschalk explained that drafts of the statement had been reviewed by "over 30 conservation organizations and agencies, including representative user groups. . . . The finished product is in accord with the majority of the suggestions made and incorporates much of the basic philosophy . . . of the Leopold Report."

This official document begins with a significant statement of philosophy that recognizes the esthetic value of wildlife resources. In addition, the statement indicates that the Bureau must cooperate with state game and fish agencies in the conservation of fish and wildlife resources for the use and enjoyment of the entire public, that control measures must remain flexible, that when control is needed it shall recognize fully the ecological relationships involved and must emphasize removal of specific offending individuals wherever and whenever possible.

The statement of policy emphasizes demonstrated need for control, selective control, cooperation with state and federal agencies, advance planning, the use of educational techniques where possible, avoidance of hazard to endangered species of wildlife, and a strong program of research "to find new, improved, selective, and humane methods."

This official policy is evidence that the Leopold report has been adopted to a very considerable extent. Only two recommendations of the report are not mentioned: the one calling for appointment of a continuing advisory board on predator and rodent control, and the final one urging far stricter legal controls governing the use of poisons, over which the Department of the Interior does not have sole jurisdiction.

NEED FOR DAMAGE CONTROL RESEARCH

The variety and magnitude of wildlife damage to man's crops and property are sufficient to demand more effective controls than are available at present, and research is urgently needed to develop them. Changes in agriculture and land use, and changes in wildlife populations and their behavior, repeatedly bring about new situations where damage by wildlife occurs. Furthermore, public attitudes toward wildlife have changed so much that it is more essential than ever that nonlethal types of control be used wherever feasible.

Federal research on wildlife damage control is being conducted in several key points in the country and many effective methods have been developed. But an accelerated program is needed for the important new problems that regularly arise; also all potential avenues to control must be explored. There is need to maintain close contact with work done on control methods in Europe, where some of the same situations have been faced far longer than in the United States.

Methods of controlling or alleviating damage fall into at least four broad categories, and studies should continue to explore all of them— biological or cultural, mechanical and electronic, chemical, and payment for damages. For each of these categories there are examples of successes in particular situations. All deserve additional study.

The biological or cultural category includes some cases, in California, where waterfowl have been lured from rice fields to areas of food planted especially for them. It also covers situations around airports, where habitats have been modified to reduce their attractiveness to birds. And it might well include the development of crop varieties that are resistant to birds, though little has been accomplished so far with this approach.

The electronic and mechanical category includes various types of scaring devices, the herding or harassing of birds, shooting, and various electronic devices, of which the most successful to date have used recorded alarm or distress calls of gregarious birds. This last technique has been used with considerable success against starlings in vineyards in Germany and France.

Chemical methods have been and are being given much attention. Several classes of chemicals offer possibilities—toxicants, repellents, soporifics or stupifacients, and the antifertility agents that are being considered as a way of holding some animal populations in check.

Payment for damages, as exemplified by the waterfowl depredation crop insurance plan used in Canada, may have applicability to some conditions in the United States. From the summary by Boyd (1963), it appears that state game agencies have had experience with this method, since 10 states were paying landowners for game damage to crops, although the programs in most cases were very limited.

LOOKING INTO THE FUTURE

Wildlife damage and nuisance situations may be expected to continue and probably to increase. The development of successful methods of controlling or mitigating damage already offers a challenge to the natural scientist or social scientist who is interested in tackling it. In the past it has been difficult to interest capable young scientists in these problems, because of the somewhat unfavorable public image of the traditional predator and rodent control programs. Those interested in wildlife management usually preferred the role of producing, rather than destroying or controlling, wildlife.

As research in bird and mammal control becomes more sophisticated, and it is more widely recognized that it draws upon many basic sciences—ecology, physiology, behavior, biochemistry, electronics—the art of controlling wildlife damage may be expected to achieve greater stature, attract more research attention, and be more frequently successful.

An example of the attention paid to bird damage and its control in Europe is provided by the discussion at a symposium held in London in 1967 (Murton and Wright, 1968). Sir Landsborough Thomson and Professor V. C. Wynne Edwards, Department of Zoology, University of Aberdeen, two of the most distinguished zoologists in the United Kingdom, acted as chairmen of sessions that reviewed bird problems on a worldwide scale. The latter concluded with remarks that are as valid in the United States as in the United Kingdom:

Given enough knowledge, rational decisions can be taken. But if people blindly take sides on questions of bird control as a matter of principle and insist on forcing the issue one way or the other by trial of strength, the decisions reached must necessarily be political decisions; and they may do quite unnecessary harm or injustice to the least appreciated interests on the other side.

Sir Landsborough Thomson's opening remarks to the session for which he acted as chairman are also pertinent:

It is to be hoped that the title, "Problems of Birds as Pests", will not lead anyone to think that this symposium has been conceived in a spirit of hostility to bird-life. Most of those taking part are in fact ornithologists or conservationists, or both. The perspective in which the topic should be viewed is that control is an aspect of conservation, requiring study like any other. In an environment where the balance of nature has been greatly disturbed, mankind has a responsibility for wildlife management; this properly includes reasonable defence of human material interests.

Birds are to a large extent economically beneficial; they are also, of course, scientifically interesting and aesthetically delightful. Yet some species tend to be harmful, and others become pests when present in excessive numbers or in the wrong places. The task is, dispassionately and objectively, to determine the facts and consider what to do.

The extent of interest in Europe in these problems also is exemplified by the organization of an international society of economic ornithologists and the appearance of its technical journal *Angewandte Ornithologie*, which deals with the positive as well as the negative economic impact of birds. It appears that in western Europe the attitudes of the public and of scientists toward wildlife damage and control have matured to a point where constructive discussion and research on the problems proceed more objectively than in the United States. The chief goal, of course, should be alleviation of the damage, rather than destruction of animals.

REFERENCES

Allen, D. L. 1963. The costly and needless war on predators. Audubon Mag. 65(2):85-89, 120-121.

Balser, D. S. 1964. Management of predator populations with antifertility agents. J. Wildl. Manage. 28(2):352-358.

Berryman, J. H. 1966. Trans. N. Amer. Wildl. and Natur. Resour. Conf. 31:246-258.

Boyd, R. J. 1963. A brief summary of game damage data and forage requirements in the United States. A report to the Colorado Game, Fish and Parks Commission. 14 p. (mimeo.)

Farmes, R. E. 1969. Crop insurance for waterfowl depredation. Trans. N. Amer. Wildl. and Natur. Resour. Conf. 34:332-337.

Fitch, H. S., and J. R. Bentley. 1949. Use of California annual-plant forage by range rodents. Ecology 30(3):306-321.

Gottschalk, J. S. 1967. Man and wildlife (a policy for animal damage control). U.S. Department of the Interior, Washington, D.C. 12 p.

Hall, R. E. 1966. Carnivores, sheep, and public lands. Trans. N. Amer. Wildl. Conf., 31:239-245.

Jahn, L. R. 1969. Migratory bird crop depredations: A naturalist's views of the problem. Presented at the Migratory Bird Crop Depredation Workshop, University of Maryland, July 15-16, 1969. 32 p. (mimeo.)

Jameson, E. W. 1958. Consumption of alfalfa and wild oats by *Microtus californicus*. J. Wildl. Manage. 22:433-434.

Kverno, N. B. 1964. Forest animal damage control. Proc. 2nd Vert. Pest Contr. Conf., Anaheim, Calif. 81-89.

Leopold, A. S. (Chr.) 1964. Predator and rodent control in the United States. Trans. N. Amer. Wildl. and Natur. Resour. Conf. 29:27-49.

Murton, R. K., and E. N. Wright (ed.). 1968. The problems of birds as pests. Academic Press, New York. 240 p.

Neff, J. A., and B. Meanley. 1957. Blackbirds and the Arkansas rice crop. Agricultural Experiment Station Bulletin 584, University of Arkansas, Fayetteville, Arkansas, February 1957, 89 p.

Paynter, E. L. 1966. Crop insurance. The Saskatchewan Government Insurance Office, Regina. 4 p. (mimeo.)

Seubert, J. L. 1966. Biological control of birds in airport environments. Interim report, Proj. Agreement FA65WAI-77, Proj. No. 430-011-01E, SRDS Report No. RO-66-8, U.S. Department of the Interior, Bureau of Sport Fisheries and Wildlife, Washington, D.C. 41 p.

Smith, C. F., and S. E. Aldous. 1947. The influence of mammals and birds in retarding artificial and natural reseeding of coniferous forests in the United States. J. Forest. 45(5):361-369.

Solman, V. E. F. 1968. Bird control and air safety. Trans. N. Amer. Wildl. and Natur. Resour. Conf., 33:328-336.

U.S. Air Force. 1966. Bird/aircraft collisions. Air Force Office of Scientific Research, Office of Aerospace Research, Arlington, Va. 15 p.

U.S. Congress. 1966. House Committee on Merchant Marine and Fisheries. Predatory mammals. Hearings before the Subcommittee on Fisheries and Wildlife Conservation, 89th Cong., 2nd sess. U.S. Government Printing Office. Washington, D.C. 255 p.

CHAPTER 8

Legislation and Administration

It has long been recognized that necessary laws and regulations constitute an important tool of resource management, particularly as a means of imposing restraints. In the wildlife field, these restraints have roots in antiquity. Indeed, restrictions on taking game were enacted in pre-Revolutionary times in all of the 13 American colonies.

Legislation and administrative regulations have served the positive role of establishing policy and promoting improvement of the environment in the interests of technically sound wildlife management. Changes in long-established cropping procedures commonly are prompted by new knowledge derived from research and may involve the removal of restrictions. Biological realism of this kind is the framework for achieving lasting productivity on land and water.

JURISDICTIONS

Under United States constitutional provisions, the states have primary legal responsibility for wildlife protection and administration, both through their administration of the well-established and recognized doctrine of public ownership of wildlife, and through police power. Neither of these functions was transferred to the federal government at the time the federal constitution was adopted; hence they remain with the states. The Constitution does, however, reserve to the federal government specific functions such as treaty-making and the regulation of interstate commerce. Both have frequently been applied for wildlife conservation purposes. These actions sometimes limit state jurisdiction in ways that affect the management of areas that are of national significance.

STATE RESPONSIBILITIES

Early assumption by the states of wildlife administration as a trust of the people was upheld by the U.S. Supreme Court in 1896 in the widely quoted case of *Geer* vs. *Connecticut*. This decision probably was influential both in the establishment in every state of a governmental unit to handle wildlife affairs, and in passage of a large and complex body of state laws or regulations.

The doctrine of "state" (public) ownership of wildlife is attributed to English common law. Now, however, in England and other western European countries the landowner has property rights in the wildlife of his land and hence, by contrast with the American scene, laws and regulations dealing with wildlife are few and simple. Responsibilities of the landowner are far greater than in America, and the functions of government are correspondingly less. As a result, Europeans have not developed such well-established units of the government concerned with wildlife (Sigler, 1956).

Although state responsibility for wildlife is widely recognized, in most states wildlife and its recreational use are subordinate to other resource interests. In many states, for example, wildlife production has not been recognized as a beneficial use of land or water, so that when conflicts arise between this and other uses, wildlife frequently receives little consideration. A major example is the administration of water law in western states (discussed later in this chapter), but others occur. The reason may well be that wildlife values are to a great extent social values, being recreational and esthetic, and are not readily measured in conventional economic terms. Although the situation is changing for the better, as wildlife values receive growing recognition year by year, in certain kinds of competition the position of wildlife is still predictably weak. When a highway is proposed along a trout stream, it is still normal for most engineers to be unconcerned about the welfare of fish. Seldom is the right of eminent domain used by either the state or federal government in obtaining a wildlife area. The Fish and Wildlife Service estimates that only about two percent of its refuge land purchases are by condemnation.

State jurisdiction relates primarily to the control of wildlife and to the manner in which hunters and fishermen may utilize the resource—not to the habitat upon which wildlife production is dependent. The landowner holds the key to production through his control of the habitat, and thus he needs to be a partner in management if the resource is to yield public benefits.

National and International Functions

The jurisdiction of the federal government over wildlife results from several specific authorities provided in the Constitution. The treaty-making power is reserved to the federal government, and under this the United States has treaties with Great Britain on behalf of Canada (1916) and with Mexico (1937) to protect and manage the migratory bird resources of North America (Magnuson, 1965a).

By 1900 it was already clear that the states could not adequately protect migratory birds. There were several efforts early in the century to make this a federal responsibility, but until the Migratory Bird Treaty was ratified in 1916, and later upheld by the Supreme Court as constitutional, there was a clear conflict with state authority. As a result of the treaties with Canada and Mexico, primary jurisdiction over migratory birds is assumed by the federal government, which has developed a strong program to implement its responsibility. The states now cooperate closely in the conservation of migratory birds, particularly in enforcing protective regulations. The common arrangement is for states to adopt the federal regulations as their own and to carry out enforcement with their own officials in state courts. The success of the North American waterfowl conservation program, which depends upon international as well as state-federal cooperation, is the envy of other parts of the world where it has not been possible to develop such a comprehensive and effective program.

Legal Basis of State–Federal Cooperation

The first important federal law in the wildlife field was the Lacey Act of 1900, which depended for its constitutionality upon federal authority to regulate interstate and foreign commerce. The most important provision of the Lacey Act declared it to be a federal offense to transport across state boundaries wildlife that had been taken illegally in any state. This law, in effect, placed the strength of the federal government behind the enforcement of state wildlife laws. At first, however, the influence of the Lacey Act was minimal because there were few protective laws to be invoked. Later, as the states increased their legal restrictions and enforcement efforts, this federal legislation became important. It played a significant role in checking the widespread illegal market hunting of that day. Gradually, however, it became evident that the Lacey Act should have been broader, and in 1926 Congress covered the black bass by a special act having provisions similar to the statute of 1900. This was amended to include certain other fishes in 1947. By the late 1960's measures were being considered to extend federal protection to the alligator, long harassed by an interstate traffic in hides.

Having assumed responsibility for migratory bird conservation under terms of the treaties, the Congress passed several laws to achieve this objective. The Migratory Bird Conservation Act of 1929 recognized a system of refuges being developed for migratory birds, and the Migratory Bird Hunting Stamp Act of 1934 was intended to raise revenue for acquiring refuge lands. Migratory bird refuges and waterfowl production areas by 1969 numbered about 350 and totaled some 7½ million acres. Many of these refuges are large and depend for their effectiveness upon dams or dikes to regulate water levels on flowages that sometimes cover many thousands of acres. Some areas within these refuges are cultivated and seeded each year to choice waterfowl food plants. Some are periodically flooded to increase mast production, as from oak.

The Lea Act of 1948 authorized acquisition and development of federal management areas for waterfowl and other wildlife in California. One objective was to develop waterfowl feeding areas on federal land that would lure ducks and geese from privately owned cropfields, and thus help to prevent crop damage. The other federal acts relating to wildlife have generally less relevance to agricultural lands.

The easement aspects of the waterfowl production area program, which is centered in the north central states, is closely related to agricultural land use. Under this program easements are purchased in perpetuity, thus obtaining the owner's right to drain, burn, or fill small water or marsh areas, so that they may be preserved permanently for the benefit of waterfowl and other wildlife. By April 30, 1968, more than 590,000 privately owned acres of waterfowl habitat had been thus preserved. This program was a partial answer to the serious problem of destruction through drainage of the pothole type of habitat, which is extremely productive of waterfowl.

The taxing authority of the federal government permitted passage by Congress of several highly important acts that have provided funds for various types of wildlife programs. In addition to the Migratory Bird

Hunting Stamp Act, there have been two important federal aid acts: The Pittman-Robertson Act of 1937, which makes funds available to the states for wildlife restoration, and the Dingell-Johnson Act of 1950, which provides cost sharing in sport fish restoration and management projects. Under these acts, excise taxes on guns, ammunition, and fishing tackle are allocated to the state game and fish departments and they must be matched in part by the states. The substance of all of these federal acts has been compiled by Magnuson (1965b).

The wide variety of fish and wildlife projects carried out in large part through federal aid includes many that relate to agricultural lands in the United States. For example, considerable research on the production of fish in ponds has been conducted under the Dingell-Johnson program. Pittman-Robertson funds have supported management work, as well as research, in the general area of increasing waterfowl and upland wildlife production through habitat improvement. Some of the states, with federal assistance, have developed large-scale habitat improvement programs that include privately owned agricultural lands. The Wildlife Management Institute and Sport Fishing Institute jointly publish an annual report, "Federal Aid in Fish and Wildlife Restoration," which describes this work. Rutherford (1949, 1953) discussed, in some detail, the Pittman-Robertson program from its inception.

The federal government owns approximately one third of the total area of the United States, and it has the same legal right as any landowner to protect its property. Under this general authority, in the 1920's and 1930's the government declared it necessary to remove large numbers of deer to protect the vegetation in certain areas. Well-known examples of these areas were the Kaibab National Forest in Arizona and the Pisgah National Forest in North Carolina.

More recently, in Yellowstone and some of the other national parks, overpopulations of elk or deer have resulted in damage to the range. Hunting is prohibited in most national parks and some national monuments. In these cases, although state and federal officials agreed that drastic reductions in big game populations were needed, the methods adopted have often given rise to controversy. To keep within the policies and regulations prohibiting hunting, the National Park Service has removed as many animals as possible by live-trapping and transplanting, and then has resorted to direct killing by its own employees. Some states would prefer public hunting under state jurisdiction, but this is contrary to the national park concept, in recognition of which jurisdiction was ceded by the states to the federal government in most of the national parks at the time they were established.

Some state control over resident (nonmigratory) game on federally owned lands has been contested by several federal agencies. In the past such conflicts have been settled in favor of the states, although the states often cede their authority to the government where to do so is obviously in the public interest, as in the case of national parks. Regulations of the U.S. Department of Agriculture promulgated in 1941 (known as regulations W-1 and W-2) are examples of the voluntary arrangements established for cooperating with the states in wildlife management. Under these regulations the Forest Service in effect pledges itself to exhaust all avenues of cooperation before calling upon federal authority in conflict with that of the states.

Several disputes between the states and the U.S. Department of the Interior may have been precipitated by the opinion of that Department's Solicitor in 1964. The following quotations from the Solicitor's opinion are among those that particularly disturbed the states, and their organization, the International Association of Game, Fish, and Conservation Commissioners. Declared the Solicitor:

... it is apparent that the United States, constitutionally empowered as it is, may gain a proprietary interest in land within a state and, in the exercise of this proprietary interest, has constitutional power to enact laws and regulations controlling and protecting that land, including the persons, inanimate articles of value, and resident species of wildlife situated on such land, and that this authority is superior to that of a state.

The opinion concluded:

The regulation of the wildlife populations on federally owned land is an appropriate and necessary function of the Federal Government when the regulations are designed to protect and conserve the wildlife as well as the land.

Following this opinion there were several years of active dispute between the states and the Department of the Interior over the jurisdictional question. Then on June 17, 1968, in an action similar to that of the Secretary of Agriculture in 1941 in promulgating regulations W-1 and W-2, the Secretary of the Interior issued a policy statement with respect to fish and resident wildlife providing:

A. In all areas administered by the Secretary of the Interior through the National Park Service, the Bureau of Sport Fisheries and Wildlife, the Bureau of Land Management, and the Bureau of Reclamation, except the National Parks, the National Monuments, and historic areas of the National Park System, the Secretary shall—

1. Provide that public hunting of resident wildlife and fishing shall be per-

mitted within statutory limitations in a manner that is compatible with, and not in conflict with, the primary objectives as declared by the Congress for which such areas are reserved or acquired;

2. Provide that public hunting, fishing, and possession of fish and resident wildlife shall be in accordance with applicable state laws and regulations, unless the Secretary finds, after consultation with appropriate state fish and game departments, that he must close such areas to such hunting and fishing or restrict public access thereto for such purposes;

3. Provide that a state license or permit, as provided by state law, shall be required for public hunting, fishing, and possession of fish and resident wildlife on such areas;

4. Provide for consultation with the appropriate state fish and game department in the development of cooperative management plans for limiting overabundant or harmful populations of fish and resident wildlife thereon, including the disposition of the carcasses thereof, and, except in emergency situations, secure the State's concurrence in such plans; and

5. Provide for consultation with the appropriate state fish and game department in carrying out research programs involving the taking of fish and resident wildlife, including the disposition of the carcasses thereof, and secure the State's concurrence in such programs.

B. In the case of the National Parks, National Monuments, and historic areas of the National Park System, the Secretary shall—

1. Provide, where public fishing is permitted, that such fishing shall be carried out in accordance with applicable state laws and regulations, unless exclusive legislative jurisdiction has been ceded for such area, and a State license or permit shall be required for such fishing, unless otherwise provided by law;

2. Prohibit public hunting; and

3. Provide for consultation with the appropriate state fish and game departments in carrying out programs of control of overabundant or otherwise harmful populations of fish and resident wildlife or research programs involving the taking of such fish and resident wildlife, including the disposition of carcasses therefrom.

In any case where there is a disagreement, such disagreement shall be referred to the Secretary of the Interior who shall provide for a thorough discussion of the problem with representatives of the state fish and game department and the National Park Service for the purpose of resolving the disagreement.

Although this policy statement appears to be cooperative and conciliatory in its tone and intent, it has not fully satisfied the International Association of Game, Fish, and Conservation Commissioners.

The Association, in a resolution adopted September 13, 1968, at its annual convention, commended the Secretary of the Interior ". . . for attempting to resolve this dispute. . ." but ". . . urges the Congress to enact legislation reaffirming the historic jurisdiction of the states over fish and resident wildlife in order to accomplish a firm and complete resolution of this dispute. . . ."

A detailed analysis of state and federal jurisdiction over fish and wildlife, including the Solicitor's opinion quoted in full, can be found in a report by Swanson *et al.* (1969:11-93). The legislation dealing with fish and wildlife is far too complex to review thoroughly here, as evidenced by the fact that a compilation of the federal laws alone fills a volume of 472 pages (Magnuson, 1965b), and that the fish and game laws of individual states commonly require 200 pages or more.

STATE CONTROL OF GAME AND FISH HARVEST

In many states the legislature has delegated to an executive or to the game and fish commission the authority to control hunting and fishing and associated activities through regulations having the effect of law. In any event, laws or regulations tend to be voluminous and complex, designed to serve many purposes. Most important are those to protect fish and wildlife resources, to provide the private landowner with protection, to provide an orderly harvest, to distribute hunting and fishing opportunity as widely as possible, and to produce the income needed for operating the wildlife department. Laws and regulations are very important management tools.

There are, however, other recognized purposes served by state wildlife laws and regulations. Some are designed to facilitate enforcement, such as those requiring the use of tags on various legally taken game and fish. Others designate fish and wildlife as recreational rather than commercial resources, including many that prohibit the sale of game, alive or dead. Still others are intended to promote gun safety; these may require training programs in gun handling, particularly by the young license-buyer, or they may cancel the license of any who have had gun accidents while hunting.

One group of laws or regulations simply discriminates between different segments of the public. Common among these are the regulations that charge nonresidents a higher license fee than residents, and those that grant privileges to certain groups. Many states, for example, permit elderly persons to fish without a license, and many permit landowners to hunt or fish on their own property without a license. A few grant nonresident members of the military services, or college students, the privilege of purchasing a resident license instead of the more expensive out-of-state permit.

Laws designed to protect the fish and wildlife resource are among the most important. Examples include those designating completely closed seasons, prohibitions against hunting and fishing during the breeding period, and establishing certain types of refuges.

Of particular importance to agriculturists are regulations designed to protect them against hunters and fishermen who may abuse the privilege of being a guest on another person's land. Some of these merit more detailed discussion, but the most significant ones, included in the game and fish laws or regulations of many states, embody provisions for posting lands against all trespass if the landowner prefers; for requiring permission of the landowner to hunt; for providing "safety zones" around occupied residential and farm buildings; for limiting the owner's liability in case of accident on his property. Still other laws permit the landowner to safeguard his property from damage by protected wildlife or provide for reimbursement of the landowner for crop damage.

Among the regulations designed to distribute hunting and fishing opportunities as widely as possible are those that establish bag limits and season limits or that limit the types of hunting and fishing by placing emphasis on recreation rather than on the amount of meat to be taken. In this category would be the prohibition against live decoys and baiting, and some of the limitations upon firearms.

Legislative delegation of authority over game and fish regulations to the state administrative agency is in general an effective form of management. It provides flexibility whereby changes can be made from year to year to meet new conditions or as need arises. The extent of such authority varies from the situation in Missouri, where it is vested in the Conservation Commission by the state constitution, to the situation, at the opposite extreme, wherein year-to-year regulations are originated by a committee and passed by the legislature.

The practice of "legislative management," which deliberately withholds from the commission discretionary powers to make regulations, is most likely to be invoked where measures favored by state technical personnel are not favored by vocal segments of the general public. Thus, appeals are made to representatives in the legislature, who are more likely to be swayed by public sentiment than by the findings and opinions of state wildlife biologists.

Under these circumstances bounties, game farms, and fish hatcheries continued to absorb a disproportionate share of state fish and game budgets long after scientific research had shown good reason for reducing or eliminating them. Handling game regulations through political and legislative channels has had its most important land-use effect in some northern and western states by keeping the controversial buck law in force and thus preventing the adequate harvest of deer herds— a situation that still exists in some states. Overpopulation of deer is likely to occur through the extensive range improvement of large timber cuttings or through fires, and by the elimination of predation as an important mortality factor. In the absence of a heavy hunting harvest, which can be accomplished only by taking both sexes, herds multiply exponentially and quickly damage their ranges.

Experience has shown that, after a developmental phase featuring "legislative management," range deterioration, and at least local decline in numbers of deer, public understanding may begin to catch up. Partial authority over regulations is then granted to administrators, as political demands slack off and informed groups of sportsmen give support to a scientifically guided program. Eventually, experience convincingly demonstrates to a controlling majority of the public and legislators that the technical agency can be trusted to handle this technical matter.

In decades past, developments of this kind have produced management difficulties and state-federal disagreements, especially on national forests. However, the controversies tend to localize and subside as information spreads and trained people take over higher administrative positions.

PUBLIC ACCESS TO PRIVATE LANDS AND WATERS

Cultivated lands are potentially the most productive of wildlife as well as of field crops, and a major proportion of the game in the United States is taken from them. The most popular species include the pheasant, quail, rabbits, squirrels, doves, and to some extent waterfowl and even deer.

In much of the United States a tradition of free public hunting on private lands is recognized by both landowner and hunter. Customs vary in different parts of the country, but the farmer is often the unwilling host to hunters who enter his land as though it were their right without the formality of asking permission. In a remarkably high proportion of cases this traditional relationship is accepted philosophically by the landowner. With increasing numbers of urban hunters, there has been a growing tendency to abuse the farmer's hospitality. State fish and game departments are appropriately concerned and invoke whatever means they can to improve landowner-sportsman relations.

Some of this effort, unfortunately, is a kind of holding action designed to maintain a relationship that is not actually appropriate under modern conditions. Today's farmer is a businessman in a competitive, highly capitalized, and mechanized industry, which is much more specialized than it was 50 years ago. At the turn of the century a typical farm included a flock of poultry, a herd of dairy cows, an orchard, some acres of feed grain, some swine, and a garden to produce vegetables for home consumption. But the general farm has largely given way to specialized monoculture, which produces much less wildlife. These changes in farming conditions and those associated with an increasing urban population, have been unfavorable to both ecological and social relationships for the sportsman seeking recreation on private land.

It is clear, however, that with appropriate encouragement, public recreation on private farms can continue at an important level. Teague (1966) has brought this out forcefully in an analysis of the conflicts and the mutuality of interests.

Trespass Laws and Enforcement

Although the states legally hold wildlife in trust for the people, the landowner has the legal right to prevent hunters and fishermen from entering his land. The sportsman's license to take game or fish does not give him access to private property without permission. The owner may, in fact, keep others out and use the land for his own exclusive hunting and fishing. Since these outdoor sports are the most common reasons for an individual to seek access to private land, the right of the landowner to prevent it is specifically included in the game and fish laws of most states.

States usually put the responsibility for restricting trespass squarely on the landowner. Arizona, Connecticut, New Mexico, Pennsylvania, New York, and Washington are among the states that require the landowner to notify hunters and fishermen either by posting signs or by word-of-mouth warning. In another group of states, represented by Colorado, Delaware, Texas, and Wisconsin, the sportsman is required by law to obtain permission from the landowner to enter his land, and in some, notably Michigan, Nevada, and West Virginia, this permission must be in writing. In actual practice, laws requiring landowner permission for entry are often ignored. With an increasing number of holdings under absentee ownership it is becoming more difficult for hunters or fishermen to secure the required permission.

Violation of the trespass laws is considered a misdemeanor, with penalties designated accordingly. Repeated offenses may result in substantial penalties. In Texas, for example, a third offense could result in a fine as high as $1,000 and revocation of one's hunting license for 3 years.

Since an owner has the legal right to restrict or prevent entry to his land in any of the states, he is indeed a key individual despite the American doctrine of public ownership (trusteeship) of wildlife. It is clear, therefore, as stated in 1930 in the American Game Policy, that the landowner's custodianship of wildlife must be recognized if this recreational resource is to be of public value (Leopold, 1930).

Programs to Encourage Access

The dilemma facing the landowner, the sportsman, and the state game and fish administrator is a difficult one. A large proportion of outdoorsmen cling to the American folkway of free and unregulated hunting, a tradition dating from pioneer times and to a considerable degree no longer appropriate. The attitude is encouraged by the fact that in many states there is a considerable amount of public land on which access for hunting and fishing still is free and unregulated, and many a thoughtless hunter tends to carry over his attitude from the public land to the private.

A farmer engaged in intensive agriculture often cannot afford to permit hunting and fishing on his land if to do so requires any of his time or if there is a possibility of other cost to him, such as damage to crops or property. Landowner situations differ widely, of course, another extreme being represented by large corporations holding forested lands for pulp or timber production. Some corporations have adopted a policy of leasing their lands to private groups for hunting and fishing, while others believe that the gain in public relations is great enough to justify throwing the land open to public use, much as if it were in public ownership.

A widespread and important need is to provide an incentive to the landowner to permit access to his lands or water for hunting and fishing; many states have tested arrangements of this kind with varying success.

State laws commonly provide for artificially stocked hunting or fishing "preserves," some of which are quite artificial, others relatively natural. This type of arrangement is growing in popularity. In California, according to Teague (1966), a pheasant-hunting club program on private land, provided for by state law, increased from 17 clubs in 1940 to 191 in 1964. Reported use of these areas by hunters rose from 30 man-days per thousand acres in 1940 to 380 man-days in 1963, and pheasant hunters in this program were paying from $275 to $350 for the right to take 40 birds under the state game bird club laws. The birds so taken were reared by private breeders who currently sell more than 250,000 pheasants for this purpose.

In California and other states, notably those in the Mississippi Valley, proprietors able to furnish good waterfowl hunting on their lands frequently have been able to sell the right to individuals or groups for remarkably high prices. Teague noted that many waterfowl hunting clubs in California have long waiting lists, and that people are willing to pay up to $10,000 for a membership. While such duck clubs furnish hunting opportunity for a limited number of license holders, the wetlands habitat they control is recognized as important in providing essential environment for a portion of the North American waterfowl population. Hunting pressure on private waterfowl clubs is usually light, so that the habitat controlled may have a positive protective value to waterfowl as well as a recreational value to hunters.

Some of the states have found that a large proportion of landowners do not demand a cash incentive, but are willing to permit their property to be used by sportsmen if they are assured of adequate protection from vandalism and abuses. One of the oldest and most successful of these arrangements is Pennsylvania's Cooperative Farm Game program, which has been in existence since 1936. Currently, it involves nearly 1½ million acres of privately owned land on more than 12,000 farms in 163 more-or-less consolidated units. In this program the Pennsylvania Game Commission provides efficient protection for the landowners through its radio-equipped game protectors. The commission staff furnishes posters prohibiting trespass in a safety zone around occupied dwellings and assures the landowner of quick enforcement if safety zones are violated.

This program inspired important features of New York's Fish and Wildlife Management Act, which has been operating since 1958. Under this act, protection is similarly provided to the private landowner who will permit hunting on his land, and more than 200,000 acres has been placed under cooperative agreement involving government and institutional lands as well as individual and corporate holdings.

In some other areas, private organizations have taken the initiative in attempting to maintain the right of free public hunting on private land. The Izaak Walton League has promoted in several states the "Hunt

America Time" or "Red Hat Program" for improving farmer-sportsman relations through education, and in Colorado and several other states a privately operated program known as "Operation Respect" has similar objectives (Johnson, 1967).

Thus, a wide variety of plans have been developed, mostly by state game and fish departments but in some cases by private organizations, designed to continue recreational hunting and fishing on private lands. Sometimes these arrangements provide the landowner with nothing but good will; others may produce substantial income from the sale of hunting and fishing rights.

The U.S. Department of Agriculture, particularly through the Soil Conservation Service but with participation by other units, has been especially active in assisting landowners to develop the recreational potential of their land. In 1966 the Cropland Adjustment Program (CAP) first offered landowners an additional fee under their cropland diversion contracts if they permitted public access for hunting, fishing, trapping, or hiking. This program, being based upon the need to regulate crop surpluses, is temporary, and no appropriations were made for new contracts in fiscal year 1969. The arrangement involves cooperation with state fish and game departments. Some of these agencies were hesitant to participate in an arrangement to pay the landowner for permitting free access to his land for recreational purposes, particularly where there was no assurance of permanence.

However, most states entered into the arrangement actively, and Boyce (1967) reported that 36,000 farmers in 48 states signed 5- to 10-year cropland diversion contracts involving a million acres. In 35 states supplemental public access payment contracts were included for about one quarter of these lands.

Michigan was particularly active, assigning staff from the State Conservation Department to participate in this program. Payments to farmers for public access were established at $1 to $3 per acre, and in 1967 farmers agreed to open more than 125,000 acres of their land to public access. These agreements were almost entirely for hunting. Fishing access involved less than 1 percent. Since a large proportion of the landowners opened all their acreage to public access rather than limiting it to acres specifically diverted under the CAP program, the first year's cost of the access program was $139,000, or $1.11 per acre. This appears to be one of the largest programs of its kind. The mechanism of the Crop Adjustment Program has been described by the U.S. Department of Agriculture (1965). Programs to encourage public access to private lands and to improve landowner-sportsman relations have been reviewed by many authors, including the following: Leopold (1940), Whitesell (1952), Hunter (1953), Gearhart (1957), Hay (1960), Kozicky (1960), Berryman (1961), Galbreath (1965), and Gilbert (1965).

Another type of access situation currently receiving much attention is that in which a private landowner who prohibits access to his own land in so doing also prohibits access to contiguous public lands that may have much greater area. The Forest Service and Bureau of Land Management are especially concerned about this problem, and in some cases they have solved it by purchasing rights-of-way or easements permitting public access through private areas to the public lands or waters lying beyond. Many of the states have similar programs for purchasing and developing access through private lands. This matter is discussed at some length in a report by Swanson et al. (1969: 148-196).

Liability Laws

A major concern of landowners is that if they permit public access to their lands for hunting and fishing, they may be liable in case of accident and injury to the hunter or fisherman. Many states, in order to meet this particular difficulty, have included in their fish and game or general laws a provision exempting the landowner from liability if he is permitting use of his land free of charge. Such laws have been adopted in part as a result of assistance from the Council of State Governments, which provides the wording of a "model law."

The typical law of this nature specifically applies only if the landowner is not charging for the privilege of using his land, but the New Jersey law, passed in 1962, does not specify, reading

no landowner . . . shall be liable for the payment of damages suffered resulting from any personal injury to, or the death of, any person while such person was hunting or fishing on the landowner's property, except that such injury or deaths resulted from a deliberate or willful act on the part of such landowner.

To landowners who charge a fee there is, of course, liability insurance available from many private companies. This subject has been reviewed by several authors, including Crews and Bird (1963), Kelsey (1964), Krauz and Lemon (1964), and Leedy (1966).

DEVICES FOR LIMITING THE NUMBER OF HUNTERS

Limiting the number of hunters on an area is important both to restrict the actual take of wildlife and to satisfy landowners who have permitted public hunting on their property. Specific studies of the matter have shown that property owners are very uneasy lest they be overrun by too many hunters. A variety of methods have been tried for limiting the number. We are concerned here primarily with those serving the interests of the landowner rather than those designed specifically for limiting the kill.

The most common arrangement is undoubtedly one under which the owner leases exclusive privileges to a group of hunters, the number being explicitly limited. The agreement usually calls for the burden of controlling the land to be assumed by the hunters themselves, so that the automobiles be left in particular parking areas where space is deliberately limited. Reports indicate that this has worked effectively.

The Province of Ontario uses a plan in the immediate proximity of large cities under which the counties require a special license issued in limited number. Methods of limiting numbers and controlling distribution of hunters have been discussed by Johnson (1943), Scott (1948), Hunter (1957), and Dimmick and Klimstra (1964).

BIG GAME HUNTING REGULATIONS

Game laws or regulations designed to accomplish an appropriate level of harvest have been developed, with many variations. Western states have pioneered in the use of effective big game hunting regulations, because public acceptance has generally been quicker there than in many of the eastern states.

As noted previously, a particularly troublesome big game hunting regulation has been the buck law, restricting hunters to deer carrying antlers of a specific size. The protection of antlerless or female big game was often justified when the population was small and the habitat in good condition. Then the objective of wildlife administrators was to permit a limited amount of hunting, but to encourage continued growth of the big game herds. The devotion of the public to the buck-law idea became so complete that when the deer population had reached a level at which it should be stabilized and kept in balance with the available forage, people frequently were unwilling to change their views. Many states in the East and Midwest, notably New York, Pennsylvania, Michigan, and Wisconsin, witnessed long and bitter controversies before the general public, including many legislators and game commissioners, was willing to accept the idea that the time had come for a larger kill, requiring the taking of antlerless deer or elk. The western states, in general, have been spared this excessively bitter type of controversy, but in California the problem is so severe that many deer ranges are still overpopulated. It is noteworthy that states that have never employed the buck law, for example, Minnesota and Maine, have generally fewer big game problems and have a better balance between the deer herd and its food and cover plants than states that have used this device.

One of the commonest arrangements that the states have used to limit the number of hunters and distribute them appropriately is that of issuing a specified number of permits for a particular area. If demand for the permits is beyond the specified number, a public lottery is held to select the successful permittees. This device has been used, particularly in the West, for almost all species of big game, including bison in those few states with a surplus to be taken by hunters. In 1967, for example, Colorado issued only three permits for shooting bison, at a charge of $200 per hunter.

Holding drawings to select hunting permittees has been used most commonly for species that are limited in numbers like mountain goats, bighorn, and pronghorn. However, where it has been necessary to limit the kill in a specific region, the permit system has also been used for the commoner deer and elk. This is an effective device for directing hunting pressure where it should be, and gearing it to the population surplus. For the purpose of distributing big game hunting pressure, many states are divided into a large number of units. Colorado, for example, has 95 game management units, any of which may have different hunting regulations from adjoining divisions, which commonly represent watersheds.

In many cases the wildlife administrator has found it desirable to encourage more hunting pressure in certain portions of his state, sometimes because a given area is relatively remote or inaccessible, and tends therefore to be bypassed in favor of easier hunting grounds by most hunters. Several means have been used to encourage heavier hunting. In Colorado the west slope of the Rockies tends to be less heavily hunted in relation to game population density than the east slope, which is nearer the larger cities. In some years hunting regulations have called for opening the season on the west slope a week or two earlier than in the east, thus attracting the opening-day pressure to the area where it is needed. For the same purpose the purchase of multiple licenses by a single hunter is permitted in Colorado's less accessible back country. Other states sometimes provide an incentive in lightly hunted areas by allowing gunners to take one or more animals beyond the normal limit—often this is a "camp deer" or "party deer" of either sex. Where a buck law has been in effect, simply opening the season to an "any deer" type of hunt will bring about a far higher kill than is possible under sex and age restrictions.

Under some conditions an any-deer season results in an excessive kill—which means that the herd falls below the level that can produce the most while conserving browse resources. Indiana had this experience when an easily accessible range was opened to liberalized hunting. Restricted hunting probably is needed in the semiagricultural regions of most states where road networks and the nature of the woodland permit heavy hunting to eliminate a high proportion of the deer. Under these conditions the states frequently issue a limited number of permits for taking antlerless animals—deer or elk, as the case may be. This practice has resulted in a more orderly hunt than can be achieved, for example, by setting a brief season of a day or two on antlerless deer at the end of the regular buck-hunting season.

From the large number of different regulatory devices developed by the states for adjusting hunting pressure in specific areas, it is clear that no one arrangement is always satisfactory, and undoubtedly more variations will be developed in years to come. It is characteristic that American big game hunters prefer a minimum of regimentation and would oppose the tight restrictions frequently applied in European big game hunts.

LEGISLATION CONCERNING PREDATORS AND NUISANCE ANIMALS

As described by Leopold (1933), predator control was chronologically second only to hunting restrictions in its development as a wildlife management measure, and also in its general popularity and adoption years ago. In North America several of the colonies established bounties for the destruction of wolves in the seventeenth century (Massachusetts by 1630, New Hampshire by 1679, and Pennsylvania by 1683). The objective of predator control was primarily the protection of domestic stock. However, the belief (very often a myth) that predation was a limiting factor on wildlife populations, and therefore an important one to control, has been widespread, and even today has many adherents.

Bounty Systems

The payment of bounties for controlling predators is still popular, despite the fact that it has been thoroughly discredited (Allen, 1962). In recent years several authors have reviewed the status of bounty payments, and Laun (1962) reported that 34 states were paying bounties for predator control in 1960, with an estimated annual cost, including administration, of between three and four million dollars. In the 23 states that supplied cost figures for 1960 the total was $1,475,000, of which the largest sum was for Michigan, where $245,000 was expended. In a large proportion of cases, counties or lesser units offered bounty payments even though the state government itself or its fish and game department had abandoned the practice. In California, the State Department of Fish and Game paid bounties on crows and black-billed magpies only, while nine counties operated their own systems of bounty payment for coyote, bobcat, mountain lion, and even bluejays. Archaic systems of bounty payment, particularly by county boards of supervisors, are conspicuous anachronisms in a period when professional resource managers so universally recognize the waste and futility of the system.

In Minnesota, for example, it was hailed by conservation groups and wildlife administrators as an important victory when in 1965 the bounty on wolves, coyotes, foxes, and lynx was finally eliminated by the governor's veto. The remnant population of timber wolves in northeastern Minnesota has officially been designated "endangered" under the program of rare and endangered fish and wildlife of the United States, and all possible protective measures are urged. Unfortunately, the 1969 Minnesota legislature reinstated bounty payments, limited by administrative discretion.

In 1967, Oregon, through its Game Commission, designated the mountain lion as a game species with a completely closed season, pending investigation of the possibility that the population was sufficient to permit restricted hunting (Oregon State Game Commission, 1967). At the same time eight counties in the state were paying bounties ranging from $5 to $15 for destruction of the animal. The bounty system, despite the evidence against it, is dying a slow death.

Protection of Predatory Animals

Passage by Congress in 1966 of the Endangered Species Act (80 Stat. 926) for the first time gave broad responsibility to the Fish and Wildlife Service to study and to recommend protective measures for rare and endangered species of wildlife. In that year the Bureau of Sport Fisheries and Wildlife published a compilation entitled "Rare and Endangered Fish and Wildlife of the United States." A single page devoted to each species includes both vital statistics and recommended protective measures. Many of the species in this category are predatory mammals and birds, including the timber wolf, red wolf, kit fox, black-footed ferret, peregrine falcon, and southern bald eagle. The attention focused on these predators and the need for their protection promises to be highly beneficial. Without adequate knowledge of a species' population and ecology, measures to protect it cannot be realistic and effective.

Hawks and owls provide a particularly good example of groups toward which public attitude, and consequently legislation, has changed over the years. General bird protection laws were widely adopted beginning about 1900 as a result of efforts by the Audubon Society to promote the "Model Audubon Law." This statement classified hawks and owls as generally beneficial (e.g., the broad-winged hawk), harmful (peregrine falcon and Cooper's hawk), or neutral (the marsh hawk). Laws passed in those days generally recognized these categories, providing token protection for the beneficial hawks and none for the harmful.

According to Chrest (1964), in 1899 only five states offered legal protection of any kind to eagles, hawks, and owls. This number has now increased to 46 states, but the degree of protection varies widely. The inadequacy of state protection of birds of prey was recognized early enough so that in 1940 Congress passed the original Bald Eagle Protection Act because the bird had been designated by the Continental Congress in 1782 as our national symbol, and because "the bald eagle is now threatened with extinction."

Soon after enactment of this act, an important weakness was recognized—namely, that a bald eagle in immature plumage is so easily mistaken for the golden eagle that many were shot by poorly informed persons in the belief, or at least with the rationalization, that they were shooting unprotected golden eagles. In 1962, therefore, the Bald Eagle Act was amended to extend legal protection also to the golden eagle, which was recognized in the enacting clause as having "declined at such an alarming rate that it is now threatened with extinction" and that it "should be preserved because of its value to agriculture in the control of rodents" and "because the bald eagle is often killed by persons mistaking it for the golden eagle."

Except for this act, birds of prey are not protected by federal law, because such species were not included in either the 1916 Migratory Bird Treaty with Canada or the 1937 treaty with Mexico. These birds, as well as certain other groups, were omitted from the treaties because attempts to include them might have delayed or prevented approval by

Congress, and thus jeopardized the protection of less controversial species. Since many of the hawks and some of the owls are clearly migratory, it would have been legally possible to gain protection for them in this manner, but emphasis in the treaty with Canada was to protect migratory game birds, as "a source of food" and migratory insectivorous birds that destroy "insects which are injurious to forest and forage plants on the public domain, as well as to agricultural crops." The justification for the later treaty with Mexico was "to employ adequate measures which will permit a rational utilization of migratory birds for the purpose of sport as well as for food, commerce and industry." Thus the birds of prey, so widely recognized now as being particularly valuable and interesting components of our fauna and in need of protection, were completely neglected in federal law.

Whether the legal protection of migratory birds is under federal law or state law, actual enforcement is primarily by state "conservation officers" or "game protectors" since federal "game management agents" are so few. Without the close cooperation of state officials, federal wildlife laws cannot be enforced effectively.

Since the states have full legal jurisdiction over all other species of hawks and owls, it is gratifying that their laws have increasingly provided legal protection. By 1965, according to Clement (1965), 19 states gave legal protection to all hawks and owls, and 26 others protected some species. Only five states offered no protection to the birds of prey. Unfortunately, enforcement of this protection usually is inadequate, but the mere fact that protection exists in the law has certainly reduced the indiscriminate shooting of hawks and owls, which was so common only a few years ago.

Species of hawks that appear to be in greatest danger of extirpation in parts of their range are suffering more from reduced reproductive success than from shooting or other direct losses (Sprunt, 1963). The osprey, peregrine falcon, bald eagle, and marsh hawk have declined alarmingly in the eastern United States (and in portions of western Europe) in the past decade, and it has become clear that the immediate cause is lack of successful reproduction. It is suspected that the ultimate cause is related to the widespread use of persistent pesticides of the chlorinated hydrocarbon group and their effect upon the calcium metabolism of the birds, and considerable research is in progress in the United States and the United Kingdom to determine to what extent this is true. (See Chapter 6 for a discussion of the effects of persistent pesticides in the environment, and for an analysis also of legislation and regulations relating to these materials.)

Legal Impediments to Blackbird Control

The depredations of blackbirds upon corn and other crops have increased in recent years to such an extent that the damage is considered "severe" in 17 states. A summary of the 1967 North American Conference on Blackbird Depredation in Agriculture (Anon., 1967) brings out many of the problems associated with control of these depredations, and state law is designated as one of the hindrances. The director of the Ohio Department of Agriculture pointed out that ". . . in Ohio, as in most other states, blackbirds may be killed only when they are damaging or about to damage a crop—except Sunday when they are protected."

As more effective control methods become available it is possible that bird protection laws will have to be so modified as to permit these methods to be used.

FUNDING OF WILDLIFE ADMINISTRATION

In most states the income that meets the costs of managing fish and wildlife resources comes mainly from sales of hunting and fishing licenses. In addition, the states receive federal aid under the Pittman-Robertson Act of 1937 for wildlife restoration and the Dingell-Johnson Act of 1950 for sport fishery restoration and management. In some states the fines from convicted violators of the fish and game laws also are used to support the fish and game department.

The tradition of providing financial support for administering the fish and wildlife resource entirely from hunting and fishing licenses is well established. It was a provision of the federal aid acts that, to qualify for benefits, a state must formally earmark hunting and fishing license income for the use of its fish and game administration.

This earmarking of funds under the principle that "the user pays" has been applied to some extent on the federal level also, under the Migratory Bird Hunting Stamp Act of 1934 and the Land and Water Conservation Fund Act of 1965. The former act was intended to raise funds for land acquisition and development and maintenance of a system of national waterfowl refuges, and the latter applies to outdoor recreation broadly, with primary objectives of encouraging long-range planning for outdoor recreation, and land and water acquisition for the same purpose.

It is now being increasingly recognized, at state levels as well as federal, that the social values of fish and wildlife are so great and so diverse that it is neither appropriate nor adequate to finance the management of this resource entirely from license holders, who comprise a small minority of the public. A few states have recognized this, and are now supplementing hunting and fishing license income with general tax revenue in order to provide more adequate support for conservation programs. The California Fish and Wildlife Plan of 1966 estimates that between 1965 and 1980 the cost of maintaining today's program in the Department of Fish and Game will total approximately $8.2 million, while new license buyers will provide only $4.2 million. It is recommended that current sources of income be augmented with general fund revenues to supply the deficit. In New York State this same situation was recognized in 1968 when the legislature provided from general revenue approximately one third of the budget of the Fish and Game Division.

The conclusion seems clear that earmarked funds, particularly from hunting and fishing licenses, will not be sufficient in the future to meet the costs of managing the fish and wildlife resource for the people at large.

WATER LAW IN RELATION TO FISH AND WILDLIFE

Water laws vary considerably from state to state and are exceedingly important in the management of fish and wildlife. The legal status of surface water is drastically different between the 17 western states (Dakotas to Texas and westward), where the doctrine of *prior appropriation* applies, and the eastern states, which employ variations of the *riparian* doctrine.

In its simplest form, the riparian doctrine permits any use by riparian landowners that returns the water to its streambed "undiminished in quantity or quality". This may be possible for certain nonconsumptive uses, such as waterwheels and fisheries. The opposite extreme is represented in western states, where frequently the entire flow of a stream is appropriated and used, leaving nothing whatever for fish habitat or recreational activities. Under this doctrine it is not unusual for a river to be completely "turned off" for a period of weeks or months.

Three features of the appropriation doctrine are in sharp conflict with fish and wildlife interests: (1) Water is legally appropriated to be diverted from its natural course; (2) most states allow the appropriation of *all* the water from a stream; and (3) fish and wildlife are not ordinarily recognized as a "beneficial use" or, if so, it is so subordinate to such uses as irrigation that the legal recognition is meaningless.

The subject of water law has been under scrutiny in all the contiguous 48 states because of conflicting demands for water and its increasing importance. Many changes have been made and are being considered. Among numerous publications on water law, several have been found particularly relevant, and they are the basis for this review. Water law in general or in relation to agricultural use has been treated by Williams (1950), Busby (1955), the University of Michigan (1955), Black (1960), Harding (1960), and Johnson (1965). The specific area of water law in the western states in relation to fish and wildlife has been reviewed by Denman (1957), Gordon (1958), Voigt (1958), Binford (1959), Lynch (1959), and Whitney (1964).

In 31 eastern states, where water is more plentiful, its relationships generally are outside the scope of this treatment. The questions of water pollution and its legal control, and of accelerated eutrophication of waters, have been treated in other reviews. The 17 western states, therefore, deserve particular attention here.

These western states have water laws based upon the appropriative doctrine, "first in time, first in right." Nine of the states included a basic water law in their constitutions, beginning with Texas in 1845 and ending with New Mexico in 1912. The other eight have statutory water law, beginning with Oregon in 1859.

Though the doctrine has been recently slightly modified in the coastal states of Washington, Oregon, and California, the basic doctrine is inimical to fish and wildlife because it assumes that appropriated water must be diverted from its natural bed, and there is no provision requiring a minimum flow. Fish and wildlife thus have no legal right to water. In dry years the water in a stream may be far over-appropriated, so that the owners of first water rights may use the entire flow for irrigation, municipal, or industrial purposes, whether or not it is used efficiently, and later appropriators (and fish and wildlife interests) have none.

It is a provision of the doctrine that appropriative rights go with the land, not the landowner, but even this feature cannot be exploited in the interest of fish and wildlife, as illustrated by the experience of the Arizona Department of Game and Fish. The Department purchased submarginal lands for the purpose of securing the water rights that went with them, but the water was to be left in its natural course as habitat for fish and game. The courts, however, ruled that since there was no active diversion of the water, the appropriative rights were invalid (Binford, 1959).

Binford also cites cases in Montana in which it was proposed to divert water from the streambed to fish-rearing ponds. This too was ruled invalid by the court because, in the conflict between irrigation and fish, the fish have lower priority. In several states efforts have been made to pass legislation that would classify fish and wildlife uses as beneficial, but these were opposed successfully by agricultural interests.

Increasing demands for recreation have resulted in some states recognizing the recreational values of water, and amendments to the original appropriative doctrine have been passed by the legislatures of the three west coast states. Each of these now has laws that provide for minimum flows in streams for preservation of fish and wildlife. Denman (1957) describes how the Oregon Game Commission, in testing the recent State Water Resources Act, requested a minimum flow of 200 cfs in the Deschutes River below the Wickiup Dam. Although granted only 20 cfs, the Commission established the important precedent of a minimum stream flow for fish and game in a western state.

In a 1957 amendment, California water law classified fish and game as beneficial users, on an equal basis with other users, and Gordon (1958) describes numerous water rights held by the Department of Fish and Game for fish hatcheries and rearing ponds, and for waterfowl management areas.

Missouri's water law requires State Conservation Department review and approval before any obstruction is built in a watercourse. If passage of fish is blocked, the department may require that either a hatchery or a fish ladder be constructed. This law has also been used as a basis for negotiating a minimum waterflow over or through a dam.

Washington's water law also places fish and wildlife on an equal basis with other beneficial users, and provides further that streambeds may not be disturbed by construction projects without consultation with, and consent of, the director of fisheries and the director of game (Binford, 1959). Pertinent sections of the amended water law of Washington are worth quoting since they are in such sharp contrast with most other western states:

75.20.050. It is hereby declared to be the policy of this state that a flow of water sufficient to support game fish and food fish populations be maintained at all times in streams of this state.

75.20.060. Every dam or other obstruction across or in any stream shall be provided with a durable and efficient fishway . . . as the director may approve. . . .

75.20.100. In the event that any person or government agency desires to construct any form of hydraulic project that will lower, divert, obstruct or change the natural flow or bed of any river . . . , such person or government agency shall submit . . . plans and specifications of the proposed construction . . . and shall secure the written approval of director of fisheries and director of game. . . .

Particularly important is Montana's Stream Preservation Act of 1964, described by Whitney (1964). Its provisions are similar to the last section of Washington's water law in that it protects watercourses from damage by such construction projects as highways. The act requires that the Montana Department of Game and Fish be notified 60 days prior to the construction of any project that might damage a watercourse.

The Department thus has the opportunity to recommend alternatives to prevent or mitigate the damage. The act has reportedly been highly successful in protecting fishery resources, but a serious weakness is that it applies only to other state agencies, not to federal or private construction.

It is clear that among the very important legislative problems in the fish and wildlife field are those relating to water, and to the preservation of streams from unnecessary damage.

THE TAX DEDUCTION INFLUENCE IN RESOURCE USE

In major decisions affecting resource management, the people act through their government by means of available political machinery. The members of Congress give support and direction to a cause as they are influenced by its proponents. They may withhold such sanction when opponent forces state their case effectively. It is inherent in our legislative process that the will of the public usually is served and that it is made known through hearings and other representations of citizens.

An acknowledged feature of this system is the right of entrepreneurs in every economic field to promote legislation favorable to their business interests. Such activities are an allowable business expense under provisions of the Internal Revenue Code. These regulations apply to the users and developers of natural resources and have long governed our public management of land and water.

Somewhat different concepts apply to the activities of citizens who attempt to affect resource decisions for reasons other than profit (see Borod, 1968). When they incorporate in conservation organizations for purposes they conceive to be in the public interest, their contributions to the organization (if eligible) are tax deductible. However, the Internal Revenue Code prohibits the use of any substantial part of that income for influencing legislation. A case of this kind came to national attention when The Sierra Club lost its tax-deductible status in 1966 for advertising in leading newspapers as part of its campaign to prevent the construction of dams in the Grand Canyon. In the year following, the club reported the loss of $125,000 in gifts (San Francisco Chronicle, March 14, 1968).

In discussing this situation, Patterson (1967) pointed out that the interests who stand to gain by certain decisions commonly have ample funds to pursue their cause, while those speaking for the general public do not. He noted that "The final irony is that the law protects itself; they cannot fight to have it changed."

Especially among the larger, more responsible, conservation organizations of the nation, there is a growing feeling that they should have similar financial privileges in working for or against legislation as their counterparts in labor and industry have.

GROWING EMPHASIS ON HABITAT

Much of the legislation discussed here has had the effect of putting a restraint on the users of fish and wildlife, and this effect will always be important. However, there have been many state laws and acts of Congress dealing with problems of environment essential to wildlife. The aim may be habitat preservation or rehabilitation, or in some cases the development of entirely new habitats. Unfortunately, destructive forces continue to increase also, as a consequence of population growth, technological developments, and social demands, so this preoccupation with habitat is well justified.

Some of the significant federal acts have been mentioned in other connections. Thus, the Migratory Bird Conservation Act of 1929 is legal authority for the system of National Wildlife Refuges, and the Federal Aid Acts (Pittman-Robertson and Dingell-Johnson) of 1937 and 1950 provided that the States might use funds from these sources for the development of habitat. Public Law 83-566, the Small Watersheds Act, though enacted primarily for flood control purposes, included provisions for creation of fish and wildlife habitat. The Federal Water Quality Act of 1965, as amended, will have exceedingly important beneficial effects upon water quality for fish in particular, because the standards it imposes are in so many cases higher than those that the states were employing. The Agricultural Conservation Program of the U.S. Department of Agriculture, effective in 1936, has encouraged wildlife habitat developments on farms and ranches through federal cost sharing and has resulted in the building of many thousands of farm and ranch ponds. The Land and Water Conservation Fund Act of 1965 provides still another source of funds that are being used in part for creation of new ponds and lakes for recreational use. Others are less direct, but still constructive, in their influence upon habitat restoration, preservation, or development, but in the aggregate they demonstrate an increasing ecologic awareness on the part of the American public.

THE FUTURE

The technologies of agriculture and of fish and wildlife management have developed so rapidly in recent decades that in most situations they are far ahead of what we can apply. Legislation and administration have lagged far behind, so that there are many examples of unresolved conflicts of interest, duplications of effort, lack of coordination or cooperation, and overlapping jurisdiction involving fisheries, wildlife, agriculture, and other land uses. The challenge of the future will be to develop legislation and patterns of administration that will make it possible to cooperate and focus a coordinated effort, giving full consideration to the many interests that are involved.

A rare opportunity to improve legislation is available to the Public Land Law Review Commission and the Congress, for the Commission was required to submit its recommendations by June 30, 1970. The recommendations were developed from a series of some 30 comprehensive studies conducted during the past 5 years. If and when adopted by the Congress and the public land managing agencies, these recommendations can have a tremendous influence on future conservation programs directly affecting approximately a third of the land area of the United States.

REFERENCES

Allen, D. L. 1962. Our wildlife legacy. Funk & Wagnalls Co. 422 p.

Anonymous. 1967. Blackbird depredation in agriculture. Agr. Sci. Rev., Second Quart., 15-22.

Berryman, J. C. 1961. The responsibility of state agencies in managing hunting on private lands. 26th N. Amer. Wildl. Conf. Trans. p. 285-292.

Binford, L. C. 1959. Western water law and policy as it relates to fish and wildlife resources. Western Ass. State Fish & Game Comm., 39th Annu. Conf. Proc. p. 41-55.

Black, P. E. 1960. Colorado water law. Coop. Watershed Manage. Unit., For. WM 90.

Borod, R. S. 1968. Tax exemption: lobbying for conservation. New Republic 159(23):14-16.

Boyce, A. T. 1967. Results of the Cropland Adjustment Program's first year in Michigan. 32nd N. Amer. Wildl. & Natur. Resour. Conf. p. 96-102.

Busby, C. E. 1955. Regulations and economic expansion, p. 666-676. *In* Water. Yearbook of Agriculture. U.S. Department of Agriculture. U.S. Government Printing Office, Washington, D.C.

Chrest, H. R. 1964. Review of literature of the bald eagle. Colorado State University Library. 121 p. (Unpub. Ms.)

Clement, R. C. 1965. Last call for birds of prey. Audubon Mag. 67(1):37.

Crews, J. F., and R. Bird. 1963. Reducing liability risks in farm recreation enterprises. Univ. Missouri Agr. Exp. Sta. and USDA Res. Devel. Econ. Div. B-801.

Denman, K. G. 1957. Water rights as related to fish and game. Western Ass. State Fish & Game Comm., 37th Ann. Conf. Proc. p. 134-138.

Dimmick, R. W., and W. D. Klimstra. 1964. Controlled duck hunting in Illinois. J. Wildl. Manage. 28(4):676-688.

Galbreath, D. S. 1965. Hunting access programs summary. Washington Game Dep., Upland Game Bird Program. p. 24-29.

Gearhart, D. 1957. "Frontiers" formed to help solve old hunter-owner feud. N.M. Wildl. 2(12):7.

Gilbert, D. L. 1965. Public relations in natural resources management. Burgess Publ. Co., Minneapolis. 180 p.

Gordon, S. 1958. Water problems and California wildlife. Western Ass. State Game & Fish Comm., 38th Ann. Conf. Proc. p. 24-28.

Harding, T. S. 1960. Water in California. N-P Publ., Palo Alto. 231 p.

Hay, H. 1960. An evaluation of Colorado's access problems. 25th N. Amer. Wildl. Conf. p. 364-377.

Hunter, G. N. 1957. The techniques used in Colorado to obtain hunter distribution. 22nd N. Amer. Wildl. Conf. Trans. p. 589-593.

Hunter, W. A. 1953. Landowner-sportsman relations. Western Ass. State Game & Fish Comm., 33rd Ann. Conf. Proc. p. 265-269.

Johnson, K. L. 1965. Analysis of state regulations of surface water development and use in Colorado. Colorado State University. Ph.D. thesis.

Johnson, L. W. 1943. Hunter distribution: studies and methods. 8th N. Amer. Wildl. Conf. Trans. p. 392-407.

Johnson, W. 1967. Operation respect. Colorado Outdoors 16(2):22-27.

Kelsey, G. L. 1964. Liability risks for hunter-hosts. S.D. State Univ., Coop. Ext. Ser. FS-241.

Kozicky, E. L. 1960. Access to private lands. Internat. Ass. Game, Fish & Conserv. Comm., 50th Conv. Proc. p. 18-23.

Krausz, N. G. P., and L. G. Lemon. 1964. Laws and regulations concerning recreation in rural areas of Illinois. Univ. Illinois, Coll. Agr., C-889.

Laun, H. C. 1963. It's time for mutiny on the bounties. Audubon Mag. 65(3): 146-149.

Leedy, C. D. 1966. Liability protection for outdoor recreation enterprises. N.M. State Univ., Coop. Ext. Serv. Circ. 385.

Leopold, A. 1930. The American game policy in a nutshell. 17th N. Amer. Game Conf. Trans. p. 281-283.

Leopold, A. 1933. Game management. Charles Scribner's Sons, New York. 481 p.

Leopold, A. 1940. History of the Riley game cooperative, 1931-39. J. Wildl. Manage. 4(3):291-301.

Lynch, R. G. 1959. Our growing water problems. National Wildlife Federation, Washington, D.C. 60 p.

Magnuson, W. G. 1965a. Treaties and other international agreements containing provisions on commercial fisheries, marine resources, sport fisheries, and wildlife to which the United States is party. 89th Cong., 1st Sess., U.S. Senate, Committee on Commerce. U.S. Government Printing Office, Washington, D.C. 410 p.

Magnuson, W. G. 1965b. Compilation of federal laws relating to the conservation and development of our nation's fish and wildlife resources. 89th Cong., 1st Sess., U.S. Senate, Committee on Commerce. U.S. Government Printing Office, Washington, D.C. 472 p.

Oregon State Game Commission. 1967. Cougar Bull., Nov.-Dec. 8 p.

Patterson, R. W. 1967. The art of the impossible. Amer. Acad. Arts and Sci. Proc. 94(4):1020-1033.

Rutherford, R. 1949. 10 years of Pittman-Robertson wildlife restoration. U.S. Fish and Wildlife Service. 14 p.

Rutherford, R. 1953. 5 years of Pittman-Robertson wildlife restoration, 1949-53. U.S. Fish and Wildlife Service. 14 p.

Scott, W. E. 1948. Methods of controlled public hunting in the United States and Canada. J. Wildl. Manage. 12(3):236-240.

Sigler, W. F. 1956. Wildlife law enforcement. Wm. Brown Publ., Dubuque, Iowa.

Sprunt, A., Jr. 1963. Bald eagles aren't producing enough young. Audubon Mag. 65(1):32-35.

Stuewer, F. W. 1953. How good is the Williamston plan? Mich. Conserv. 22(5): 23-26.

Swanson, G. A., J. T. Shields, W. H. Olson, et al. 1969. Fish and wildlife resources on the public lands. A report prepared for the Public Land Law Review Commission by Colorado State University; available from Clearinghouse for Federal Scientific and Technical Information, U.S. Department of Commerce, Springfield, Va.

Teague, R. 1966. Recreation potential on farmlands. Internat. Ass. Game, Fish, & Conserv. Comm., 56th Conv. Proc. p. 128-133.

University of Michigan. 1955. Water resources and the law. U. Mich. Law Sch., Ann Arbor. 614 p.

U.S. Department of Agriculture. 1965. Cropland Adjustment Program for 1966 through 1969. Washington, D.C. 13 p.

Voigt, W. 1958. Water policy problems, east and west. Western Ass. State Game & Fish Comm., 38th Ann. Conf. Proc. p. 5-23.

Whitesell, D. 1952. Analysis of farmer-hunter relationships. 17th N. Amer. Wildl. Conf. Trans. p. 533-539.

Whitney, A. H. 1964. Montana's first year with a stream preservation act. Western Ass. State Game & Fish Comm., 44th Annu. Conf. p. 229-231.

Williams, M. B. 1950. Water law in the United States of America. United Nations Food & Agriculture Organization, Geneva. 161 p.

CHAPTER 9

Evaluation and Conclusions

There is, in the histories of communities in relation to their resource base, a period of learning how to reach the resource and use it, followed by a period of rich enjoyment which seems endless in that happy time; then there comes a choice of working out the resource and losing it, or learning the art and science of conservation that the resource may be perpetuated by wise use. (Darling and Eichhorn, 1967)

Many of the uses of land described in this report seem to represent the critical ecological transition in the history of man on this continent. If our criteria of living standards are to include space, scenic, and recreational values, then certain practices cannot be sustained and should be subjected to replanning and control.

In this sense the destruction of "outdoor" resources has reached a critical point. Irreversible changes in fauna and flora (except possibly of local populations of species otherwise secure) should be permitted, if at all, only after the most searching study. Such a policy is necessary, since the demands of a burgeoning population are, actually and potentially, unlimited.

THE POPULATION VARIABLE

It appears inevitable that unchecked population growth will bring about a "bread-alone" level of living in North America, as it already has in much of the world. Population controls are an essential part of the operation of every natural ecosystem, and the development of a durable homeostasis for mankind on this continent includes the abridgment of demand as a concommitant of conservative resource use. For the present, it is too much to ask just how many people should be planned for at just what point in the future. But to accept a doubling of population between 1960 and 2000 and to mobilize all natural assets to meet the "need" is self-defeating. Areas strategically suited to industrial and population buildup are being heavily used. Large public investments to replace open spaces with new communities means a further expansion of population, increasing drain on resource reserves, and more of the pollution overload that is becoming a national emergency.

If present trends were to continue, population growth would eventually be checked by shortage and hardship, but the fund of native wealth would have been irretrievably damaged. From this perspective, the inadequacies of our present social and economic guidance were recognized by Udall (U.S. Department of the Interior, 1967).

One could contemplate the United States a century from now with equanimity if our growth rates and growth patterns reflected a mature, purposeful national will. Arrogant events and the headlong pace of material progress have left us little time to ask what people are for, or to agree on long-term societal aspirations. We have learned neither how to grow, nor at what pace, and that is our failing and our future trouble.

It is evident that population planning is a part of resource planning. The following conclusions are based on the assumption that public programs will of necessity be developed toward optimizing human numbers by controlling birth rates, as death rates continue to decline. Without this, it is impossible to plan for continuing resource management.

HIGHEST USE AND SOCIAL NEED

It has been largely implicit in our discussions of land and water use that one works "with nature" and requires of any area the kind of yield that represents the most continuing human benefits. Usually this is the highest biological productivity of an area—e.g., it would ordinarily be poor business to maintain a hardwood forest on soils that could raise corn efficiently.

On the other hand, the extent and distribution of various land types on the continent are fortuitous, and blind adherence to the principle of highest potential yield can lead to oversupply in one commodity and scarcity in another. This is particularly true where one kind of produce is marketable and another is not. In terms of public policy, someone must reach a judgment between the productive potential of an area as determined by physical capability and what actually should be done with it to serve best the majority of citizens. The first is a biological problem, the second entails social and economic analysis.

These issues are a mark of the present, because earlier in our history "highest use" was nearly always synonymous with the greatest dollar return. In a sparsely populated continent this was the practical and workable approach. Today's complexities include the alternatives of the free market versus artificial price supports and the contentions of people who "got there first" in the use of land and water.

Modern planning for resource use is much concerned with opposing doctrines, both of which are revered as part of the American way. The one defends the free enterprise system and the constitutional rights of individuals. The other centers on guardianship of the public interest, which means a conservation policy—"the greatest good of the greatest number over the longest time." A proper balance of interests will not be achieved easily or quickly, but to seek it is the unavoidable responsibility of an enlightened society. The burden of a sometimes unpopular policy must fall on the elected representatives of the people. It is inherent in the nature of the situation that causes of the future may have few advocates to oppose the numerous advocates of the short-term interests of today and tomorrow.

AN OVERVIEW

In the following sections we synthesize what appear to us certain broad policy principles that apply to land-use issues and trends. It is not by chance that these encompass the husbandry of all renewable resources, with wildlife taking its place among other benefits yielded by the environment. This is not intended as a summary of the entire report; important questions on many land and water operations are treated only in the text itself.

We adopt this presentation to avoid any suggestion of a piecemeal approach to resource management. It is notable that the government has not had a disinterested mechanism for appraising resource uses or developed any overview that could monitor the management of our continental ecosystem along lines of true improvement for the future. This is a problem in the environmental biology of man, and planning at any lesser level of integration must inevitably continue and magnify the errors of the past.

The Worth of Wildlife

The interpretations in this report fortify a view that wild animals and, in general, the natural scene have far-reaching significance for human welfare. The dimension is a social one, not measurable fully, or even in large part, in dollars or other economic terms. We believe that to preserve the quality and variety of the American out-of-doors is justified by assumption and principle, rather than by economics. Against an encompassing materialistic attrition, the burden of proof has been on the defenders of every outpost of nature, until after a short 300 years, little of the truly primitive remains. The unique features of our remaining wildness should be inviolate to every impinging claim.

Management of Brushlands

The development of basic knowledge on the ecology and values of brushlands, especially several types that occur in semiarid regions, appears to have been slighted. Subsidized eradication operations appear to be going forward without an adequate knowledge of the effects on fauna of the resulting plant successions.

In land-use research programs, high priority should be given to acceleration of fact-finding on brushland management in relation to wildlife, livestock, and other values. Federal and state land management agencies should be urged to review current policies and regulations that bear on requirements for joint planning between land managers and wildlife biologists prior to the initiation of brush manipulation operations. Relationships should be established to assure adequate protection of public wildlife values. Special attention is needed in public assistance programs toward providing incentives that will make it feasible for landowners to benefit wildlife as they go about their brushland management programs.

Control of Birds and Mammals

It is essential that the control of wild birds and mammals undertaken to reduce economic damage be based on a systematic and scientifically verified method of collecting stock and range damage information. This

fact-gathering is logically the responsibility of government wildlife research agencies and should not be a part of the mission of operational
control groups. Where feasible, handling damage through a landowner
insurance system, such as that used for waterfowl problems in the Prairie Provinces of Canada, is to be recommended. An ecological approach
that makes clear the relationship of crop or livestock losses to land-use
practices is fundamental in setting control policies and gauging public
responsibility for compensating programs. Extension and demonstration
should be emphasized as a way of aiding landowners on a self-help basis.

Recognition of the status of large predators as vanishing species
within the United States—especially the grizzly bear, grey wolf, and
puma—requires that these species be given special protection through
appropriate state-federal cooperative arrangements. The natural relationships of predators to game species need to be better understood as
being generally beneficial or innocuous and not as justifying public programs for the reduction of carnivores. Taking abundant predators as
game, under appropriate regulations, is preferable to any alternative
kind of control. It should be basic to the design and application of control techniques that they be used specifically on local problems rather
than generally against populations or species. Widespread experience
with the bounty system indicates that it tends to be indiscriminate and
self-perpetuating and has no place in public management.

The great and increasing public interest in predatory birds and mammals is evidence of their exceptionally high esthetic value. In this connection, the protection of all birds of prey, as now practiced in more
than half the states, is to be encouraged.

Protection of Waters and Wetlands

Aquatic habitats are critically important to many forms of wildlife that
represent a major public interest. These habitats have been subject to
long-standing attrition and degradation, and they are still being destroyed at a rate the nation can ill afford. Wetlands may properly be
designated as an ecological disaster area in need of emergency action.

While the drainage of properly used agricultural lands is essential, the
"reclamation" of new crop acreage through public subsidies of any kind
should be terminated. By every feasible means, landowners should be
encouraged to preserve headwater marshes and small waters, and incentive programs should be developed to improve and restore such
areas in the public interest. Such measures should be given high pri-

ority in the planning of small-watershed programs, and the present emphasis on drainage and channelization of streams is in need of review and change. The states should be urged to establish and enforce more stringent regulations governing the dredging and filling of natural water areas. Coastal brackish waters are the most productive habitats of living things on land or sea, and their critical significance to marine resources and other coastal wildlife is largely ignored. Regulation of filling operations, canal building, and other activities that damage bays and estuaries should be an immediate issue and might properly be made a responsibility of the Secretary of the Interior.

River Basin Policy

We regard the "total" development of river systems as a misbegotten concept stemming from early assumptions that economic expansion must outgain population—now a patently erroneous premise. A much restructured, artificial hydrology will result in the mass decimation of wildlife and natural areas, will foreclose future management options by bringing about irreversible changes, and will create problems of unpredictable magnitude through siltation and eutrophication. Most overflow lands can be used most securely and economically within the limits of their natural flood dynamics, through a policy of public information and zoning. The view that it is the destiny and right of every backcountry area to establish at public cost a big-city industrial culture by major changes in river systems or by other means is not ecologically realistic for the nation as a whole.

The Open Lands

Areas of sparse human population should be valued as essential space, and in some measure as a counter-balance to the huge megalopolises that are taking over great sections of the continent. For millions who must live under the stress of concentration, the still-open lands will be a retreat offering some measure of social refreshment and privacy. In keeping with this growing value, forests, ranges, marshes, and seashores can yield their multiple benefits to best advantage under informed ecological management. Water, timber, forage, wildlife, and recreation are commodities under increasing demand. They are the products of extensive areas that also help dilute the accumulated atmospheric and waterborne wastes that degrade the quality of life in population centers. We conceive that spaces extensively used are an asset to be recognized in the American way of life.

REFERENCES

Darling, F. F., and N. D. Eichhorn. 1967. Man and nature in the national parks. Conservation Foundation, Washington, D.C. 80 p.
U.S. Department of the Interior. 1967. Man . . . an endangered species? Conservation Yearbook 4. U.S. Government Printing Office, Washington, D.C. 100 p.

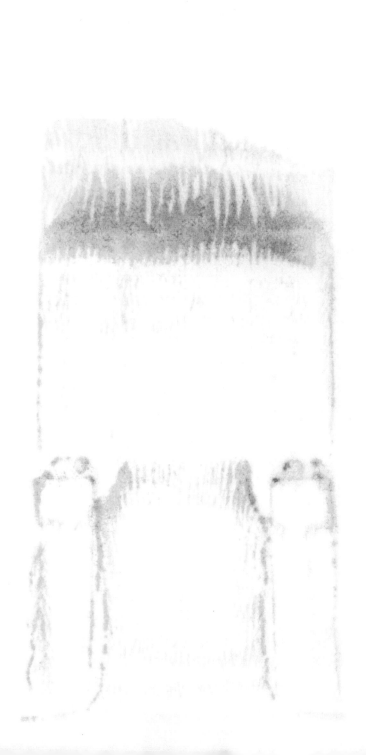